FLORIDA

Population Change, 1950-1960

Figure 1

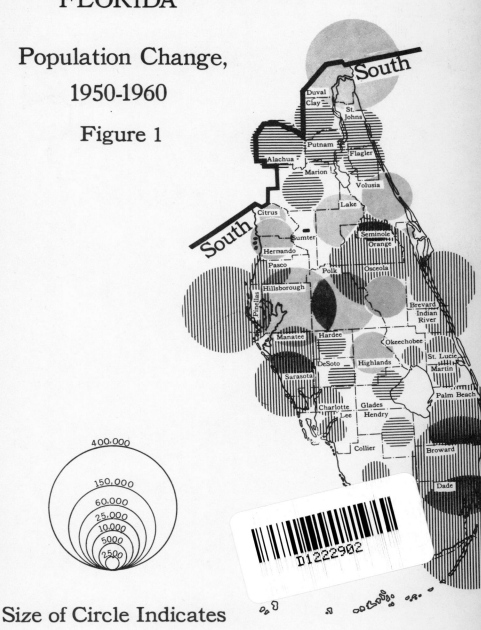

400,000

150,000

60,000

25,000

10,000

5000

2500

Size of Circle Indicates
Gross Increase

The Politics of Mis-Representation

William C. Havard
Loren P. Beth

The Politics
of Mis-Representation

RURAL-URBAN CONFLICT
IN THE
FLORIDA LEGISLATURE

Louisiana State University Press

Preface 5 4/09

IN most respects the study which follows is self-explanatory, but it may be important to say something about the time involved. The authors were both living in Florida during the period from 1953 to 1958, and as political scientists were especially interested in the activities of the Florida legislature. One of us was immediately concerned because of his position as director of the Public Administration Clearing Service at the University of Florida, the other as a teacher of the legislative process.

The 1957 session of the legislature was observed very closely, at first hand, from beginning to end. By necessity, the 1955, 1959, and 1961 sessions were studied from the outside and in less detail and have been used mainly to check our conclusions.

Since the decision in the case of *Baker* v. *Carr* in March of this year, actions affecting state legislative apportionment have occurred with such astonishing speed that observers have had difficulty keeping abreast of them. On July 23, while this book was in page proof, a three judge federal district court in Miami ruled that action must be taken by the Florida legislature to remedy the "invidiously discriminatory" apportionment plan now in effect if the state is to avoid a reapportionment by judicial decree prior to the 1963 session. The broadly framed decision was interpreted by Governor Farris Bryant as rendering invalid both the existing constitutional provision and the proposal for amendment that was to have been voted on in the November election (described in Chapter III). Governor Bryant responded by calling the legislature into special session on August 1 for the purpose of reapportioning.

After eleven days of what the St. Petersburg *Times* referred to as "bitter wrangling" the legislature proposed another reapportionment amendment which would raise house seats to a total of 135 and the single-member senate districts to 46. The effect of the change was hardly as sweeping as the increase in size would imply. Each county would continue to have a representative, and, even though Dade (with 12 additional seats) and the other large counties would have substantial increases in representation, a house majority could still be elected by about 27 per cent of the state's population. In the senate the change is much more limited; under the proposal, slightly more than 13 per cent of the population would be able to elect a majority of members of that chamber. The consensus seems to be that, if adopted, this change would break the rural county hold on the house but would leave the senate power structure very much as it is. The general view also seems to be that few of the dissatisfactions arising in the large counties are relieved by the plan. The struggle is thus by no means at an end as this volume goes into the printing stage. The proposal is under the scrutiny of the court; and the senate arrangement, in particular, is strongly objected to by the plaintiffs.

If substantial changes should be forthcoming immediately this book may well be history rather than analysis of a contemporary political problem. However, two important qualifications should be made regarding this possibility. The first is that something less than a complete change in the apportionment system may be permitted by the courts, at least for the time being. Of more importance, however, is the fact that political habits long indulged in are slow to break, so there is no reason to suppose that the legislative power structure which we have described will vanish overnight even if drastic reapportionment should take place in time for the 1963 session.

Acknowledgments

IN addition to our observation and study of the legislature in action, we had a great many interviews with observers, politicians, and scholars. For political reasons most of these cannot be named; in any case, there were far too many of them to list. Although they remain anonymous, our debt to them is heavy and our thanks are warm. Newspapers and official documents were also of great help. The conclusions we have drawn may seem extreme to some readers: they are, in any case, our own, and no other person named or unnamed is responsible for them.

After we left Florida, the assistance of the Public Administration Clearing Service and its Director, Professor Gladys Kammerer, was very kindly extended, with the consent of our friend Manning Dauer, Chairman of the Department of Political Science at the University of Florida. We have been greatly assisted, as well, by research grants extended over a period of years by the University of Florida, the Louisiana State University, and the University of Massachusetts. Finally, the Public Administration Clearing Service has been kind enough to give us permission to incorporate sections of our monograph, *Representative Government and Reapportionment: A Case Study of Florida,* published in 1960 as No. 20 in its Studies in Public Administration. Likewise, acknowledgement is due the *Journal of Politics* for allowing us to use some of the text and tables from our article, "Committee Stacking and Political Power in Florida," which appeared in the issue of February, 1961.

WILLIAM C. HAVARD
LOREN P. BETH

Contents

Figures

Tables

xiii

Chapter 1

Introduction

THE state of Florida, in common with a great many other places, has been characterized as a land of change. However, few persons who used the phrase as a capsulated description of Florida's history prior to World War II could have realized the extent to which they were speaking predictively rather than simply retrospectively. For the rate of change in most sociological features of the state has greatly accelerated during the past two decades. In many respects the South has emerged during this period as the nation's urban frontier; it is the sector of the United States whose economic development requires most in the way of application of human and capital resources and at the same time is so open to development that its projected dividends in terms of fulfilling the American dream of an urbanized technocratic society seem to be virtually unlimited. For a variety of reasons Florida has been penetrated earlier and more extensively than the other states of the deep South in the attempt to exploit this new frontier.

The 1940–1950 population growth in Florida (873,891; 46.1 per cent) was far greater than any other southeastern state both in terms of gross increase and ratio, and every subsequent projection indicates an even more rapid rate of growth in the past decade. More than two million inhabitants were added between 1950 and 1960 (an increase of 79 per cent), and the population in 1960 was almost five million.

The proportionate rate of urbanization has paralleled the phenomenal growth of population. From 1920 to 1950 Florida's rural-urban ratio reversed itself, changing from two-thirds rural to two-

1

thirds urban. By 1956 Dade County (Miami) alone contained more than double the number of urban residents of the entire state as of 1900. Florida is the most heavily urbanized state of the South and is thirteenth among all the states in proportion of urban to rural inhabitants. Not to be forgotten in all this is the fact that Florida's per capita annual income ($1,949 in 1960) is the highest in the South. This achievement (which is also fairly recent) offers strong support to the new economic psychology of the South, which foresees its particular fulfillment of the American idea of progress in a rapid assimilation of the region to the urbanized and industrial condition of the North.

However, the tables of statistics which bring joy to the hearts of directors of local chambers of commerce may merely afford preliminary data on a new set of problems for the political analyst. Political systems have a disagreeable tendency to remain static in the face of sociological change, and it is quite possible for the degree of resistance to political adjustment to manifest itself in direct proportion to the intensity of social change. Such has apparently been the case in Florida; state politics there still reflect to some extent the predominant characteristics of southern ruralism (exhibiting, of course, particular local variations), and the main response of its practitioners to the challenges of the paleotechnic age has been a posture of defensive intransigence. Like the other southern states, Florida continues to practice an ambivalent one-party politics which has its origins in the Civil War and Reconstruction and sustains itself by the evocation of an elaborate *mythos* through which those events are interpreted. As has been apparent since the United States Supreme Court handed down the decision outlawing racial segregation in the public schools, the single-issue traumatic politics on which southern leaders have relied intermittently since Reconstruction can still be used with considerable effect in Florida, although the 1960 gubernatorial campaign indicated a trend toward moderation in this respect. The present dramatic social changes in the state, then, must be seen against this historical backdrop if the full dimensions of contemporary Florida politics are to be appreciated.

In many respects the understanding of the way in which sociological change has created a new set of political problems is simplified by the fact that there are really two Floridas, which may be roughly distinguished as Peninsular and Continental Florida. Continental (or North) Florida is typically southern, predominantly rural and ethno-centric. Any attempt to draw arbitrary lines separating this area from southern Florida, however, immediately involves the observer in contradictions immanent in the process of change itself. Despite the indeterminate nature of the transitional region between the two parts of the state, certain preliminary differentiations may be made at this point which will serve as a basis for later elaboration and qualification.

In the ante bellum period the settled portion of Florida (except for Key West) was North Florida, and the heart of North Florida was the territory between the Suwanee and Apalachicola rivers. This area, then known as Middle Florida, contained the bulk of the state's population and was its economic and political mainstay. In 1860, Negroes constituted about 45 per cent of the state's population, and the black belt, too, was defined largely in terms of Middle Florida. Slavery reached only as far south as Marion County as it spilled over the Suwanee River and on into the counties adjoining the St. Johns River, and it hardly touched the counties west of those bordering the Apalachicola.

South (or Peninsular) Florida was thus, in a sense not comparable to any large contiguous area within any other state of the deep South, excluded from the historic experience which forms the basis of southern one-party, race-oriented politics. As late as 1880 Peninsular Florida (excluding Key West) contained only 10 per cent of the state's population. With few exceptions, the cities in South Florida whose populations exceeded ten thousand in 1950 do not appear in the census before 1900 and only Key West, Jacksonville, and St. Augustine (if we may for this purpose include the latter two in South Florida) show up before 1890. South Florida is thus (like some of the western states) an actual twentieth-century frontier in ways other than those characteristic of the new urbanism of the South as a whole.

The map which serves as the end papers for this study provides ample evidence of the type of population change occurring in South Florida. Today well over 70 per cent of Florida's population lives outside the areas reached by slavery, and included among these counties are the ones whose growth and urbanization are most unprecedented. The nature of that growth, too, is worthy of note. The usual characterization of South Florida as tourist-oriented and Yankee-dominated is based on an unmistakable impression. In 1950 slightly over half the inhabitants of Florida were born outside the state, a ratio of non-native to native population that was exceeded only by five states of the Far West. Florida's net gain through interstate movement as of 1950 was just short of 950,000, which was larger than any state except California, and well over half a million of these interstate immigrants originated in nonsouthern states. Naturally the overwhelming bulk of the newcomers have settled in the urban agglomerations on the east and west coasts of Peninsular Florida, thereby establishing themselves as the most important factor in the inflation of the population in those sectors.

Even the most casual observer in Florida cannot fail to be impressed by the extent to which this area has succeeded not merely in conforming to the patterns of urbanism of the Northeast, but in establishing a concrete representation of the futuristic dream of such a society. The polyglot accents of the residents (which are indistinguishable from those of the tourists), the continuous expression of unbridled optimism about economic possibilities of the region, the intensity and pervasiveness of commercialism and even the determined concentration on an exclusively contemporary style of architecture give ample testimony to the spirit of innovation that pervades every aspect of life in urbanized South Florida.

There is little in this atmosphere to sustain the type of politics that Florida shares with the other states of the deep South. Many of the newcomers are from regions that practice two-party politics, and a sizeable number of the new inhabitants are Republican by family tradition and preference. There is no evidence there of the hazy, brooding sense of tragic history that has been such a boon to the southern politician's capacity for using diversionary tactics to maintain personalized rule at both the county and state levels. Nor can the race issue be used to unify these new urban residents into a collectivity, obsessed by the fear of integration to the exclusion of all other political and economic problems.

The accent on initiative and lack of concern for the past does not mean that urbanized Florida is unaware of the necessity for an appropriate governmental role in these new developments. Despite a pronounced tendency to overindulge in the usual shibboleths about the harmful effects of governmental intervention, there seems to be a clear recognition of the necessity for positive collective action if the bright promise of the future is to be realized. Consequently, adaptation of governmental machinery and activities to the problems at hand has been characterized by the spirit of innovation exhibited in other types of endeavor. City-manager government has had a field day in Florida; experiments in local planning and zoning have been launched with great fervor, and there can be few places in which consultants on problems of local government have found their services more in demand or their counsel more readily accepted. The fact remains, however, that the types of problems faced by urban Florida cannot be handled by local initiative; the bigger issues require state action in the form of general legislation. Since the new urbanism does not stop at county lines drawn fifty years ago, the habitual practice of settling area problems through mutual back-scratching by local legislative delegations no longer serves even as an expediential substitute for more comprehensive programs. Only a coherent policy based on appraisals of the state-wide effect of various alternatives can cope with such state functions as highways, taxation (including sources, exemptions, and reservations of adequate sources for local levy), planning, and conservation (particularly of the water resources on which so much of the state's economy depends). And the new factor of urbanism is probably the most important determinant of the conditions under which these problems may be satisfactorily resolved.

We have centered this study on the obvious contradiction between the dominating, irreversible trends in the social composition of Florida (with all that these changes portend) and the all but imperceptible effect that these factors have had on the state's overall political style. To be sure there have been piecemeal changes in certain political institutions and activities, some of which have already been noted in passing. Perhaps the most conspicuous alteration at the state level has been in the governorship. It is now generally accepted that the political type who occupies that office will exhibit characteristics of sophisticated urbanity in appearance, manner, speech, and promises held out as inducements to popular support. In many respects this situation is an acknowledgement of the state-wide preponderance of the urban electorate. The cracker politician, in the form of either a race-baiting demagogue or a populist-oriented economic reformer, is conceded little chance in a gubernatorial campaign; only a completely unforeseen turn of events could result in the election of a Sidney J. Catts or a Fuller Warren as chief executive. But by the same token, the office of governor as an effective agency in the complex power structure of the state seems to have diminished appreciably, both in respect to the exercise of legislative leadership and in relation to the independent components of a checked and balanced executive branch; Florida, as will be amply demonstrated, has a "weak" governor.

Other questions relating to the persistence of nineteenth-century politics in Florida force themselves on our consideration. Why, in a state which has voted Republican in the last three presidential elections, returned a Republican to Congress at the last four congressional elections, strongly challenged at least one other congressional seat, and established what amounts to a Republican majority in certain urban counties, has the Republican party had so little success in breaking the stranglehold of one-party politics on Florida generally? Again, why has a state whose population changes have reduced the Negro population to the smallest proportion in any deep southern state (less than 20 per cent) and whose areas of greatest population density lie outside the black belt both geographically and ideologically, vied with its neighboring states in the severity of its legislative attempts to preserve segregation? Above all, if American politics is explainable largely in terms of the interest group struggle and if there is a tendency toward equilibrium in the countervailing pressures of these groups (as many political scientists imply), why have the urban areas of Florida, with their economic advantages, unity of purpose on many questions of public policy, and an informed and articulate leadership, had so small an impact on public policy decisions and almost no access to positions from which direct power is exercised?

For a variety of reasons we have concentrated on the legislature in assaying answers to these and other questions about contemporary Florida politics. In the first place, casual observation had already led us to the tentative conclusion that the legislature (or at least a certain rather amorphous coalition within that body) constitutes the most important determinant of the political pattern as well as the content of public policy in Florida. In other words, the main institution through which political power is exercised seems to be the legislature. It is obvious that the use of political power to secure a program that is relatively consistent depends on the creation and maintenance of a stable and systematically functioning political organization. And the type of consistency exhibited in Florida makes it questionable that the perfection of human nature upon which anarchy rests its demand for the abrogation of political institutions has occurred in that state. At the same time it is equally certain that no overt-political machinery in the form of a party or factional system built on state-wide popular support forms the basis of cohesion on which governing authority rests. The struggles for control within the institutional structures (and the power relationships which are created within the government apart from the electoral process) appear to provide an answer to the problem of how the prevailing system is maintained in Florida and the relative success of the legislature in its recent struggles with the executive point to the representative assembly as the main locus of power.

Even if these considerations were not so compelling, the particular characteristics of the legislature mark it as the logical point of departure from which to move toward an understanding of the process as a whole. For the legislature is the "policy-making branch" in a government based on the separation of powers principle and, in addition, it is the branch which, by reason of organization and function, is best fitted to assume the representative quality demanded of popular government. That it has not always done so does not vitiate the common conception of its special qualities and responsibilities.

We have attempted to set our analysis of the Florida legislature against the standards of organization and performance which seem to be inherent in the common sense conception of the way in which the American system of representative government operates.

Our presupposition is that any workable political tradition implies the existence of a certain consensus about the way in which the system is supposed to work. Although such a consensus is never universal, never fully articulated, and never wholly free from internal conflict, manifest deviations from its standards are invariably accompanied by elaborate apologies and an appeal to the "true" conception of the institution. Certain components of this ideal type may be set forth here without the refinements and elaborations that will be required in the later analysis of the actual situation in Florida.

The first and most important attribute of the American representative structure is popular sovereignty. No historical or ideological justification is necessary to recall the hold that this idea has on the imagination of American citizens. A concomitant of the idea of popular sovereignty is the conception of the right of each individual to participate in the selection of representatives unless there are valid reasons for disqualifying him. Furthermore, equality of influence among the individual participants is stressed, thus leading to the various constitutional devices (for example, periodic reapportionment) for adjusting representation to changes in the sociological structure.

The problem of translating a fairly clear ideal of popular sovereignty into a workable set of institutions involves movement into an area in which agreement in principle is less certain. Historical experiences supervene in any given case to raise problems about the representative function and the relation of the representative to his constituents. A certain ambiguity exists in these matters; virtual representation appears to be anathema to the electorate, yet the idea of a "public interest" which is more than a natural harmony of local or special interests seems to be inseparable from the conception of responsibility which the representative assembly is called on to sustain.

In one sense the particular type of party organization which is thought to be dominant in the American system compromises the conflicting claims on behalf of direct, instructed representation on the one hand and the development of a form of parliamentary majoritarianism necessary for positive government on the other. Thus the functions of the political party as a unifying agency, an educational instrument, and a means of translating the right to vote into the opportunity to make the vote effective in terms of genuine choice appear to be recognized and accepted. And the two-party system, with its tendency to promote clear legislative majorities while retaining the guarantee of nonobstructive criticism is widely regarded as the model arrangement toward which the system is directed. At the same time, however, an abstract emphasis on governmental negativism, the primary method of nomination, and the pervasive spirit of federalism (which extends far beyond the division of powers between state and national governments) work against any attempts to interpose the party between the representative and his constituency and tend to disperse effective organizational control among the smaller units in the political geography of the country. The acceptance, then, of the real or presumed advantages of two-party politics always seems to be offset by a suspicion of the oligarchic tendencies of political organization, and there is considerable opportunity for the promotion of party disintegration in the institutional arrangements of American government.

On the level of legislative organizations and functions the surface pattern is much more coherent. It is commonly expected that legislative bodies will be bicameral, that they will rely heavily on the committee system, and that their deliberations will be controlled by certain standard procedural arrangements. Even in matters on which there are wide variations among the states—size of houses, length and frequency of sessions, pay of members, etc.—criticism of the particular arrangement is likely to gravitate toward a common set of standards, such as a "wieldy" chamber, membership as a full-time occupation, and unlimited sessions. The appropriate functions of legislatures may be defined, too, in terms of certain traditional expectations, among which law-making by means of open and exhaustive deliberation and surveillance over administration are the most important. Latterly, of course, the role of executive leadership in the development and co-ordination of public policy and the budget has been taken for granted.

The manifold aspects of legislative organization and activity and the complicated interrelation among these several determinants of legislative performance are the immediate objects of our analysis.

The study is generally directed toward an understanding of the manner in which a representative system operating within a particular historical and social context adjusts (or fails to adjust) to vast changes in its sociological matrix. In a larger context, we are concerned with an explication of the overall political process in Florida and the tensions created out of a substantial divergence between ideals and practice.

Chapter 2

The Political Background:
Florida Politics

IN his pioneering study of the realities of southern state politics V. O. Key found that in Florida it is "every man for himself."[1] If there is any one thing which sets the tone of Florida politics, this is it. The fact that there are no permanent state-wide political organizations of any significance colors the whole range of political practices in the state, and not least its legislative politics.

Although usually appearing on the Democratic ticket, every man runs for himself, whether his office be a local, county, or state one. Only seldom does a candidate for one office publicly support any candidate for another. In political campaign rallies the most common statement made by the candidates is to the effect that "I am not a member of any machine"—by which is meant "slate" or "ticket." Candidates for Congress do not publicly support candidates for state offices: candidates for the legislature do not (except rarely) support gubernatorial hopefuls.

As might be suspected, the result is that such political factions as exist in Florida politics are temporary and shifting ones based on the personalities of leading politicians and/or loose coalitions depending on community of economic or political interest. Politics are personalized to an uncommon degree. And further, such a situation gives rise to the fact that state-wide candidacies tend to show highly regional voting patterns, localized around the areas where each candidate is best known. It is somewhat rare for a politician to become in the real sense a "state figure," for his political support is too localized; he must depend on certain areas for most of his votes.

The foregoing general statements about Florida's politics are too categorical to go without some attempt at proof. And their effects on the legislature need particular examination.

Florida's Political Parties

While Florida shares with the rest of the "Solid South" a general attachment to the Democratic party, it has often been remarked that in many respects the Sunshine state's politics more closely resemble a "no party system." Within the broad and vague contours of the party are encompassed all the varied political viewpoints which, in our system, generally find uneasy accommodation in the two parties. But the dominance of the Democrats in Florida has led to an obscuring of policy politics and an extreme emphasis on "office" politics: not only is each man for himself, but rather than standing for a clearly defined viewpoint, each normally is interested primarily in attaining office. The voter is left with little real idea of what he is voting for other than personality.

It is true that both political parties have the usual state-wide organization, and in many areas of the state there also exist county party groups. But in fact these are supernumerary organisms; they usually exist more or less without reference to the office-holding politicos. They are skeletal in nature and without important functions. While one might suppose that such organizations would at least handle the presidential campaigns, even this is not uniformly true. In 1956, for instance, Adlai Stevenson's campaign was deliberately kept free of the "regular" Democratic organization. The reason apparently was that the state committee of the party was not regarded as being capable of running a state-wide campaign utilizing to the full the opportunities presented by television. While by 1960 there were apparently determined efforts to bolster the state organization, these have not so far borne much fruit.

In campaigns for state and local offices, the party organization is disregarded except in certain minimal features. A too close identification with the regular organization might tar the candidate as a "machine man"—which is regarded in Florida politics as a factor that contributes more often to political defeat than to victory.

As is normal in one-party states, the primary elections assume a dual function, for they not only serve as the device for nominating the Democratic candidate, but in most parts of the state also as the real election. Normally, the winner of the Democratic primary is assured of election in the fall. In the primary campaign he runs against his opponents, who are also Democrats—so that the party organization must be officially neutral. As for the general election, the usual candidate need not campaign at all, a fact which goes far toward explaining the atrophy of the regular party as a campaign mechanism.

There are restricted areas of the state where this does not hold true, for instance Pinellas County (St. Petersburg), Sarasota County (Sarasota), Orange County (Orlando), Brevard County, and (to an increasing extent) Lee, Manatee, and Dade counties; in 1960 Charlotte County might have been added to the list. Representative William C. Cramer has been sent to Congress four times by the Republican voters of the First Congressional District, which includes St. Petersburg and Tampa; the Fifth District, including both Orlando and Brevard County, saw a close two-party race for Congress in 1956, but Democrat Sid Herlong won re-election; and Representatives James A. Haley and Paul G. Rogers had reasonably stiff competition in their west and east coast districts in 1960. Orange County in 1955 and 1961, Pinellas, Sarasota, and Brevard counties in 1957, and Charlotte in 1961 have had some or all of their state legislative delegations composed of Republicans. One might say, then, that at least four counties—Orange, Sarasota, Pinellas, and Brevard— have already developed functioning two-party systems. It is hardly accidental that these are all counties in which the population is largely composed of Yankee immigrants and that they are also comparatively heavily urbanized counties.

Nevertheless, a real two-party system is apparently far in the future for Florida, despite the fact that she favored Eisenhower in both of his campaigns and Nixon in 1960, a fact possibly related to the organizational weakness of Florida Democrats and to the defection of large numbers of Negro voters (Duval County, which has the state's largest Negro registration, went for Eisenhower by a narrow margin in 1956[2]). Outside of the counties named, Republican

candidates for state or local offices were few and far between, even
in 1956.

Regional Alignments

Both the development of Republican party strength and the
Eisenhower votes show a strong regionalism. A line drawn south-
west from Jacksonville to Cedar Key would separate rather neatly
the parts of Florida that voted for the General and for Nixon from
those that did not; it would also include all the counties mentioned
above in which Republican registration is significant. Perhaps more
important, the primary votes for United States Senator and for governor show the same regional pattern. In the gubernatorial primary
of 1948, South Florida supported Dan McCarty for governor, while
the winner, Fuller Warren, was strongest in the north. The same
alignment brought victory to South Florida's favorite, LeRoy Collins, in 1954 and 1956,[3] and with some changes in proportion the
pattern showed once more in the Bryant-Carlton second primary
in 1960.

There is some indication, however, that the pattern of voting,
at least in state politics, is less a regional affair than it is an
indication of a rural-urban conflict. In 1948, for instance, Warren
carried most of the South Florida counties which are predominantly
rural; but the only urban counties he carried were Escambia (Pensacola) and Duval (Jacksonville) in North Florida, and Hillsborough
(Tampa). He lost the entire tourist area on the east coast. In the
1956 primaries, Collins received over 35 per cent of the vote in
every urban county and over 50 per cent in all but Escambia and
Duval counties; on the other hand, he received less than 50 per
cent in nineteen of the nonurban counties south of the line described
above.[4] In 1960 this pattern was confused by the fact that the
"liberal" candidate, Doyle Carlton, was from rural South Florida;
consequently he received heavy support all over South Florida.

South Florida appears to be moving north, for voting trends in
the "border counties" in 1956—counties which Key, Herbert Doherty
and Hugh Price have included in North Florida—showed significant
strength both for Collins and for Eisenhower.[5] These counties are

Duval, Clay, Alachua, and Marion particularly. Nixon also had a majority in Alachua, while he had over 45 per cent of the votes in Duval, Clay, and Marion. It is significant that Duval is a highly urbanized county, while both Alachua and Marion have recently

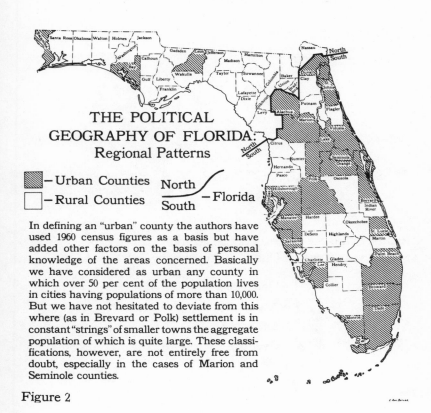

THE POLITICAL
GEOGRAPHY OF FLORIDA:
Regional Patterns

– Urban Counties North
– Rural Counties ——— – Florida
                 South

In defining an "urban" county the authors have used 1960 census figures as a basis but have added other factors on the basis of personal knowledge of the areas concerned. Basically we have considered as urban any county in which over 50 per cent of the population lives in cities having populations of more than 10,000. But we have not hesitated to deviate from this where (as in Brevard or Polk) settlement is in constant "strings" of smaller towns the aggregate population of which is quite large. These classifications, however, are not entirely free from doubt, especially in the cases of Marion and Seminole counties.

Figure 2

found that their county seats have become rather large towns with a majority or close to it of the counties' populations. Gainesville (Alachua) has a clear population majority and is the seat of the state university, which gives it a somewhat cosmopolitan and urban feeling. Ocala (Marion) is a growing and important tourist center, with the motel-restaurant interests which are so typical of South Florida.

The rural-urban pattern is not entirely unambiguous, however, for obviously the voting tendency in Duval and Escambia counties has not been affected as strongly as the South Florida urban centers. As a matter of conjecture, it seems probable that in these

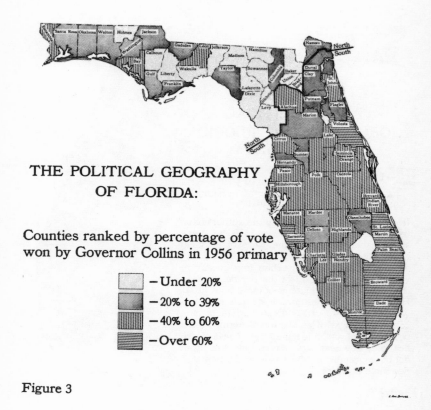

THE POLITICAL GEOGRAPHY
OF FLORIDA:

Counties ranked by percentage of vote
won by Governor Collins in 1956 primary

    — Under 20%
    — 20% to 39%
    — 40% to 60%
    — Over 60%

Figure 3

urbanized counties the "Old South" historical and social background is still strong enough to prevent the dominance of clearly urban interests, partly because the new settlers are mostly from rural Georgia and Alabama. Thus the effect is one of a combination rural-urban and North-South political cleavage.

This cleavage can be shown in other ways than by examining the votes in state-wide campaigns for public office. For instance, Price has shown a striking similarity between the pattern described above and attitudes on the Negro issue,[6] and our studies of the legislative votes on segregation questions in 1957 very clearly reveal the same phenomenon. The accompanying maps attempt to show in a composite manner the regional pattern on segregation issue votes

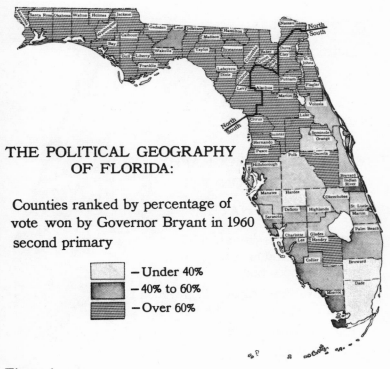

THE POLITICAL GEOGRAPHY
OF FLORIDA:

Counties ranked by percentage of
vote won by Governor Bryant in 1960
second primary

- Under 40%
- 40% to 60%
- Over 60%

Figure 4

in the 1957 regular session of the Florida legislature. The first of these issues was an interposition resolution.[7] In the senate there were eighteen votes indicating an opposition to the resolution. Of these, only two came from north of the base line used above, and of twenty senators representing at least partially urban districts, fourteen voted against interposition. In the house vote on the same issue, seven of twenty-eight North Florida representatives opposed interposition as against twenty-two of sixty-seven South Florida delegates—not a very significant regional differentiation. But on a rural-urban basis, a very significant pattern showed up, for only six of forty-seven representatives of rural counties voted against the resolution, while twenty-three of forty-eight urban representatives took that step.

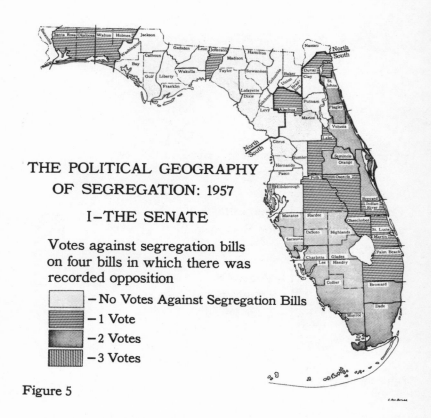

THE POLITICAL GEOGRAPHY OF SEGREGATION: 1957

I—THE SENATE

Votes against segregation bills on four bills in which there was recorded opposition

— No Votes Against Segregation Bills
— 1 Vote
— 2 Votes
— 3 Votes

Figure 5

The same distinction shows up clearly in a study of the votes on reapportionment in the 1955 special session. Considered on the basis of a strictly North-South cleavage, these votes do not indicate too much. For instance, on Senate Bill 9-X, the senate on June 10, 1955, passed the measure by a vote of twenty to eighteen. This particular proposal did not meet with the governor's approval and was unsuccessful in the house. North Florida senators voted four-

teen to six in favor of the bill, while South Florida opposed it sixteen to two. On a rural-urban basis, fifteen rural senators voted for
the bill, only three against; and fifteen urban senators opposed it, while
only five favored it.[8]

In the house vote on House Bill 6-X (which probably repre-

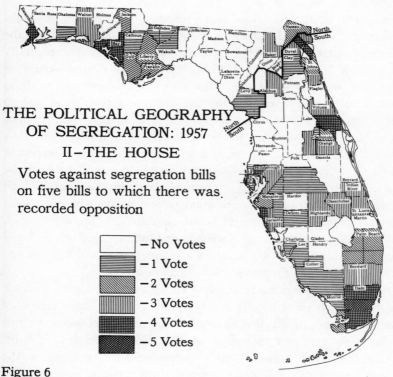

THE POLITICAL GEOGRAPHY
OF SEGREGATION: 1957
II—THE HOUSE

Votes against segregation bills
on five bills to which there was.
recorded opposition

— No Votes
— 1 Vote
— 2 Votes
— 3 Votes
— 4 Votes
— 5 Votes

Figure 6

sented the governor's viewpoint), taken on a tabling motion, the
rural-urban cleavage showed up even more prominently. North
Florida representatives opposed the bill twenty-nine to four, while
South Florida supported it only thirty-seven to twenty-one. But representatives from rural counties opposed this reapportionment measure forty to four while urban legislators favored it thirty-seven to ten.
(Three of four abstentions were urban representatives.)[9]

What emerges from this analysis of regionalism in Florida
politics is a significant but complex combination of rural versus
urban political interests with an older and possibly diminishing conflict of North Florida—representing the old ante bellum slave-own-
ing South—and South Florida, which is "New" Florida, Yankee-
dominated and tourist-centered. These two patterns of conflict cut
across each other in a complicated fashion, but some of the
effects are clear. More and more, the major state-wide elections
reflect the voting dominance of urban South Florida, and the
result is that the governor in recent times—and this is particularly
true in the cases of Dan McCarty and LeRoy Collins—tends to
represent the interests of the urban voters. Even rural or semi-rural
candidates like C. Farris Bryant in 1960 are forced to appeal to
the urban vote if they are to have any hope of success. This does not
mean that governors are likely to be political liberals, but they
are likely to stand for the needs and desires of the urban centers as
against the hostility to those desires found in the rural parts of the
state. This is likely to mean, in practice, governors who sponsor high
taxes, better highways, governmental reform at the state and local
levels, the institutionalizing of county government, legislative reapportionment, constitutional revision, and an acceptance of racial
integration (or if not an acceptance of integration, at least an unwillingness to take the more drastic steps to prevent it).

It is well, however, to be cautious enough not to assign a monistic
factor as the basis of Florida politics. Many political issues inevitably
cut across the rural-urban cleavage. But more important at this
point is the fact that the urban areas of Florida are strikingly different *from each other,* as, to a somewhat lesser extent, are the
rural zones. These differences, existing within the framework of a
general similarity, may produce striking divergences of interest and
political action.

One can easily point to several illustrations of these differences:
among the urban areas, Pensacola is an industrial center and the
home of a large naval base; Jacksonville is the leading seaport and
rail center of the state as well as an insurance center of great
importance, and yet it retains a good many "Old South" attitudes;
Miami thrives on the great winter tourist trade from the North; while

St. Petersburg is a haven for northern-retired people and has little industry. Differences of interest between these urban areas are inevitable. In the rural areas there are the significant differences presented by the fact that while one region is a center of ante bellum cotton culture, another raises tobacco, while still others concentrate on cattle raising, citrus production, truck farming, or the raising of slash pine for pulp.

Such heterogeneity prevents the growth of a duopolistic political factionalism as striking as might exist in a state in which there is only one large urban center arrayed against a largely rural hinterland which is fairly homogeneous.

In consequence, the comments herein concerning the rural-urban political cleavage in Florida should not be taken as a simplistic explanation of a political system which is far too complex to be explained so casually. Nevertheless, it is our opinion that the rural-urban cleavage is at once the most basic and the most far-reaching aspect of present day politics in the state.

Given the fact (to be examined thoroughly in a later chapter) that the legislature is stacked in favor of the rural counties by the apportionment system, it is practically inevitable that there is going to be conflict between the governor and the legislature—more of it than would be accounted for by the separation of powers or by the mere fact that the governor speaks for the entire state while each legislator speaks only for a small part of it. As a matter of fact, it seems probable that the executive-legislative conflict will increase rather than diminish in the future, at least until such time as some effective reapportionment takes place and the race problem diminishes in importance.

Another result is that the pressure *against* reapportionment becomes nearly insuperable. For the combination of North Florida with rural dominance in the legislature makes it almost inconceivable that any real change in the balance of legislative power will ever be permitted unless it is forced from outside; any apportionment legislation or amendment has to be approved by the very people who will lose power if it *is* approved.

The urban South Florida representatives, then, find themselves in a permanent minority status even though they represent a substantial majority of the state's population. For this reason, the rural-urban cleavage does not show up as clearly on many issues as one might expect, for the urban legislators are forced to fit themselves into the pattern of rural politics: they must horse-trade on a personal basis since their factional strength is not great enough to achieve very much. Horse-trading, of course, means that for every act to benefit urban interests the legislator must agree to support legislation favored by the "pork chop gang," the county courthouse clique, the economy bloc, or some other such group.

Factions—Personal and Otherwise

It is well known that electoral factions are almost nonexistent in Florida politics. This does not mean, however, that a candidate runs without support or opposition from other politicians. In practice, he may be publicly supported or opposed by politicians who are not at the time holding or running for elective office. Brailey Odham, for instance—a man who had been ·defeated in a previous try for the governorship—strongly supported LeRoy Collins in the 1956 primary campaign, as did "Ted" David, the retiring speaker of the house, who was (rightly) suspected of harboring gubernatorial ambitions for 1960.

Locally, candidates for the legislature often have the behind-the-scenes support or opposition of the other members of their legislative delegations. As in one instance, it is said (without verification) that Representative Ralph Turlington of Alachua County was opposed for re-election in 1954 by Senator "Bill" Shands of the same county. There is a good deal of authority also for believing that Shands and several other "porkchoppers" converged on St. Augustine in May of 1956 to work for the opponent of Senator Verle Pope, perhaps the ablest and certainly the most articulate of the urban-bloc representatives in the senate. Such claims are difficult to verify, however, since there is a pronounced attempt to keep opposition or support strictly non-public.

Under such conditions, each candidate is forced to conduct his own hunt for votes without the aid of a party or factional ticket and without the help of other prominent politicians in any public sense. He must find his own financial support—a circumstance which may make him easy prey to pressure groups willing for reasons of their own to finance his campaign. Old legislative hands tell of the time when a substantial number of legislators had their campaign expenses paid by a leading lumber corporation, and the story goes that the lobbyist for this corporation had these legislators' votes in his pocket in the ensuing session of the legislature.

The election expense laws make it possible to make some shrewd guesses as to which private interests are supporting candidates. It was well known in 1956 that General Sumter Lowry's primary campaign was being financed by DuPont interests. C. Farris Bryant was forced to curtail his 1956 campaign because of lack of funds— a defect induced, no doubt, by the fact that the sources of money were sure he could not win and did not wish to waste their money on his candidacy. In the same campaign it was said that Fuller Warren was financed by the race-track interests.

The nearest thing to "party control" in political campaigns seems to be the practice in county campaigns of having the party organizations sponsor rallies at which all the candidates will appear. Typically, however, at these rallies the air is filled with disclaimers of any political alliances.

The most a candidate can do under such conditions is to build up his own personal political organization. Most such organizations, however, are extremely unstable and transient. They must ordinarily be rebuilt before each election campaign. They are not transferable— Key, for instance, points out that the political support of a candidate for one office is not often transferable to campaigns for another office by the same person.[10] Key's statement, however, is limited to state-wide offices and does not apply to the legislature, where it is quite common for a house member to be able to use his voting support to transfer to the state senate. What is unusual is for a governor to be able to keep his support after his single term in office. It is rare for him to be able to hold it over four interim years and come back to the gubernatorial mansion, and equally as rare for him to be able to transfer it effectively enough to jump into the United States Senate. This is evidently another element in the general weakness of Florida governors. For not only must they depend on and cultivate personal political allegiance, but they also must do so in the knowledge that if they wish to run again or for a different office they will have to do the job all over again. In addition, such electoral support as a successful gubernatorial candidate may build up is subject to two principal defects after he settles down in Tallahassee. First, much of his support evaporates the day after the election; second, so much of his support nowadays usually comes from populous urban South Florida that it is never more than partially transferable into legislative support either in terms of prestige or of power.

This lack of permanent political alignments has a pronounced effect on the way the legislature operates. It obviously means comparatively weak leadership from the chief executive. More than that, it means that factional alignments are built up *inside the legislature after the election.* From the standpoint of democratic responsibility such a system has little to recommend it. The general public is buying a pig in a poke when it votes, for it knows not what sort of alignments will be made. While newspapers speak rather loosely of the "pork chop gang" or the "economy bloc," the average voter is in no position to find out who belongs to these groups, for not only are they informal, but they also shift at each session and with each issue. A governor must build up a new group of supporters for each bill he sponsors—including new floor leadership; any legislator trying to get a bill passed must scurry around the floor picking up his support as he may by skillful compromise and trading. There is no organization through which to work. Personality thus becomes unusually important, as do the positions of the presiding officers of each house, for to them are given the powers, usually residing in the majority party, of picking committees and their chairmen. Being a friend or trusted ally of the presiding officer is a valuable asset to a legislator. It was often pointed out in 1957 that the election of Representative Tom Beasley as speaker-designate for the 1959 session (he was formally elected the first day of the 1957 session) and his position as 1957 Rules Committee chairman put the other members in a position where they had to be very careful not to offend him, for he would be in a position to discriminate against them in committee assignments in 1959.[11]

The lack of organization has still another important effect, especially when combined with the inevitable rush of a short session and the consequent inability of the legislature to study bills thoroughly; it leaves a rather pronounced political vacuum into which the lobbyist is only too happy to rush. E. E. Schattschneider has remarked that the legislator "escapes from the authority of the party only to fall prey to the organized special interests."[12] Unable to rely on party leadership or support, the legislator tends to take at face value the claims of pressure interests, especially when he believes they are strong in his constituency. This is nowhere more obvious than in Florida attitudes on race questions: no one knows how many legislators have voted for white-supremacy legislation because of the fear—assiduously cultivated by small groups of highly vocal people—that they might be thrown out of office by their voters. Only Representative John Orr of Dade County was willing to put this to the test; his re-election in 1956 was not reassuring to the other members because he came from an atypical district and clearly and openly relied on the disaffected labor and minority groups for his support (in addition, he was defeated in 1958). A strong party organization might be able to take a stand of some sort on such a question and thus give the legislator some political and moral backing. Lacking such support, the representative turns to the readiest available source of information and of persuasion: the pressure group.

Issue-Politics in Florida

V. O. Key gives only minor importance to issue divisions in Florida politics.[13] It is the feeling of the present authors, however, that issues and issue-oriented factions are of somewhat more importance than Key believes. It is true that such factions are neither clearly organized nor readily identifiable, but they may be of some importance even so. The difficulty is that there is no simple, clear-cut liberal versus conservative split; the actual cleavage is at least a four-way one with all the complexities implied by such multiplicity.

One may illustrate by reference to the experience of former Senator Claude Pepper. Pepper was an extreme liberal (at least for Florida) who served in the United States Senate from 1936 to 1950. In 1958 he failed miserably in an attempt to regain his seat; the common feeling was that his defeat came because "he can be attacked in South Florida for his tough attitude toward business and in North Florida for being soft on the Negro problem." Price concludes that "the integrated social and economic liberal . . . has little chance" in Florida politics.[14] But the situation may be different locally, for Pepper was able to gain nomination for a new seat in Congress from Miami in 1962.

What this seems to mean is that Old Florida still retains enough of the old Populist feeling so that an economic liberal—antimonopoly type—can appeal successfully to its voters on such issues. New Florida, however, is heavily business-oriented but not industralized enough for labor to act as an effective counterweight to business conservatism. Tourism is the major industry of New Florida, but it employs few of the type of workers who would be interested in union activity. Consequently except for a few of the large metropolitan districts—principally Tampa and Miami—labor is an almost negligible factor. In state-wide elections it is the South Florida conservative Chamber of Commerce type candidate who stands the best chance, for that is where the votes are.

At the same time, however, the 1956 and 1960 primary campaigns for governor seemed to indicate that a candidate cannot successfully appeal to the South Florida vote on a platform solely or primarily consisting of racial segregation appeals. Yet such appeals may strongly attract the North Florida voters of the ante bellum slave-holding counties, especially when combined with a certain personalized social welfarism. Price sums this up strikingly in the following words:

> If the color line can only be maintained at the cost of adverse national publicity, a weakened school system, decreased business confidence, higher school bond rates, and the other likely results of extremist action, then that is the price that many people in North Florida are willing to pay. South Florida, which would stand to suffer the most from the repercussions of an extremist policy, may not favor desegregation but is certainly not willing to make every sacrifice to avoid it.[15]

We find then a complex issue lineup in Florida. The liberal of South Florida is likely to be a social liberal but not an economic liberal: a point illustrated in the Florida legislature by such men as Senator Verle Pope of St. Johns County or Senator (former Representative) Sam Gibbons of Hillsborough. On the other hand the North Florida liberal is likely to retain at least a slight Populist tinge in economic matters but is completely intransigent on social change— a type perhaps well illustrated by Senator John Rawls of Marianna County and Representative J. S. Alexander of Liberty County.

Is there such a thing as a thorough-going liberal or conservative in Florida politics? Such a liberal as Pepper stands little chance in a state-wide election today, as was illustrated in his 1958 primary campaign against Senator Spessard L. Holland. However, his localized success in the Democratic congressional campaign in Miami in 1962 illustrates how shifting the sands of regional politics are in the state, for Pepper was heretofore the darling of the Populist, cut-over pine woods sectors. There are perhaps a few isolated localities where local politicians can win even though they are such liberals—the case of Representative John Orr of Miami was an outstanding example until his defeat in 1958. On the other hand, the integrated social and economic *conservative* can, to some extent, make the best of both worlds. Governor Collins has illustrated the technique by which this is done: you simply emphasize your business conservatism, which attracts the South Florida vote, and add enough segregationism so as not to alienate too many others. The combination of race prejudice and conservatism is quite common in the legislature. Representative C. Farris Bryant, now governor, was a prominent example in the 1956 special session; Representative "Bill" Chappell, 1961 speaker, and Representative Mallory Horne, speaker-designate for 1963, were prominent for this feature in 1957. This type of conservatism has been well described by Jasper Shannon, who points out that "as an order, the Democratic party has a creed inherited from the non-industrial past, . . . but the ancient institution is not a going concern which presents alternative programs to that offered by a big business dominated Republican party."[16]

As in all politics, one must speak of tendencies rather than certainties. There will always be some exceptions to the general statements made above. And the more so in Florida during the past decade, for the state is in a pronounced transitional period. Although it has recently become a predominantly urban state, its urban population is not yet—if it ever will be—like that of the North. For one thing, there is no pronounced industrial working class; for another, many of the city people have recently left the farms of Florida, Georgia, and Alabama, and have not yet lost the habit of thinking in rural patterns. Yet again, there are large numbers of Northerners who have come to Florida either to engage in tourist enterprises or to retire. Their conservatism is pronounced and unreflective, particularly in economic affairs; many of them, it has often been noted, also assimilate southern racial attitudes very rapidly.

If one can speak in terms of political types, the rising generation of Florida politicians is best exemplified by such men as former Governor Collins and Senator George A. Smathers, and in the legislature by Representatives Chappell and Horne. These are what might be called "Chamber of Commerce" types—smooth, outwardly sophisticated, skilled in the modern political techniques of radio and television, and making a virtue of a conservative moderation on the Eisenhower model. The cracker politician like Fuller Warren or Claude Pepper is dead except in certain local areas. The new politician tends rather strongly, we believe, to play down issues unless he is certain of their public acceptance—a characteristic which is only different in degree from those of his predecessor, perhaps, except that the Madison Avenue touch which lends itself so well to television campaigning makes it much more effective than it used to be.

If the race question is regarded as a temporary political issue which will be more or less settled within the foreseeable future—a diagnosis which may now be considered as more than a hope— then it may be possible that a real issue-politics will develop in Florida at least to the same extent that it exists in other states. It will foster the growth of a two-party system and will at the same time be a beneficiary of that growth. Up to now, however, the race question has cut so strongly across all politics that it has inevitably blurred any factions which might otherwise be built up along issue lines: except for John Orr, no Florida politician has had the political courage or vision to favor integration.

The Negro in Florida Politics

The race question, then, at present cuts across all factionalism in Florida politics; all groups participating in elective politics are segregationist in some degree except perhaps the Negroes themselves. To what extent segregationist policies express the real convictions of such leaders as Fuller Warren and LeRoy Collins is problematical, but as politicians they apparently feel they have been forced to more extreme positions than they would take as private citizens. The extremism of Sumter Lowry colored the entire 1956 gubernatorial campaign, and it pulled Collins so far from his earlier moderate position that it is really doubtful that the result was a victory even for moderation, much less for acceptance of the necessity for integration. It was very noticeable that Collins' real attitudes were subordinated in this campaign, for once he was elected and had become ineligible for re-election, he became a moderate again.

This might seem to indicate that the only role the Negro plays in politics is a negative one. Such a diagnosis, however, is at best partially true; for Negroes do vote in Florida in relatively large numbers and consequently play a rather important part in elections, particularly in certain local areas of heavy registration. In general, however, the place of the Negro in politics is a peripheral one, since it is confined to voting (no Negro holds elective public office in Florida today) and even in voting the peculiar nature of Florida politics tends to restrict somewhat the importance of the Negro vote. Hugh Price, who has written an excellent study of this subject, contends that politics, "by its tendency toward a fluid sort of factionalism . . . makes balance of power politics impracticable" on the part of Negroes, "there being no fixed centers of power to be balanced."[17]

Enough Negroes register and vote in Florida to constitute a major, though largely imponderable, force in politics. In 1960 almost 10 per cent of Florida's registered voters were Negroes—a significant proportion of the electorate in any close campaign. There seems to be little difference, by and large, between rural and urban areas in this registration, although until recently there was a strong tendency for the counties which once had more Negroes than whites —counties mostly situated in North Florida between the Suwannee and Apalachicola rivers—to show very low registration. In addition to active leadership by Negroes, there appear to have been some cases —especially in Duval and Dade counties—where white politicians have had something to do with fostering the Negro vote. This process has gone farther in Duval (Jacksonville) than anywhere else; since 1947, according to Price, Negro voters have been playing a "decisive" role in elections there, as may be indicated by the fact that for the first time in its history Duval County plumped for a Republican presidential candidate in 1956.[18] But the major importance of the Negro vote in Jacksonville seems to be in local elections. As Price points out, a candidate elected with substantial Negro support is likely to be responsive to Negro interests to some extent; at the same time, the immediate stake for Negroes is likely to lie in the performance of the duties of the sheriff and other local offices which touch their lives intimately. As a result more political interest is shown in such offices—particularly if one candidate has a reputation for discriminatory or cruel treatment of Negroes.[19]

Significant though the Negro vote may be in a few local areas and in state-wide campaigns, it is nevertheless true that it plays little part in legislative elections.[20] It is true that there are a few counties where the Negro vote seems to have a significant impact on legislative conduct: again, Duval County provides the chief example, since the Duval delegation as a whole seems less extremely segregationist than many despite the presence of many Negroes in the county. But only one representative has consistently voted for the extension of Negro rights. He was John Orr of Dade County. While Orr seemed to rely heavily on the Dade County Negro vote, this does not explain why other politicians from his own county and from others with heavy Negro votes do not do the same. Even Orr did not publicly court the Negro vote, and Senator Pepper was defeated in 1950 partly because of charges that he did. Apparently the Negro vote is not large enough in most counties to make a sig-

nificant impact, or else the difference between candidates on the
Negro issue has been so slight that the Negroes themselves are split
and do not know whom to support. In addition, the fact that the
majority of the legislators come from rural counties where, all
things considered, Negro voting is less of a factor, may explain the
intransigence of the legislature on the subject. The weakness of
the Negro at the ballot box is indicated by the fact that there is
little or no correlation between legislative attitudes and the proportion of the Negro vote to the total vote in the legislative districts.

These attitudes plus the malapportionment which throws control
of the legislature into rural North Florida hands give the Negro
little to hope for from the Florida legislative process, and the
string of race legislation which was passed in the 1956 special
session and in the 1957 and 1959 regular sessions would seem
to justify colored voters in paying little attention to legislative campaigns. It seems inevitable, as Price concludes, that groups which demand things which the apportionment system makes the legislature
bound to reject will "eventually turn to the popularly elected executive or to the courts for action. The long-run result is lower prestige
for the legislature and conflict between executive and legislature."[21]

Such intergovernmental conflict over the race problem has already appeared in Florida. In the 1956 special session the legislature,
under the leadership of C. Farris Bryant (now governor) was obviously willing and eager to go farther in passing restrictive legislation than was Governor Collins; only a timely dissolution of the
session by the governor prevented the passage of an interposition
resolution.[22] In 1957 the resolution was one of the first pieces of
legislation to be passed,[23] and the legislature then went on to consider seriously even more drastic legislation: to try to restrict Negro
access to the courts[24] and even to authorize the closing of the public
school system under certain conditions.[25] The governor retaliated by
threatening to veto such laws.[26] It should, however, be noted that
extremism builds up its own opposition, even in the legislature. It
was notable that the 1956 measures passed almost unanimously
through both houses; they were sponsored by a study commission
and approved by the governor. But the more extreme measures of

the 1957 session, which were sponsored by extremists in the legislature and opposed by the governor, were passed, if at all, by greatly reduced margins.

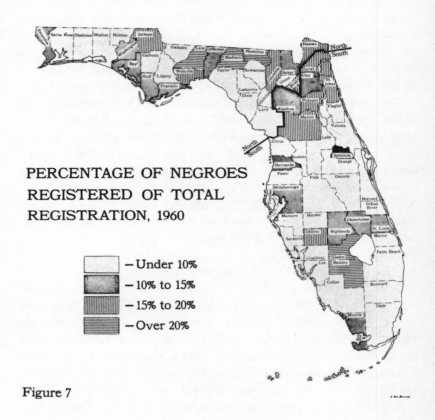

PERCENTAGE OF NEGROES
REGISTERED OF TOTAL
REGISTRATION, 1960

— Under 10%
— 10% to 15%
— 15% to 20%
— Over 20%

Figure 7

The Legislature and the Courthouse Clique

In view of the fact that members of the legislature are elected from counties, it would be natural to expect that they would be identified with the courthouse politicians in their home counties, especially in the rural areas. While this connection cannot be definitely established, the incomplete available information indicates that at least half of the 133 legislators have held previous public positions indicating some such identification.[27] Our assumption is that quite a few more have actually risen through courthouse politics. If this is true, legislative politics is likely to reflect to some extent the nature of politics in the counties, and further, it would seem a logical presumption that in matters on which the rural county politicians feel strongly the legislators would be likely to accede to their desires.

Jasper Shannon has written a stimulating essay on the nature of the governing classes in southern county seat towns.[28] He points out that after the Civil War the locus of political power in the South shifted from the plantations to the county seats, accompanied by a drastic change in the nature of this leadership. The county seat politicians were dominated by business ethics and the desire for pecuniary rewards.

> The creed of this banker-merchant-farmer-lawyer-doctor govern-
> ing class is worthy of study. It explains more about southern
> politics than any analysis of structure can possibly do, though it
> is the decentralization of power into these semirural units which
> makes its existence possible. . . . The member of the governing
> group will be a joiner. He will probably belong to the church,
> in many cases be a leading member, probably an officer. He will
> observe the religious forms and pass the collection plate on Sun-
> day. During the rest of the week his religion may be stored away
> unless he sings in the choir or belongs to the quartette which
> sings at funerals. Occasionally he may attend a church convention,
> and, upon demand, he can pray acceptably in public, frequently
> making up in quantity what his supplications lack in quality. He
> may even pray about the brotherhood of man, but in his day-to-day
> activities he may like others overlook his conscience in the interest
> of business. "This is a business proposition, you know" will be
> his approach to a client and his reproach to a meddlesome con-
> science.[29]

The county seat elite, moreover, is practical—which translated means conservative, "accepting current political and social behavior without questioning its major premises."[30] It is probusiness and anti-labor; it is anti-intellectual and wants its schools old-fashioned and inexpensive. A member of this elite "offers lip-service to the demo-cratic credo of liberty, equality, and majority rule, but to his way of thinking liberty has nothing to do with labor leaders or college professors, and equality does not include people with black skins."[31]

There is, however, a certain amount of ambivalence in this social background, for the governing class "is caught between the industrial and agrarian mores."[32] Its rural background leads it to distrust and dislike the industrial way of life—it may strenuously resist the idea of attracting factories to the county seat. But on the other hand as business men the members of this class must fit themselves into the ethics of a business society. They have an extremely strong respect for property, says Shannon, without any real aristocratic *noblesse oblige,* for the elite "is not incapable of a *beau geste* in a community chest drive or at a charity bazaar, but it is careful to keep its assessments low and thereby contributes to low standards of schools and other public services."[33]

"The leaders control the election process and thereby keep political and economic power alike in their own hands. In this fashion they keep assessments down, tax rates fixed, and the schools in proper hands."[34] Thus does Shannon sum up the position and values of the county seat governing class. While his analysis is confined to the South, and ours to Florida, northern readers may detect a striking similarity to their own rural and small town politics. The pattern is an American one rather than a regional one.

It is plain that the ethics of the county seat as here described is also the ethics of the Florida legislature, or at least of the dominant North Florida rural majority. There is nothing about the so-called "pork chop gang" or the "economy bloc" which is inconsistent with the set of values herein described. "Porkchopism" means favors to the ruling groups; "economy" means keeping taxes low—especially those taxes which fall on the same group. Spending by government is bad because it means higher taxes—unless the beneficiary of the spending happens to be the local businessman rather than workers or public school children. There is nothing much wrong with a sales tax, but property owners are already being bled to death by the property levies. This is the state of mind with which many legislators approach their problems. The poor deserve no help from government—else why are they poor? But the well-to-do, having demonstrated their deserving qualities, may properly apply for and receive benefits from government.

Several incidents taken from Florida politics may serve to illustrate the influence of the "county seat mentality" on the Florida legislature. One concerns the rather numerous bills appearing in the 1957 session having to do with party loyalty. It seems that in one east coast county a tax collector, having emerged victorious from a close race against a Republican opponent who had apparently just turned Republican in order to make the campaign, pledged himself to "get a law through the legislature" preventing candidates from running on a party ticket unless they had been members of that party for some time! Since such situations have not been uncommon in recent years in those counties where Republicanism is growing (Representative William C. Coleman of Orange County, who sat in the 1955 session, had always been a Democrat prior to his successful campaign on the Republican ticket), the legislature has responded to this and similar pleas by considering party loyalty bills and some approach to stricter primary laws.[35]

Another incident goes back several years. A sheriff had died in office, and under Florida law appointments to vacancies in county elective offices are filled by the governor. Florida has developed a sort of minor-league version of senatorial courtesy, in which the county delegations have a strong say as to whom the governor will appoint to fill such vacancies. But apparently the courthouse clique has a great deal to say about it, for in this case the state senator went into hiding so as to isolate himself from courthouse pressure until he had gained some idea of who he himself would favor for the position!

It was, moreover, extremely noticeable in at least one bill before the 1957 session that the Florida legislator often pays great heed to the desires of his county's political leaders. The proposal was to have the state take over the burden of paying for rights of way for state highways—a rather onerous load which had been theretofore paid for by the counties. In the debate on the proposal, which would cost the state an estimated $30,000,000 for the biennium, almost every speaker (both pro and con) referred to the attitudes on the bill of his county commission, and the opposition claimed to have secured the assent of Lewis Hall, the legal representative of the state association of county commissions, to a compromise proposal.[36]

Then again, Florida is one of those states still placing no serious limitations on local bills. The result is that general laws are often negated for particular counties because of courthouse pressures, and in general that county legislative delegations feel almost obligated to support in the legislature any bill desired by their courthouse politicians. Since local bills traditionally are not questioned if they have the unanimous support of the county delegation, their passage is normally assured—which means in practice that the county seat politicos can get from the legislature pretty much what they want.

Political Effects of the Cabinet System

Florida's cabinet system is a unique and in some ways an anomalous institution. No other state has an institutionalized cabinet which exercises power as a collective body. This unusual body has a pronounced effect on legislative politics, in terms of its collective capacity, of its individual members, and of its effect on the governor's leadership powers.

As a body, the cabinet is composed of the six elected executive officials of the state: the governor, secretary of state, attorney general, commissioner of agriculture, superintendent of education, and comptroller. Among these, the governor, while theoretically most important, actually is likely to sit as a junior partner. For while a governor can serve only one term, all the others are eligible for indefinite re-election. It is usual for the governor to be the youngest man, both in years and in executive service, on the cabinet. The older members tend to regard him as a political tyro and as a temporary phenomenon, to be suffered with patience during his short tenure. Commissioner of Agriculture Nathan Mayo, who served in this capacity from 1923 to 1960, saw approximately nine governors come and go. The governor's vote in the cabinet counts for no more than anyone else's. His influence is perhaps less than that of each of several other members.

The political longevity of the other cabinet members—only four times since 1885 has one of these gentlemen failed to get himself re-elected if he wished to be—gives them an unparalleled opportunity to build political machines. In addition, most of them have rather specific "clienteles" upon which they can count for all-out political support. The commissioner of agriculture is in a strong position because his support among the farmers and farm suppliers is concentrated in the same areas from which the majority of the legislators come—the rural counties. Commissioner Mayo took care to keep his fences mended; he published a newsy "swap sheet" which circulated heavily in farming areas. The superintendent of education has the support of the county boards of education and the teachers' organizations, which are unusually potent in Florida. The comptroller and the treasurer can count on the bankers to stand behind them. The attorney general can bank on the county courthouse officials.

Not only does this kind of support mean easy re-election, but it also makes it possible for these cabinet members to exert a surprising amount of influence in the legislature. Veteran legislators tell of receiving phone calls from all the bankers in their districts when the comptroller was putting on the pressure. It is almost axiomatic in Tallahassee that the legislature will pass any legislation which is seriously pushed by one of the more powerful cabinet officials. So powerful are they, in fact, that they are often able to dictate to the governor the choice of their successors—in which case they may resign in the middle of a term so that the successor will be able to build up his own political support before he must submit himself to the electorate. Perhaps their negative power is even greater than their positive power; it is seldom that a cabinet member must submit to a bill which he has opposed. And if it comes to a test of strength between the governor and the cabinet—or even part of the cabinet—it is not at all certain that the governor will win. In the 1957 legislature the governor sponsored a central purchasing bill, which went sailing through the house committee in a matter of a half-hour; but when the house found that the cabinet—or some of it—opposed the bill, it was recalled by the committee and amended so as to meet the objections.[37] The governor had to submit as gracefully as possible to the partial emasculation of his bill.

On the other hand, the cabinet system has this strong point: when the members stand together they become a political influence which is very difficult for the legislature to resist. The cabinet finds strength in unity. If the governor, then, can mass the rest of the cabinet behind him on particular proposals, he may feel fairly confident that the legislature will accede to his suggestions.

State Politics and the Legislature

In this chapter an attempt has been made to consider the major aspects of politics in Florida and to draw the connections between politics in general and politics in the legislature. It may be well to summarize some of the major politicial influences which help to determine what kind of legislative process the people of Florida get.

The lack of well-organized parties is responsible for several rather unusual characteristics of the legislature: this unorganized state politics is reflected in the representative body in the absence of organized party groups or factions and the resultant dominantly personal mode of operation. The weakness of party organization is also a contributing factor in the general debility of executive leadership, so that the legislature is either left leaderless or is forced to depend to a marked degree on the activities of pressure politicians or the leadership of a few unrepresentative but long-lived legislators. It has also been found that the unique cabinet system contributes to the weakness of the governor and that the race problem seems to draw together many of the disparate personalities and splinter groups in the legislature.

The Citizen's Role in Florida Politics

Although, as in all democratic polities, a great deal of lip-service is paid to the importance of the individual in Florida, it is to be feared that his actual significance is not as great as much democratic theory presupposes. For in modern mass democracies the individual tends to be submerged in the competition of private groups and political organizations; a citizen who wishes to be of even minor political significance finds he can ordinarily do so only as a member or representative of some group which for any of a number of reasons can exert influence in politics.

Even the minimal duty of the individual citizen—voting—loses much of its significance when considered in the light of Florida politics. This is true not least because of the absence of effective party competition at most levels and particularly in state and local politics. It means that much of the time no electoral contest is fought over differing issues or ideologies, and often, that there is little to choose between the incumbent Representative Scylla running for re-election, and the challenger Mr. Charybdis, who for no apparent reason except personal ambition wishes to replace him in Tallahassee. Faced with such an absence of choice it is not surprising that large numbers of voters even in contested elections fail to exercise their franchise. It should perhaps be noted, however, that this voluntary self-disfranchisement makes the votes of those who do turn out more significant. It is not unusual for less than a fourth of the population to vote: in Alachua County's legislative election in 1956 only a sixth voted even in the one contested election.

The peculiarities of Florida politics account also for the fact that some votes count more than others. If a Floridian wishes to maximize his voting power, it is wise for him to make sure that he is: (1) white, (2) a Democrat, and (3) a rural resident whose county has a traditionally low voter turnout. If, in addition, he can control the votes of a large number of relatives, he may be able to play a large role in deciding who will serve in county offices as well as in the state's house of representatives. It is obvious that the urban voter thus loses in significance both absolutely (because of the large number of urban voters) and relatively (because of the disproportionate strength of the rural areas at least so far as the legislature is concerned).

The decentralized and unorganized nature of politics in Florida, moreover, means that the average citizen loses to a large extent the chance of taking intelligent and informed citizen action, whether in voting or in activities of other kinds. Bewildered amid a maze of independently elected offices which are not even loosely tied together by a party or faction; lost in the intricate personalized politics of the legislature; and stymied by the lack of meaningful choices in elections, only the exceptional citizen is in position to take *any* intelligent political action. He cannot "throw the rascals out" because he has no effective means of finding out who the rascals are. He is forced to "vote the man not the party," but has no real notion who the best man is. The democratic responsibility of the officeholder becomes a meaningless shibboleth, and the democratic idea that the citizen through his vote is responsible for policy becomes merely one of the great American myths in the absence of effective ways of making it an actuality.

If there is one thing that has impressed (or depressed) us in this study, above anything else it is the certainty that any correspondence between legislative action in Florida and the majority will is largely accidental except on noncontroversial matters. This is the basic fault of Florida's legislative system. It leads to a host of other evils which are discussed in this book, not the least of which is the forced abdication of the individual from his rightful and honored place as the responsible citizen of a self-governing state.

Chapter 3

Legislative Apportionment

LEGISLATIVE apportionment really involves two factors: the basis of the apportionment and the method by which it is carried out. In Florida the basis of apportionment is as follows: in the house of representatives seats are assigned to the counties on a fixed numerical basis. The five most populous counties each have three seats, the next eighteen counties (by population) are allowed two representatives each, and each of the remaining forty-four counties elects one member. The basis of senate apportionment is quite different. The constitution provides for thirty-eight senatorial districts, "such Districts to be as nearly equal in population as practicable, but no county shall be divided in making such apportionment, and each district shall have one Senator; . . ."[1] Where senate districts are composed of more than one county, the counties making up the districts must be contiguous.[2]

The method of apportionment used in Florida establishes the legislature itself as the apportioning agency. The legislature is required to reapportion decennially at the regular session of years ending in the number "five." The constitution also provides that if the legislature fails to reapportion at the prescribed session, it shall be the continuous duty of the succeeding legislature or legislatures to reapportion. If the legislature fails to reapportion in accordance with this provision, the governor has the duty of calling it into extraordinary session and such a session is "mandatorily required to reapportion the representation. . . ." An extraordinary reapportionment session cannot consider any business other than reapportionment and the normal time limits imposed on special sessions do not apply.[3]

Despite the democratic presumption which favors the use of population as the sole determinant of apportionment and despite the fact that the constitution does not specify the use of any other basis, the conditions imposed by the apportionment article mean that geography has come to play at least as important a role in determining the allocation of legislative seats in Florida as population. The rigid use of county areas for electoral purposes is basic to the plan, and its corollaries—the guarantee of one seat in the house to each county no matter how small, the limitation of a maximum of three representatives to a single county no matter how

Table 1
House Seats In Terms of Population

	No. of Seats	No. of Counties	1960 Population	Percentage of Total State Population	Average of Population Growth, 1950-1960 (Percentage)	No. of Counties with Declining Population	No. of Counties Below Average State Growth (79 Per Cent)	Percentage Range of Population Change
Upper Quartile of Counties According to Population	23	9	3,357,500	67.8	107.9	0	4	+49.8 to +297.9
2nd Quartile	24	13	925,800	18.7	105.4	0	7	+29.9 to +371.1
3rd Quartile	24	22	496,500	10.0	51.5	2	16	—11.1 to +193.8
4th Quartile	24	23	171,800	3.5	12.7	11	22	—32.2 to + 86.0

large, the fixed number of senatorial seats, and the limitations on the assignment of them—combine to produce wide variations in the number of people represented by members of the legislature from county to county. The statistics on this question could be taken through a practically endless number of combinations to show the effects of these limitations, but the accompanying bar graph and tables contain most of the relevant information.

The deviation from a pure conception of population-based apportionment is striking. On the basis of the 1960 population, more than one hundred people are represented by each member of the house of representatives from Dade County (the largest county) for every person represented by the member from the smallest county. In the senate the disproportion in the number of people represented by the senator from the largest as compared to the smallest district is almost one hundred to one. Even more revealing is the fact that the six largest counties contain over half the state's population and elect

Table 2
Senate Seats In Terms of Population

	No. of Districts	1960 Population	Percentage of Total State Population	Average of Population Growth 1950-1960 (Percentage)	No. of Districts with Declining Population	No. of Districts Below State Average Growth	Percentage Range of Population Change
Upper Quartile of Senate Districts by Population	9	3,357,500	67.8	107.9	0	4	+49.8 to +297.9
2nd Quartile	10	1,055,400	21.3	89.3	0	5	+29.9 to +229.2
3rd Quartile	10	372,900	7.5	19.3	2	10	−13.1 to + 52.7
4th Quartile	9	170,900	3.5	28.1	3	9	− 9.2 to + 71.3

less than one-fifth of the members of the house and less than one-sixth of the senate; while counties containing less than 15 per cent of the population elect a majority of the members of the house of representatives, and districts containing less than 13 per cent of the population elect a majority of the senate. Compared to the other states Florida ranks forty-third in the percentage of population required to elect a majority of the upper house, forty-fourth (of forty-six) in the percentage of population required to elect a majority of the senate, and last in terms of an index which combines the two houses.[4]

It should be remembered, too, that not only the basis but also the method of reapportionment used in Florida has contributed to this imbalance in the distribution of seats, although perhaps in a more secondary fashion. Exclusive reliance on the legislature for securing a reapportionment has meant that only moral force could be

HOUSE OF REPRESENTATIVES

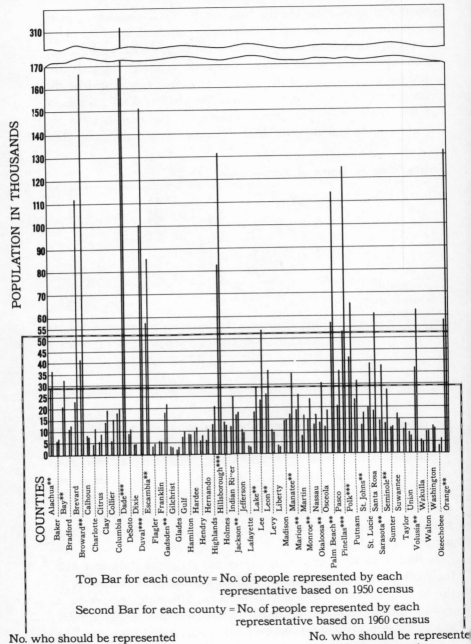

Top Bar for each county = No. of people represented by each
representative based on 1950 census

Second Bar for each county = No. of people represented by each
representative based on 1960 census

No. who should be represented
by each representative
per 1960 census
Approx. 52,000

** two representatives

*** three representatives

No. who should be represente
by each representative
per 1950 population figures
approx. 29,000 +

Figure 8

applied to secure compliance, and when moral obligation alone
comes into conflict with the necessity for certain members to divest
themselves and their areas of political power in order to allow reapportionment, the moral force is frequently insufficient. The ten-

SENATORIAL DISTRICTS

1960

Figure 9

dency to try to avoid or minimize reapportionment is more often the
rule than the exception. In a technical sense, too, the five-year gap
between the reapportionment act and the census on which it is
based is unrealistic in terms of the contemporary rate of population
change, even if other circumstances did not impose so many restrictions on the practical realization of an ideal reapportionment.

It is also of importance to note the legal situation. Some cases
are recorded in which state courts have invalidated reapportionment

SENATE

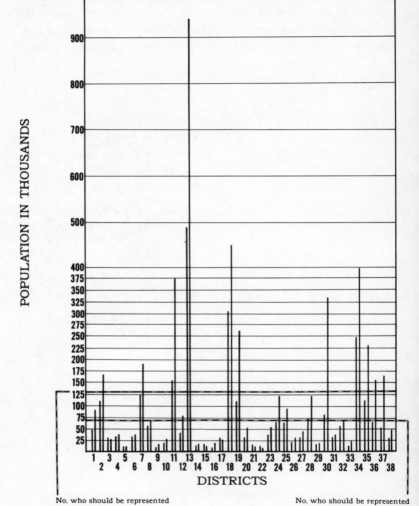

No. who should be represented
by each Senator per
1960 population figures
Approx. 130,000

No. who should be represented
by each Senator per
1950 population figures
Approx. 73,000

Top Bar for each district = No. of people represented by each Senator
based on 1950 census

Second Bar for each district = No. of people represented by each
Senator based on 1960 census

Figure 10

acts passed by legislatures on the grounds that they have not satisfied the constitutional requirement of that particular state.[5] But this does not seem to be the essential problem in Florida, for the districts as apportioned by the legislature seem to be about as equal in population as one could reasonably expect under the formulae laid down in the constitution. Until recently no court, apparently, has felt that it had the power to order a legislature to reapportion or to do the job itself,[6] except in those relatively few states in which the constitution specifically calls for such action.[7] It is evident, then, that in Florida the main problem is that the constitutional reapportionment formulae are defective and that the legislature controls the amending process. The result is that constitutional amendments are subject to a legislative veto and that no reapportionment is possible without the present malapportioned legislature's consent. As Anthony Lewis has pointed out, "voting for a fair apportionment bill would in many cases mean voting oneself (or one's friends or political interests) out of office. That is too much to ask of most politicians."[8]

Lewis suggests that the state and federal courts actively intervene to force fair apportionment. He feels this could be done without the necessity of amending state or federal constitutions. Since his article appeared in the *Harvard Law Review*, it appears to have had some influence on judicial actions. For the present, however, Florida is strait-jacketed by the nature of her amending process.

The effects of the recent U. S. Supreme Court decision in the Tennessee apportionment case, *Baker* v. *Carr*,[9] are at this time imponderable. Yet it seems likely that an almost immedate result will be some new cases brought by urban Florida citizens. Since, even after the recent reapportionment, Florida's districting is markedly worse than that of Tennessee, court relief of some kind is a distinct probability. In fact, several attempts to gain court aid were made, unsuccessfully,[10] even before *Baker* v. *Carr;* another such attempt has been reported at the time of this writing, the results of which we may only guess.[11]

The Crisis Over Apportionment:
Background and Recent Developments

The distribution of legislative seats in Florida has always created a serious problem. Even in the period before the state was admitted to the union difficulties were involved in the apportionment of the territorial council. Interestingly enough, the controversies were waged along much the same lines that they are today; the problem of area as opposed to population as the basis of representation was very much at issue, and even then there were patterns of regional influence at stake, although the rural-urban division which looms as the most important factor today was not present. The precedent for political maneuvering to prevent equality of representation for what amounts to the predominant populational and sociological development of the state was thus established very early. Since that time this precedent has been faithfully followed.[12]

Since the adoption of the first constitution, certain practices inimical to a population-based apportionment have been in effect. In the house these have included a fixed limit on the number of representatives and the guarantee of representation to each county; while the senate has had to be elected from single-member districts, with the proviso that no county may be divided in setting up these districts.[13] Since Florida's admission to statehood other practices have been gradually but steadily developed which further restrict the possibility of an equitable apportionment. The use of the silent gerrymander is notable; a reapportionment has been included in each constitution and only on rare occasions has the legislature abided by the constitutional mandate to change this original apportionment decennially. Reluctance to deprive a sitting member of his seat by transferring it to a more populous area seems to account at least partially for this development.

The legislature has also adopted the tactic of proposing a constitutional amendment rather than reapportioning by statute when pressures for reapportionment have reached the point at which they cannot be ignored. For the most part these amendments seem to have been directed toward vesting control of the legislature more firmly in the group which is in power and toward preserving this imbalance in legislative strength through constitutional formulae which narrowly circumscribe the possibilities of a shift to a populational basis of representation. Even when these measures have failed of adoption by the people, they have offered to opponents of reapportionment the advantage of long delays (and often a complete avoidance) in complying with constitutional stipulations on the question.[14]

In 1923 the amendment technique was successfully invoked to enact the present "automatic" provision relative to house seats. In retrospect it may seem surprising that the larger counties should have overwhelmingly accepted such a constrictive formula. However, it should be recalled that the spectacular urban growth of South Florida has occurred only since 1920. The 1920 census indicated Duval (Jacksonville) as the only county in Florida containing more than 100,000 residents.

It was only in the post World War II period that the areas of greatest growth in Florida realized what a bad bargain they had made in accepting this compromise. In the 1945 session, Governor Millard Caldwell became the first governor to invoke the constitutional power to call the legislature into extraordinary reapportionment session and hold it in session until a reapportionment act had been passed. After fifty-three days, a bill was passed to which the governor felt he could give his consent. As had become customary, the change was minimal—the house seats were reallocated on the basis of the constitutional formula and a token gesture was made with respect to the senate. Since that time the problem has intensified and additional complicating factors have appeared.

The relation of the governor to the legislature on the question of reapportionment in the 1945 session and in the session of 1955 (which is discussed below) points up the extent to which the governor's role today is accepted as being that of state-wide representative, while the legislature is conceived as an agglomeration of representatives of local areas. Since there is neither party nor strong factional cohesion to hold the members together and to secure some solidarity between the legislature and the governor and since many of the features of the separation of powers doctrine are totally divisive in the absence of the party or some other organizational catalyst, the reapportionment question can produce more intense conflict between the governor and the legislature than almost any other. And the tensions built up by this conflict can very easily spill over into other issues, causing antagonisms which may completely destroy the effectiveness of that executive leadership which appears to be so vital in contemporary government at all levels.

All the stops were pulled out on the reapportionment theme in 1955 and the cacophony was appalling even to the ears of people accustomed to considerable disharmony. It is difficult to think of a move known to the history of the reapportionment struggle in the state that was not employed, and several additional ones were especially invented for the occasion.

The governor was committed to press for a rather extensive change. During the summer and fall of 1954, while he was governor-elect, LeRoy Collins appointed twenty-eight citizens' committees to study and make recommendations on various state problems. One of these committees was on reapportionment. Although the committee report very carefully stipulated that its efforts had been directed toward working out a compromise between the extremes of population and geography and that it was not prepared to violate the prevailing tradition which required both to be taken into consideration, its recommendations received little attention. The proposals of the commission were very moderate: thirty-eight senatorial districts would have been created and an additional senator would have been added for each major fraction of 300,000 population in a county above the first 300,000. The proposals also included a requirement that the three senatorial districts having the least population be included in the territory to be revised in any future reapportionment. The counties were to be assigned house seats on the following basis:[15]

(1) Under 25,000 population—one representative.

(2) 25,000 to 75,000 population—two representatives.

(3) 75,000 to 175,000 population—two representatives plus an additional member for each 50,000 population (or major fraction thereof).

(4) Populations over 175,000—four representatives plus an additional representative for each additional 100,000 population (or major fraction thereof).

Such an apportionment plan would have had the immediate effect (on the basis of 1950 population figures) of adding a second senator for Dade County, removing the upper limit on the number of representatives from each county, and establishing an increasing ratio of population for assigning additional members to large counties, with a leveling out at one additional member per 100,000 when the population of a county exceeds 175,000. Although Dade County would have had seven members in the house, Hillsborough and Duval counties five members, and Pinellas County four members under this plan, the overall change would have been slight. Twenty-two per cent of the state's population could still elect a majority of the house of representatives and, unless by some extraordinary change in its attitude the legislature should decide to make drastic shifts in the senatorial districts, very little alteration would take place in senate apportionment under the plan. Although certain features of this arrangement were incorporated into some of the reapportionment measures subsequently introduced, the legislature for the most part ignored these suggestions and attempted to thrash out the problem within its own ranks.

It was apparent even before the 1955 session began that a number of legislators were moving toward the idea of a constitutional amendment which would give each of the sixty-seven counties its own senator and offset this feature to some extent by making representation in the house reflect the population principle to a greater degree than at present. Some of the members who were opponents of reapportionment seemed to favor this move as a means of circumventing a reapportionment fight under the present constitutional arrangements. An early introduction and passage of the proposal would have allowed them to get the jump on the opposition and use the pending referendum on the measure as an argument against any reapportionment bill that might alter the composition of the legislature to any appreciable extent. If the proposed amendment were accepted by the people, it would have only the effect of assuring small-county control of the senate with limited concessions in the house; while if it failed, it was always possible that the whole question of reapportionment could be passed over until the next decennial period. The tactics were simple and the men who employed them were masters at the art of attrition. They had the advantage of small county dominance of the two houses; it was always possible to pick up a scattering of votes among the lukewarm by offering concessions on other measures or by appealing to the desires of certain members to avoid commitment on controversial subjects, and once the constitutional proposal was passed, it could be used as a bulwark for defense against other apportion-

ment bills. In addition, the idea of a populationally apportioned
house and a geographically apportioned senate has the superficial
appeal necessary to attract a few real (if somewhat ponderous) advocates of reapportionment long enough to slow the initial momen-
tum of the attack on malapportionment.

Thus it was that Senate Joint Resolution 7, embracing these features, was introduced at the very outset of the 1955 regular session
and was never really headed. As it was originally passed by the senate, the proposal called for a single senator for each county and for
members in the house to be assigned to the counties in descending
scale according to population rank order, with the three most populous counties each receiving six seats, the next two getting four, the
next five getting three, the next eighteen obtaining two, and the
remainder one each. The measure was amended in the house, with
the senate concurring in the amendment, to provide a house membership based on the following formula: the number of representatives was set at 135 and each county was allowed at least one representative, with the remaining 68 seats being allocated to counties
having populations in excess of 8,000. Units were established by
dividing 68 into the total population of the state in excess of 8,000
in each county (2,286,033 on the 1950 basis). The quotient yielded
by this division was 33,618, which formed the unit of population
required to obtain each additional seat. The population of each
county in excess of 8,000 was then divided by this unit to determine
the number of seats to be assigned to the particular county.

Although this house arrangement appeared fairly liberal when
measured in terms of alternative suggestions, the retention of the
guarantee of one representative to each county meant that the
formula would soon become regressive insofar as a population-based
apportionment is concerned. On the basis of the 1950 population,
for example, the formula would raise the population required to
elect a majority of the house to 30 per cent, which was a considerable
advancement over the existing figure of less than 18 per cent. However, the 1955 population estimates indicated a decline to less than
28 per cent under the new formula, and further declines could be
projected in terms of the type of growth the state was experiencing. In
1950, eighteen counties each contained less than 8,000 people, six of

these counties had moved above the 8,000 mark by 1955 and several other slightly larger counties were declining toward this figure. In the meantime, the population of the state as a whole has grown so rapidly that a reapportionment based on 1956 figures would have required the use of a quotient of more than 54,000 for the assignment of the 68 seats remaining after each county had been allocated its member. Even the house, then, would not have been equitably apportioned under this plan; and when it is considered that a majority of the senate would have been elected by slightly over 10 per cent of the population based on 1950 figures (with a decline to 8 per cent by 1955), it is hardly surprising that the plan was strongly opposed in the more populous areas of the state. In the November, 1956, general election, the proposal was defeated by a vote of 288,575 to 187,662, with practically all of the larger counties (Duval and Bay being the significant exceptions) voting heavily against the amendment.[16]

If the opponents of reapportionment had hoped by the proposal of this amendment to forestall the pressure to reapportion under the existing constitutional provision, they were doomed to disappointment. That such a hope existed is indicated by the fact that, although half a dozen reapportionment bills were introduced in each house, none was agreed upon by both houses during the regular session. Following this failure to reapportion during the 1955 regular session, the governor promptly resorted to his constitutional power to convene the legislature in an extra-ordinary reapportionment session. Technically, this session, which met on June 6, 1955, did not terminate until the terms of the members of the 1955 legislature (except for holdover senators) expired following the election of November, 1956.

The lines were fully drawn for the battle; the governor had substantial support in the house (at least for his minimum asking point), while the senate presented an unyielding majority in opposition to changes as extensive as those demanded by Collins. The fight was almost entirely big county versus small, with a few exceptions which are explainable in terms of the individuals concerned or the advantages to be gained for particular counties as a result of the various proposals at issue. Each side appeared to become more

adamant as time passed. The governor very early indicated that the
minimum apportionment acceptable to him would allow Bay County
a separate seat in the senate and split the ninth district, which is composed of Citrus and Hernando counties and has the second smallest
population among the districts (all parties seemed agreed that the
smallest district—Jefferson County—would be shifted in any reapportionment that might occur). Later evidence shows, however,
that the advocates of fairly extensive reapportionment wanted to
constitute Bay, Monroe, Sarasota, and Manatee as single county districts. Such a proposal was objectionable to the majority of the
senate, apparently because the shift would favor urban South Florida,
and the senate was willing to do no more than make an even trade
by allowing Bay and Monroe to become single county districts.

Only one positive action resulted from the special session—a
separate bill (4-X), reapportioning the house according to the constitutional formula, was passed. Its only effect was to increase the
representation of Monroe and Okaloosa counties from one to two
members each:[17] a change which actually meant an increase of one
representative for rural North Florida. The battle over senate reapportionment, on the other hand, settled into a sort of trench
warfare. Fourteen or fifteen reapportionment measures were introduced in each house, ranging from rather drastic changes in the
districts, to a constitutional amendment designed to call an election
on Senate Joint Resolution 7 of the regular session within ninety
days, to a senate concurrent resolution (17-X) declaring that in
the opinion of the legislature the senate was already apportioned
as nearly equally as was practical. Several measures were introduced
which were designed to end the extraordinary session, including motions to adjourn sine die and motions to recess until a date following the general election of November, 1956.[18] On two occasions the
governor requested advisory opinions from the state supreme court:
one raised the question whether the governor was precluded from the
use of the veto on apportionment bills, and the other sought to
determine whether the governor could call a special session (under
his general power to convene special sessions) which would meet
during a recess of the extraordinary session. The first opinion was
requested because some members of the legislature who were deter-

mined to bring matters to a head had publicly stated that the gubernatorial veto power did not extend to apportionment questions. The
supreme court advised, however, in a four to one opinion that the
veto power was operative.[19] In the second instance the governor
sought advice from the court when he decided that a special session
was needed to consider the report of the "Fabisinski Committee" on
segregation and certain other problems, including additional financial support for various state institutions. The court was unanimous
in its opinion that the calling of such a special session during a
recess of the extraordinary reapportionment session was within the
power of the governor.[20]

Two senate reapportionment bills were agreed to by both houses
during the extraordinary session (H.B. 10-X and S.B. 18-X), but
were vetoed by the governor. These bills were identical in form,
except that the senate bill (which was passed later) added a proviso indicating that the redistricting contained therein was as nearly
equal as practical. The main effect of these bills was to make Bay
and Monroe single county districts, while a few other counties were
shifted in order to compensate for these changes. On the whole the
plan provided for a minimum unsettling of incumbent senators and for
a balancing of North and South Florida. In his veto messages (July
13 and August 5, 1955), the governor conceded that some reapportionment would result from the bills, but the changes were
not sufficient to satisfy constitutional requirements. He pointed out
that Manatee and Sarasota counties were still combined in one district,
as were Seminole and Brevard, with the result that the bill would
provide sixteen districts (including four single county districts) with
populations less than Manatee alone, eleven districts (two of them
single counties) with less than Sarastoa alone, nine districts (two
of them single counties) with less than Seminole, and eight with less
than Brevard (again including the two smallest single county districts).

Although subsequent legislation was introduced, it was recognized
after the second veto that a hopeless deadlock existed. The governor,
however, continued to press for a reapportionment based on the
principles outlined in his address to a joint session on June 30, 1955:
constitute single districts for Bay and Monroe, separate Sarasota from

Manatee, break up and reconstitute the three smallest districts, and give relief to the three largest multicounty districts.[21]

The longer the fight dragged out, the more bitter it became, and the effects were apparent throughout the 1957 session. As the argument grew hotter the opposing forces became less restrained and many of the deep-seated frustrations and fundamental political divisions which had been covered with a thin veneer of comradeship and verbal attestations of harmony began to show up quite clearly. The old question of dividing the state was raised again, and many of the tensions between urban and rural county and North and South Florida were evident. Twenty-nine members of the house who were supporters of extensive reapportionment offered a detailed explanation of what they thought was involved in the question, including a brief history of apportionment in Florida, reapportionment in 1955 and why it was necessary, refutations of arguments against reapportionment, and the underlying reasons for its defeat. After arguing that the fears of certain members were completely unfounded, these members concluded with the following strongly-worded expression:

> After these many days of labor in endeavoring to give the people of the State of Florida fair representation in their Senate, we have been forced to the firm conclusion that the underlying reasons for defeat of reapportionment are the refusal of some members of the Senate to give up their personal political control over state, city and county government, and their personal political control over laws affecting large segments of the business interests of the State.
>
> We have concluded that it is our duty to give the full facts to the House of Representatives, the Senate and the people of the State of Florida. We herewith rededicate ourselves to continue this struggle until the victory for the people has been won.[22]

Several of the signatories of this communication later suffered from the public and private expressions of rancor of those who were opposed to them. Reprisals took the form of direct attack, loss of support on measures on which advocates of reapportionment might otherwise have received additional votes, a decline in prestige in the house brought about by niggling opposition to them on every occasion, opposition in elections, and private expressions of dislike, distrust, or disdain. Despite the fact that some local ties between individual house and senate members were strengthened, the overall separation between the two houses probably increased rather than diminished as a result of the fight. The division in both houses was very close (less than five votes difference appeared in many crucial roll calls in each house), and resentment on both sides tended to build up against opponents in the opposite house even more perhaps than among members who were in closer proximity. In addition there was a strong feeling among opponents of reapportionment in the senate that neither the governor nor the house of representatives should have anything to say about the redistricting of the senate; the tendency toward the narrowest possible exclusiveness of function was stimulated to a considerable extent by the fight over reapportionment.

One of the worst outcomes of the long struggle was the strain placed on legislative-executive relations, although once again the respective positions of the governor and the legislative majority illustrate the increasing necessity for the executive to assume a special representative function when the composition of the legislature lags behind sociological change and no longer reflects the ecological balance of the state. Some of the more powerful members of the senate were already prepared to do battle with Collins because they had been supporters of Senator Charley Johns in the gubernatorial race against Collins in 1954. It should be remembered that Johns's strength lay in just those counties which enjoyed the advantages of overrepresentation, so that there was a close relation between the individual support of the senators (and representatives) from these districts and their interest in retaining an older, personalized, rural type of politics in Florida. The present apportionment or something as close to it as possible is one of the finest weapons in the armory of these politicians. By contrast Collins was, as has been indicated, a master in the use of mass media of communications; he commanded great support in the urbanized areas (particularly in South Florida), and his tenure of office was characterized to a considerable degree by the displacement of personalized government in favor of institutional patterns of administration.

The tendency on the part of some legislators to distrust Collins expanded under the pressure that he brought to bear on the question of reapportionment. In an address delivered to a joint session on September 27, 1955, the governor clearly indicated his tactics:

> There can be only one recourse then for me, and those who fight with us in every corner of Florida, and that is to take the issue to the people in the elections next spring. The people will become aroused. I predict the organization throughout Florida of citizens groups crusading for fair representation. Candidates for all elective offices, statewide and local, will be required to take an open stand for fair representation or for the status quo. It matters not whether I am a candidate for governor. I will, God willing, be Governor, and the full weight and force and influence I possess and can honorably use will be thrown into this fight for fair play for all the people of Florida.[23]

The fact that Collins was willing to appeal "over the heads" of the legislature directly to the people was a source of irritation to members of the legislature who thought these matters should be settled in the privacy of the governmental family. In the face of the governor's imprecations they became even more adamant and sought refuge in a greater attachment to extreme localism. Even today many of them will insist that the governor "should have taken what he could get," rather than press a hopeless case to the point at which he completely isolated some of his opponents. It is strongly alleged in some quarters that, as a result of Collins' stand on reapportionment, certain members resolved to fight every measure the governor backed; and judging from the behavior of a few legislators in committee and on the floor in the 1957 session, it is not difficult to accept such allegations as true. The attempts (quite often successful) to emasculate the governor's proposals on such matters as the allocation of additional funds to purchase highway rights of way, race relations, changes in certain regulatory bodies, and administrative reorganization frequently appeared to have been made again and again by the same people more for opposition's sake than by reason of strong conviction. There can be little doubt, too, that the increased sense of unity among the small counties and the intensification of their distrust of the large counties has affected legisla-

tive-executive relations adversely. They have done so directly because the governor was automatically lumped with the "big county
boys" in the minds of the small county bloc, and indirectly harm
was done by virtue of the fact that many large county leaders on
whom the governor relied for advancement of his program saw their
influence wane in the face of these new developments.

Even some of the governor's staunchest supporters on the reapportionment question expressed dissatisfaction with the way he
handled the issue. A few seemed to feel that the governor could
have won over the two or three senate votes necessary to pass a reapportionment bill that would have satisfied his minimum demands
by simply making generous overtures—such as a personal appeal
and possibly an arm-around-shoulders photograph—to a few members who might be inclined to waver. Others, and these seem the
more numerous, felt that Collins did not wield a big enough stick
to beat certain members in line after threatening to use virtually
every legitimate power at his disposal to get reapportionment through.
The latter groups felt that pressures could have been brought to
bear in the way of restriction of road construction in certain areas,
the threat of the use of the veto, and the denial to legislators of
patronage voices in appointments made by the governor in their
respective areas. Many of these same people also indicated that the
governor could have gone much further than he did in the 1956
campaign to fulfill the vows he made in the address to the legislature cited above. There apparently was no permanent estrangement
between the governor and the legislators who felt this way, and
many of them would concede that stronger pressure by the governor might have meant an even greater impairment of his effectiveness with the legislature than had already occurred. These attitudes
on the part of his closest followers are good illustrations of how
debilitating the reapportionment struggle can become when so much
heat is aroused, especially in a state in which there are so many
forces working against any political cohesion which has a positive
purpose.

Reapportionment remained a dormant issue throughout the greater
part of the 1957 session. Everyone concerned seemed to be of the
opinion that the proper time for taking up the question was during

the legislature's consideration of the draft of a constitution submitted by the constitution advisory commission, and the legislature
did not go to work seriously on this report until very near the end
of the session. The only reference to reapportionment in the governor's message to the legislature was to the effect that the commission's proposals seemed to him to meet the fundamental requirements necessary to place apportionment on a better basis and to
avoid future stalemates.[24] The constitution commission included
among its thirty-seven members the eighteen legislators who com-
prised the Florida Legislative Council plus a sufficient number of
former members of the legislature to afford a fairly heavy majority
of people with a legislative background and orientation. Former
Senator (now Appellate Judge) Wallace Sturgis, who had served
as chairman of the governor's committee on reapportionment, was
chairman of the constitution advisory commission, and the provisions for reapportionment contained in the commission's draft closely
resembled those that had been presented by the reapportionment
committee.[25] This plan called for the reapportionment to occur at
the regular session of 1959 (following the presumed adoption of
the article) and again in 1963 and decennially thereafter. The
number of senatorial districts was raised to forty-two. These were
to be single-member districts; multicounty districts were required
to be contiguous; no county was to be divided; and the three smallest
districts were to be revised as an incident to each reapportionment.
House seats were to be allocated to the counties on the basis prescribed by the reapportionment committee, except that the population increment for each additional representative for counties above
175,000 was raised from 100,000 to 150,000. The most important
change was the inclusion of a provision which permitted the governor, after an extraordinary reapportionment session had sat without
effective result for a period of sixty days, to adjourn the legislature
and certify to the supreme court the failure of the legislature to reapportion, following which the court would reapportion and return
the results to the secretary of state.

The legislative majority was no more disposed to accept these
recommendations than it had been to adopt the plan of the reapportionment committee. Their stalemate victory in 1955 had apparently
strengthened the opponents of extensive reapportionment. When the

legislature met in the fall of 1957 to complete its consideration of the commission's proposed constitution, it came up with a reapportionment provision that differed rather sharply from the commission formula.[26] For the most part the legislative version hewed very close to the line of the existing house plan, with a fixed membership, a guarantee of one representative to each county and a variation in the number of representatives from the counties according to population rank. Under this proposal house membership would have been increased to 114, with the five most populous counties having five representatives each, the next two four each, the next seven three each, the next twenty-three two each, and the remainder one each. The plan was ingenious in allowing almost precisely the same proportion of the state population to elect a majority of the house as the existing formula. Furthermore, the decline of the proportion of the population required to elect this majority from 1950 to 1956 was the same as that experienced under the prevailing plan.

Although the senate reapportionment policy offered by the legislature as part of its proposed constitution cannot be appraised with precision because it did not contain an enumeration of districts, several of its features conformed strikingly to earlier patterns of action on the problem. The number of senators would have been increased from thirty-eight to forty-five, and the provisions for single-member districts and for not dividing a county in apportioning the senate were retained. As might have been expected, the legislature did not seriously entertain the constitutional commission's idea of allowing the supreme court to act as an apportioning agency, and the legislative draft left the power to reapportion exclusively to the legislature.

At least two other features of the plan tended to weaken the possibilities of change for the future. The power of the governor to hold the legislature indefinitely in reapportionment session was drastically curtailed by a provision allowing the legislature to adjourn such a session after sixty days. Furthermore, a clause was added to the senate provision which would have allowed reapportionment of that body to be "based upon population and such other pertinent factors as may be determined by the legislature."

The proposed constitution which embodied these principles of apportionment was to have been submitted to popular vote at the

November, 1958, general election in the form of a series of amendments, each of which embraced an article of the constitution. The proposed articles were tied together on the ballot, however, by a "daisy-chain" stipulation whereby rejection by the voters of any one of the articles would have resulted in the defeat of the entire draft constitution. This method of constitutional revision was successfully attacked in the courts,[27] with the result that the voters never had an opportunity to express themselves on the question. For the second time in the decade of the 1950's, the attempt to satisfy the demand for reapportionment by amending the constitution was thwarted.

Proponents of the constitutional amendment method of settling the reapportionment question were not discouraged by these failures. The 1959 regular session was again confronted with the reapportionment problem, but the attacking forces seemed to have exhausted themselves in the long struggle, and the defensive alignment displayed the magnanimity expected of so powerful a foe. The resulting search for an honorable truce was characterized by a surface calmness attendant upon the backstairs diplomacy leading to a settlement. After some backing and filling in which both sides presented their asking points and negotiated from them, a proposed constitutional amendment was passed by the legislature over light opposition from each side.[28] The amendment was declared to be of an emergency nature so that a referendum could be held on its passage at a special election in November, 1959, rather than have the proposal carry over until the general election of November, 1960.[29]

In most respects the 1959 reapportionment plan followed the previous formula, with the main deviations corresponding to the lines laid down by the legislature in attempting to revise the constitution in 1957. Thus, the changes proposed in 1959 continued the practices that have generally characterized the previously discussed historical experience with reapportionment in Florida. Both the house and the senate were increased in size, and the plan was drawn in a manner calculated to provide a minimum upsetting of incumbent members. Care was also taken to see that the counties were not deprived of their existing representative strength. House membership was set at 103, and the seats were allocated as follows: five representatives to the most populous county in the state, four representatives to each of the next two most populous counties, three representatives to each of the next six most populous counties, two representatives to each of the next fourteen most populous counties, and one representative to each of the remaining counties.

Under the plan the senate was to be increased to forty-four members. The main regulative provisions were carried over from the previous plan, including the stipulations that only one senator be elected from each district, that multicounty districts be composed of contiguous counties, and that no county be divided in creating a district. Two significant changes were incorporated into the amendment with regard to the senate. The first established an additional condition of reapportionment by prohibiting the inclusion of more than three counties in a district. The second deleted the requirement that the senatorial districts ". . . be as nearly equal in population as practicable. . ." and substituted for it the prescription that "such apportionment shall provide fairness and equity among districts based upon population, geographic area and economic affinity."

The amendment also made certain general changes in the apportionment plan. Under its provisions decennial reapportionment would take place at the first regular session after each federal census (1961, 1971, etc.) rather than in the fifth year of each decade. However, the amendment specified that the first reapportionment under the plan be adopted by the legislature at the 1959 session and take effect in 1961. Furthermore, the new provision required that the house of representatives be reapportioned again in 1961 on the basis of the 1960 census, but that the senate apportionment of 1959 not be changed until 1971. The old constitutional provision for an extraordinary reapportionment session in the event the legislature fails to reapportion at the appointed time was included in the proposal, but the legislature followed its earlier lead by adding a clause allowing either the governor or the legislature itself to adjourn the session sine die after sixty days.

The reapportionment enabling act necessitated by the amendment and intended to go into effect at the 1961 session was duly passed.[30] In the case of the house of representatives, the act simply added the

seats created by the amendment to the counties in the top population
brackets. In the senate, provision was made for the six new senate districts by splitting several two-county districts into single-county districts and by shuffling the counties that had belonged to the four-
county districts under the former apportionment. Only seven of the
old thirty-eight districts were affected; all of the existing single-
county districts (including Jefferson, with a 1950 population of
10,400 which has since declined to 9,500) continued to be single-
county districts and only one previously two-county district (the
third) had a third county added to it.

An analysis of the apportionment policy proposed in 1959 in
terms of its immediate effect on the representative character of the
legislature and its flexibility in providing a means of adapting the
representative system to sociological change reveals a pattern that
is all too familiar. The main advantage or concession cited by
those who supported the plan was the addition of eight representatives from the urban areas. To the extent that additional voices
from the large cities might have added to the clamor for more attention to the problems of these areas and to the state problems
which have resulted from social change, the plan contained features that might commend it. On the other hand, a few elementary
computations reveal the extent to which the prevailing imbalance
of representation was preserved. Under the reapportionment of 1955,
the forty-six smallest counties contained 18.7 per cent of the population as of 1950 and elected a majority of the 95 member house.
On the basis of the 1958 population estimates these forty-six counties contained 16.3 per cent of the population. Under the apportionment proposed in 1959 the forty-eight smallest counties would
elect a majority of the 103 member house and, in terms of 1950
census figures, contained 20.3 per cent of the population. On the
basis of the 1958 estimates, the proportion of the total state population living in these counties had declined to 18.9 per cent. Furthermore, if the seats involved in the 1959 reapportionment were allocated on the 1958 population basis, the decline would be even
more pronounced, for the proportion required to elect a majority of
the 103 member house would then be only 17.2 per cent of the
population. Since the prevailing population trends have continued,

any reapportionment in 1961 under this plan would reveal a situation in the house that would very closely approximate the 1959 situation. By way of further contrast, the six largest counties in the state (1958 estimates) contained 54.8 per cent of the population and would have elected 21.4 per cent of the 1961 house under the 1959 plan.

The situation with respect to the senate is similar. Under the existing apportionment (1945) the twenty smallest districts elect a majority of the upper chamber and contain (on the basis of 1950 figures) 17.7 per cent of the total population. By 1958 the proportion of the state population residing in these districts had declined to 13 per cent. Under the 1959 apportionment the twenty-three smallest districts would elect a majority of the senate. Based on the 1950 census figures (to the extent that population was a factor, the 1950 data were apparently used in the 1959 proposals for reapportionment), 17.7 per cent of the population resided in these districts. According to 1958 estimates the proportion of the state's population in the twenty-three smallest districts had declined to 14.2 per cent. And in the senate the six largest districts (in terms of 1958 figures), containing a majority of the population, would have had a smaller proportion of senate seats (13.6 per cent) than they would have had under the existing apportionment (15.8 per cent). Considerable comment was made in the press and elsewhere about the fact that the great urban agglomerations actually would have suffered a proportionate loss of representation as a result of the addition of six seats. None of the proposed new districts, for example, contained a population equal to the representative ratio necessary to qualify as a separate senatorial district in an apportionment plan based on a proportionality of population. In fact, Brevard County alone among the new districts came close to the requisite population for a senate district based on proportionality. Examination of the 1959 act from the standpoint of areal interest groupings, however, reveals that four of the six proposed seats are in rapidly growing urban areas, and that the change would have produced a net gain of two senate seats for South Florida over North Florida. Once again the observer is forced to the conclusion that the only improvement offered by this plan was

an increase in gross representation from the urban areas, and even
this advantage was offset by the additional obstacles erected against
a more equitable apportionment in the future.

Several of the determinants of reapportionment newly established by the amendment were obvious barriers to effective change.
The senate reapportionment of 1959, for instance, was frozen for
twelve years, and the basis for senate apportionment was a blatant
reversal of the old formula which at least paid lip-service to the
idea that population should be the fundamental criterion of representation. In addition, the limitation of the governor's power over
extraordinary reapportionment sessions would have deprived him,
in his representative capacity, of a powerful institutional means
of rallying public opinion against a violation of constitutional responsibility by the legislature. In terms of the possibility of adjustment of the representative structure in the future, the arrangements prescribed by the proposed constitutional amendment of 1959
appeared to be retrogressive rather than progressive.

The adjective "compromise" was used by a wide variety of factions in the legislature as the appropriate characterization of the
reapportionment settlement. It is fairly typical of the prevailing
mores in the Florida legislature with respect to the sanctity of the
counties that representatives from the larger counties obtaining additional representation (particularly those securing separate senate
seats) tended to join the small county bloc in mutual self-congratula-
tion on their accomplishment. On the whole, Representative William H. Boyd of Manatee County probably gave the most accurate
view of the attitude of a great many proponents of reapportionment
when he said: "I think the boys of the majority bloc have made
us a little better deal. They are at least trying to work out something. This helps Manatee, because we are in for a senator. It is
hard to admit, but these boys are going to give us whatever they
want. If you are hungry, why hold out for a steak? Go ahead and
eat humberger [sic?]."[31]

The battle over the 1959 reapportionment amendment was heavily
joined during the campaign preceding the November 3 referendum.
Most of the newspapers along the lower east coast, except for the
Miami *Herald,* were opposed to the plan, as were the St. Petersburg

Times and the *Independent*. In the urban areas on the east and west coasts, committees were organized under various labels to fight against the amendment in the name of fair representation. In Pinellas County (St. Petersburg) the Republican party organization (the majority party in that county) came out strongly against the proposed amendment. Other newspapers in various parts of the state supported the plan, as did certain civic organizations, including the League of Women Voters. Governor LeRoy Collins, perhaps somewhat reluctantly, indicated that he was backing the amendment, while several potential gubernatorial candidates from urban South Florida opposed the plan, took the governor to task for his stand, and indicated that reapportionment would be a major issue in future statewide campaigns. Few political issues of recent years have received attention comparable to that displayed on the 1959 reapportionment question.

The proposed amendment was defeated in the November election by a vote of 177,955 against the proposal to 146,601 for it. The geographical pattern was fairly clear: the lower east coast counties from Indian River to Dade County voted against the proposal, as did Volusia, St. Johns, and Duval counties further north along the coast. On the west coast only Pinellas County voted against the amendment. Although the voters in the other urban counties voted their approval of the measure (except in Escambia) the heavy majorities in Dade, Broward, Palm Beach, and Pinellas counties were more than sufficient to offset these favorable votes. In several urban counties the possibility of becoming single-county senatorial districts seems to have been a predominant influence, but in Hillsborough, Orange, and Polk the appeal must be put down to a combination of the desire for a settlement by compromise and to gains (or at least protection against possible loss) of seats in the house of representatives. A sizeable number of North Florida rural counties also voted against the plan, apparently because the concession to urbanism and to South Florida was deemed too great. Seven of the North Florida counties whose electorate returned a majority against the proposal declined in population between 1950 and 1960. A total of forty-three of the sixty-seven counties in Florida delivered majorities in favor of the amendment.

The most recent chapter in the long story of "reapportionment by the 1950 census" started during the 1961 legislative session and is not yet finished. The legislature adopted a "compromise" scheme developed by Governor Farris Bryant, which would enlarge the senate to forty-five members, deprive Jefferson County of its senator and make it a part of a multicounty district, and allow single senators to all of the twenty-three largest counties plus Santa Rosa (because it would by this plan be geographically separated from any possible multicounty district). Thus Bay, Okaloosa and Santa Rosa (all North Florida counties, the latter two primarily rural) would gain senators. At the same time, Seminole and Brevard would be separated, each having a senator, as would Manatee and Sarasota. These new seats would come into existence before the 1963 session, provided the amendment is approved by the referendum in November, 1962. Again, the major urban daily newspapers are opposing the plan, as are a good many citizen's organizations.

As for the house, the Bryant plan envisaged an increase to 105, with Broward County gaining two members to a total of four. The rural members of the house balked at such generosity (even though it is estimated that Broward will have a million residents by 1970) and cut the total to 104. This would mean nine new seats, apportioned as follows: the largest county (Dade) would gain two (to a total of five); the next three largest counties (Duval, Hillsborough, and Pinellas) would each gain one (to a total of four for each); and the next five counties would each have three seats (Polk would thus be unchanged, while Broward, Palm Beach, Orange, and Escambia would each gain one seat); the next fourteen counties would each have two seats (under this provision Brevard and Lee would each gain a seat, twelve other counties would remain at two, and Jackson and St. Johns would each lose a seat).

This plan had two outstanding improvements over most of the earlier schemes. It would, in the first place, make population a major factor to be considered for both houses (although the senate provision speaks only of "equitable representation," and in neither house would proportionality be enforced); in the second place, it would for the first time actually mean a loss of some existing seats, and thus an unseating of some incumbents. These are real gains, and while in many other ways the plan closely resembles the 1959 amendment which the voters rejected, these new gambits by the rural leaders may be enough to account for a favorable referendum vote when the issue comes before the electorate.

On the other hand, the new plan is a long way from achieving proportionality or urban control. For one thing, many of the new seats, both in the senate and in the house, would go to counties which are not urban or are only semiurban. Thus the balance of the two houses would be disturbed only minimally. But more important, the new proposal makes almost no change in the basic fact that a small minority of the population would elect a majority of both houses. Under the new dispensation, using 1960 census figures, 13.5 per cent of the voters would elect a majority of the senate (the figure for the present apportionment is 12.3 per cent); and 17.7 per cent would elect a majority of the house (the present figure is 14.7 per cent). These are, to begin with, hardly striking improvements; and the population trends are such that by the time the new apportionment took effect in 1963 the figures would be as bad as they are under the present apportionment. It is hard to escape the feeling that the urban areas are again being asked to buy a scheme which does not do much to meet their basic needs, especially since the amendment provides that all counties which reach 50,000 population will automatically qualify for a second seat—a provision which practically guarantees that the smaller counties will always control the legislature.

This sketch of the history of legislative apportionment in Florida reveals much of the source of today's problem. Despite the American constitutional presumption in favor of a populational basis of representation, this state has never used the criterion of equality as the sole basis for the allocation of legislative seats in either house. The legislature originated from a time when representative inequalities were defined by geographical areas. These geographical identities received constitutional sanction and protection, and the pattern has never been broken, although the areas of over and underrepresentation have naturally altered with the development of the state. To a considerable extent, in fact, the situation was worsened, not only from a standpoint of the declining number of people who can elect a majority of each house, but also from the increasing inflexibility of the constitutional formulae for reapportioning. The minimum spread which exists today between the number of representatives who can be returned in the larger as compared to the smaller counties, the single member senatorial districts coupled with the prohibition against dividing the counties in forming senatorial districts, the political sanctity of county boundaries, and the unalterable conviction that electoral districts should be coeval with county lines appear to be almost insuperable barriers to reform. Even with the best will in the world it is difficult to see how the application of the present constitutional formula could provide an apportionment anywhere near a theoretical standard based on proportionality of population. At the same time, the opponents of reapportionment seem to be increasingly adamant in setting extremely narrow limits on what they will offer by way of constitutional adjustment of the situation. The proponents of reapportionment, on the other hand, are equally determined to reject propositions that hold out the form of change without its substance.

The inflexibility of the institutional arrangement and the hardening of the attitude of the legislators from the overrepresented areas have unfortunately paralleled a change in the sociological structure of the state which makes a reallocation of legislative seats more imperative than ever. From the adoption of the 1885 constitution until the mid-1920's there was a gradual increase in the number of counties so that areas which were developing rapidly received additional increments of representation as a result of the creation of these new administrative districts. During this time, too, the growth of the state did not bring with it any basic change in the makeup of the population. As late as 1920 two-thirds of the people lived on farms, and the largest city in the state was only slightly over 100,000 in population. The relative homogeneity of the population and economy meant that the discrepancies in the population sizes of legislative districts did not work any great representative hardship. Although it does not appear that there was as much verbal adherence to the idea of virtual representation then as there is now, there was in fact a much better case to be made for it. Today the position is reversed; over two-thirds of the state is urban, and the differences between the areas of over- and underrepresentation in terms of socio-economic conditions are striking. As one sociologist puts it:

> It is for this reason that the thirty year period since 1920, approximately a sociological "generation," is of great import to everyone concerned with public affairs in the state. The men and women in the age groups at present carrying the greatest load of civic responsibility were born and grew to maturity before the great urban surge began to show its social and economic effects, and consequently all may not always be aware of the degree to which the sociological character of their state has changed, or of all the implications of that change.[32]

The author of this quotation went on to point out that the unrepresentative nature of the Florida legislature is the fundamental political problem resulting from this change. The implication is quite clear: no longer is the question of reapportionment an academic one of merely adjusting the representation to accord with the population distribution of a people whose economic patterns, mode of life, and governmental requirements are very similar if not uniform. Instead the question that faces the state is the substantive one of trying to provide a legislative assembly which reflects the experiences and needs of an overwhelmingly urban population. A prima facie argument can be made for the simple principle of equality for equality's sake in an American state constitutional system, but the very foundation of representative government rests on the supposition that the representatives will reflect the character of the society sufficiently to allow the legislature to make its decisions on the basis of the aspirations and needs of the entire community. Pure majoritarianism may be nebulous in theory and hazardous in practice, but the actuality of institutionalized rule by a minority is even more difficult to defend in terms of the ideology of American democracy, and its practical consequences hardly bear out the claims of those who insist that it reflects the general will and does no violence to public policy.

The Arguments and the Consequences

The arguments offered by the opponents of reapportionment are surprisingly simple in structure and appear to be easy to refute both

logically and empirically. They are, however, put forward with great
persistence and fervor. In addition they are nearly always delivered
with an oratorical flourish calculated to bolster the convictions of
the speaker while they are winning the audience. Stripped of this
paraphernalia, they may be stated as follows: (1) The present apportionment (or something like it) must be maintained or the large
counties (and particularly the cities) will gain unlimited control
and completely ignore the interests and needs of the smaller counties, especially those of the rural areas. (2) Political control in
the metropolitan areas is almost invariably in the hands of corrupt
city machines and dominance by such groups would be far worse
than any faults resulting from the present apportionment. (3) The
"federal" argument is presented in support of equality of representation in the senate, i.e., an analogy is drawn between the relations of
the states to the United States and the counties to the states. (4)
It is frequently argued that the present system provides for the welfare of the entire state and that no advantage would accrue from a
change. (5) An increasing number of rural county members have
been putting forward the argument that since the urban counties
elect the governor, the small counties must retain their dominance
in the legislature. (6) The argument from legal prescription is a
last resort of the legal-minded opponent of change; the fact that the
present system is imbedded in the constitution is treated as proof
positive of the moral and practical importance of the principles it
follows. Finally, underlying this to some extent, although never
mentioned, is the fear that reapportionment would give additional
power to those urban areas which are least resistant to racial integration.

The first two arguments derive from a closely related set of
presuppositions and emotional attitudes which are inherently interesting to the observer of politics. In the first place, there is a strong
implication that the rural life provides a better natural training
ground for political responsibility and infuses into the character
the basis for stricter adherence to moral precepts than does an urban
background. Although little evidence can be adduced to support such
a conclusion, it hovers in the background of the pronouncements
which attend this line of argument. Underlying the argumentative

support of the system of rural overrepresentation, too, is an in-
grained distrust and fear of the cities and city residents, a distrust and
fear which holds that the city-slicker is out to fleece his simpler but
more upright country cousin.[33] Further, there is a fallacious presumption that the cities are monolithic in their interests and power
structures, rather than diverse and grouped into agglomerations of
competing forces.

The argument that the less populated areas must be given a
majority of representation to protect their interests against the physical majority is a *reductio ad absurdum* of the proposition that minorities have a right to representation. A logical extension of the
argument would hold that representation of any group should be
in inverse proportion to its size in order to prevent encroachment
by numerically superior groups. And in the pragmatic sense, it can
be shown that the vote of the urban representatives on questions
respecting the economic interest and general welfare of the rural
populace is, for the most part, as responsible as the vote of rural
representatives and certainly bears no comparison with the discriminatory vote of the small county majority on questions in which
the urbanized areas have a vital stake.

Although never openly advocated in this connection, the idea
of functional (or occupational) representation seems to be implicit
in the demand for an imbalance of representation in terms of population. For the most part this attitude appears to be related to the
idea that the agrarian interests of the state should receive special
consideration in any apportionment plan that might be considered.
However, even a cursory investigation of the contemporary economy
of Florida is sufficient to reveal the mythological elements in the
assumption that the present apportionment provides for such functional representation. As of 1957, agriculture produced only 4.9
per cent of Florida's personal income, as against the 40.6 per cent
produced by trades, services, and related industries. The geographical
sector that we have designated as "North" produces only 12 per
cent of the total personal income of the state and only 0.8 per
cent of the agricultural income of the state. Thus the counties for
which overrepresentation is most often demanded (perhaps in protection of agricultural interests) actually produce a very small share

of the agricultural income of the state. Furthermore, these counties are almost as diverse in their sources of income as other sectors of the state: no county in North Florida received more than 50 per cent of its gross personal income from agriculture; in all but a few of these counties the combined income from government and trades, services, and related industries represented more than 50 per cent of personal income; and income from either of the two latter sources exceeded that from agriculture in well over half of the North Florida counties.[34]

Finally, the suggestion of the dominance of machine politics not only has a nostalgic appeal that is more closely related to the 1890's than the present, but also ignores the institutionalization of politics which has been necessitated by contemporary economic and social conditions. Machine politics and bossism smack much more of the personalized approach to government and social welfare characteristic of the small county courthouse gang than of the present day municipal organization. The institutionalized politics of the urban era may throw up a type of political action that is as bad or worse than anything of the past, but it is doubtful that it will repeat the forms taken by organizations adapted to an entirely different set of circumstances.

The "federal" argument is one which can be used quite handily to trap the amateur constitutionalist. It ignores, however, the fundamental fact that the county's relation to the state bears no comparison with the relation of the states to the central government of the United States. The counties are administrative creatures of the state and their powers can be altered by the state, while the constitutional division of powers between the states and the nation is based on a conception of the sovereignty of each unit. In fact, the political, legal and psychological sanctification of the county is an ex post facto attempt to invest the county with attributes that make it possible to claim area representation for it.

The contention that the present system of apportionment, even though not based on population, provides a government and laws which are completely adapted to the needs of the entire state and the whole of its people will be considered in its practical aspects later. But the character of the argument itself is such that no opponent of reapportionment would accept its full consequences, for to do so would be to admit the validity of the broader concept of virtual representation. The position can be maintained only by insisting that the quality of representation rests not on mere numbers, but on an overriding concern on the part of the representatives with the general welfare to the complete exclusion of the instructed mandate and of all political ties that would prevent complete independence from local influence. To argue thus means not only that the entire argument for the protection of local interests is violated, but also that the principle of direct representation and its usual corollary, the instructed mandate, must be invalidated. The opponent of reapportionment is hardly concerned with these refinements, however, for his expression on the question is ordinarily designed to appeal more to the heart than to the head. He is much more likely to suggest that there is really no basic conflict between the large and small county delegates and that some of his "best friends are big county men." And if he is really subtle, it is likely that he will suggest that the whole reapportionment issue is no more than an attempt by a disgruntled minority to upset the harmonious relationship that generally prevails throughout the entire assembly.

The argument which holds that since the governor's selection is determined by the large urban areas (particularly those in South Florida), the small counties have a right to hold a majority of the legislative seats is one which adds a new dimension to the separation of powers doctrine at the state level. Separation of function is apparently overshadowed by the idea of securing a balance of areal forces regardless of the distinctions between the types of office by which the respective forces are represented. As has been pointed out, the governor has assumed in the eyes of many people a new representative quality, but this development has occurred largely because the majority has been denied an adequate voice in the legislature, and the limitations imposed by the nature of his office on the governor's power to influence or control the making of law are too often overlooked. This use of the separation of powers as a defense of the present apportionment discloses an antimajoritarian sentiment of the baldest sort.

The legal argument is one which is very familiar because it is used as a defense of the status quo in almost all public issues. It ignores both the cause and effect of the existing legal arrangement and claims for it a prescriptive right whose superiority even over popular sovereignty is implied. It amounts to a declaration that "whatever is, is right." But here, too, the radical conservatism on which the contention rests finds expression in elliptical forms such as an appeal to the elemental fact that "we are doing all right under this formula and have operated the system for a long time to good effect, or at least without hurting anyone."

If all of these arguments are considered as part of one pattern some interesting results follow. In summary it might be said that there is a fundamental logical inconsistency between two points of view ordinarily held in combination by the opponent of reapportionment in Florida. In order to justify his refusal to accept an apportionment on a purely populational basis, the supporter of the present system must insist that the interests of the nonurban areas can be protected only by allowing these areas a disproportionate share of representation. At the same time, the defender of rural overrepresentation is far more likely than others to insist on an instructed mandate, or in other words, to argue that the primary function of the representative is to reflect directly the interests, views, and opinions of the particular area he represents. This latter attitude implies the presence of strong sentimental attachment to the nearest thing to direct democracy based on local preferences that is compatible with a representative system. But this conception conflicts in the most apparent fashion with his implicit denial (as expressed in his attitude on the need for inequitable apportionment) of the right of the urban areas to be so represented. The only reconciliation of the two points of view lies in the innate conservatism and the advantageous power position of the man holding such views. It is to his advantage and to that of his constituents not to relinquish his hold on the reins of state power.

This cleavage is characteristic of a persistent conflict in American thinking which can be traced all the way to the revolutionary period. On one side of the fence stood the radicals who supported a majoritarian view of government bolstered by theories of equal representation based on universal manhood suffrage, while on the other were the conservative Federalists with their distrust of popular majorities and their search for constitutional and other legal arrangements that would secure a balance of interests, a check on mass rule, and a limitation of suffrage. From the standpoint of the early American political groups, these principles coincided perfectly with their respective egalitarian and elitist conceptions. But when these two independent heritages (radical democracy and antimajoritarianism) are united in a single person, as they appear to be in the contemporary advocate of rural domination, it is small wonder that he appears disturbed by the problem of reconciling these disparate ways of thinking. His arguments are ingenious in their simplicity, while his capacity for constructing legal arrangements designed to stave off the demands for equal representation is little short of extraordinary. One wonders sometimes whether, except in the moments when the intense emotionalism of his oratorical powers succeeds in sweeping aside all reservations, he has convinced himself, or whether he is simply forced to fall back on the simple premise that his power position must be maintained without regard to moral or logical niceties.

The political consequences of malapportionment in Florida are so extensive as to reach into almost every aspect of governmental organization and policy in the state. The fact that no simple cause and effect sequence can be ascribed to the influences of the apportionment system does not bear out the claim that the system has no substantive effect on public affairs; instead it indicates that the influences are in most cases subtle and deeply embedded in the structure of government. One of the gravest obstacles to reapportionment is the power structure which has been built up within the framework of the system, many parts of which would be affected by an apportionment according to population.

Perhaps the most important indication of the extent to which reapportionment would affect most aspects of Florida government is the amount of controversy which it has aroused. The only other contemporary issue that can produce as much concern as reapportionment is racial integration. If reapportionment would have as little practical effect as some opponents maintain, it is extremely difficult to see why both sides are so exercised about it.

The type of apportionment which exists in Florida contributes to an anomic[35] situation in the state's politics, some characteristics of which were presented in Chapter 2 and alluded to in the foregoing discussion. By focusing attention almost exclusively on the counties as geographical determinants of representation and as the entities whose interests must take first place in affecting the individual representative's vote even on state-wide issues, the system creates a narrowness of outlook that precludes a broader conception of the function of representation. The conducting of the state's business on the basis of mutual back-scratching has become so habitual that to suggest a different approach to state politics is blasphemous.

In this framework, the legislator is tied hand and foot to local power groups, to patterns of local political behavior, and to methods of fulfilling his obligations to the local area which leave him little opportunity for viewing problems in their state-wide context. Members so oriented can unite more easily for negative than for positive purposes, except when they are united through the offering of mutual advantages to their respective local areas. The absence of any general interest conception (however vague it may be) also encourages the pressures of large economic interests, who see their opportunity to fill the power gap left by this type of political thinking. Parties, and even strong factions, are not allowed to develop because they might destroy these local ties and reconcile some of the conflict over interests and issues within the organization, rather than leave them to ferment until they reach the legislature iself.[36] Such state-wide machines as exist in Florida (including state organizations of county officials and groups who are united into an effective force because they form the clientele of one or the other of the cabinet members) have their roots in the system and are dedicated to the idea that their power should be used to perpetuate it. In a very direct sense, the disintegration of the executive authority implied by the cabinet system, the increasing difficulty of the relations of the governor and the legislature, the anomolous patterns of legislative leadership, the refusal to accept institutionalized practices of administrative operation such as a state-wide merit system, and other existing or emerging methods of political action are certainly conditioned by legislative apportionment.

The fact that legislative apportionment plays a part in so many

aspects of the politics of the state does not mean that if reapportionment is sought first all these other things will be added. Too many
of the legislators and potential legislators from the large counties have
received their political education in the traditions of the present
system to allow them to break radically with it. In addition, there are
several points of contact between economic interests and the present
system which are fully accepted by many of the urban county representatives and for which a place would be found in any new organizational form.[37] Even so, there are unquestionably general differences
in personality type and in outlook between the present representatives
from urban and rural areas which would have an effect on the structure of politics as well as on issues if more urban members were returned. Although the generalizations are by no means unlimited, the
urban representatives tend to display a sophistication about the diver-
sification of groups in society, an understanding of the necessity for
formalizing large scale governmental organizations and processes, and
less reluctance to resort to new techniques in administration than do
most of their rural county colleagues. An apportionment, therefore,
which brought to the legislature a sizeable increase in members possessing these characteristics would certainly make some impact on
the method of getting elected to the legislature and on the tone of
its houses even if not on more fundamental matters.

Of equal if not greater importance would be the effect of such a
change on the handling of certain major issues now before the state.
A few years ago a student of the problem of reapportionment polled
a wide variety of politicians, legislators, and political scientists on
the connection between apportionment and the politics and public
policy of the states concerned. The results for Florida are very interesting: it was agreed by all the individuals polled that apportionment
in this state had produced significant controversies between the major
political parties, between rural and urban areas, between geographical
regions without regard to their urban or rural characteristics, and
between metropolitan and nonmetropolitan areas. On the questions
involving issues of public policy, the correspondents from Florida
were unanimous in their agreement that the present apportionment
of representatives influenced the support of public education, highway
fund distribution, social welfare programs, and taxation and public

finance. In addition, some of the individuals polled indicated that
apportionment entered into the attempt to resolve problems in the
fields of labor and management relations and local government sub-
sidies and support. Unanimous affirmative answers were also forthcoming from Florida on the following questions: "Is legislative apportionment, in your state, symbolic of cleavages sharp and decisive
in other relations than legislative behavior and votes themselves?
Would there be significant changes in the political complexion and
policy in your state were an actually equitable apportionment in
theory and practice obtained?"[38]

It would be extremely difficult to catalogue in a brief space all
the areas of policy in which a substantial change might occur if
equitable reapportionment could be achieved. Illustrations drawn
from the fields of race relations, finance, and labor legislation, however, afford a good insight into the types of differences that could
follow such a change.

After several radical pieces of legislation aimed at preserving segregation had been staved off during the 1956 special session, the legislature passed some very stringent measures in 1957. Included among
these was an interposition resolution (H.C.R. 174). Although much
parliamentary maneuvering attended the passage of this resolution,
an analysis of two important votes indicates what might have happened had a population-based apportionment been in effect. On April
5, the house of representatives passed the resolution, with the record
vote being taken on a motion to defer the bill temporarily. The
motion to defer received twenty-nine favorable votes (those voting
favorably may obviously be considered as opposed to interposition),
fifty-nine votes were cast in opposition to the motion, and there were
six absences. The twenty-nine representatives who were not in favor
of interposition were drawn from areas containing over 52 per cent
of the state's population on the 1950 basis and nearly 55 per cent
of the population based on 1956 estimates. When a record vote on
the resolution was taken in the senate (in this case on a motion to
re-commit to committee), the result was seventeen ayes (the ayes
may be taken to be opponents of interposition) and twenty-one nays.
One of the nays, however, changed his vote from aye to nay in order
to move for reconsideration, and so may be taken as an opponent of

interposition. The senators opposed to interposition represented over 64 per cent of the population on the 1950 basis and over 69 per cent in the terms of the 1956 estimates. From this and other votes, it appears almost certain that the more extreme types of segregationist legislation depend for their support in Florida on a legislative apportionment which denies to a majority of the population its full share of legislative seats. The margin in the senate was such that, even allowing for considerable bias, interposition would have been killed had representation been on a proportionate basis.

The way in which the problem of overrepresentation of certain areas limits flexibility in fiscal and other types of policy was also clearly illustrated in the 1957 legislature. Among many other problems of finance, the state was faced with the fact that many counties were no longer able to build needed secondary roads because most of their highway funds were being expended to acquire rights of way for the construction or improvement of the state primary road system. The bill which came before the house (as committee substitute for H.B. 721) provided relief for the counties by stipulating that the state road department be required to meet 60 per cent of the costs of procuring primary rights of way. The bill included an appropriation of thirty million dollars for this purpose for the ensuing biennium. As the bill stood, it was estimated that the road department's share of the costs of rights of way would be covered by the appropriation, and the money would be applied by the department to the roads that it was planning to construct during the biennium. A group of small county representatives (with their support largely drawn from the rural areas) managed, however, to amend the bill so that the money would be allocated among the counties according to the formula used for dividing the seventh cent of the gasoline tax. The formula provides that the money shall go to the counties on the basis of three equally weighted factors—area, population, and mileage of roads contributed by the counties to the state road system by 1931. It is patently obvious that such an allocation has no relation to the location of projected highways, the variation in costs of rights of way, or any of the other factors which enter into the planning of a major highway system. The only plausible explanation of this action is that many small county delegates are unwilling to permit any funds to be distributed except in a manner that follows the principle of disproportionality characteristic of the representative system itself. The house action on this measure is an excellent example of the use of county lines as determinants of state expenditures, a practice which in this case (and in many others) handicaps the effectiveness of a major state department and penalizes the urban areas in which the costs of rights of way are higher and the need for interconnecting highways greater. It should be noted that the measure was not enacted into law.

A final example, drawn from the field of labor legislation, has a more hypothetical quality than the two issues discussed above. In 1943, the legislature proposed a "right-to-work" amendment to the Florida constitution (Declaration of Rights, Section 12) which was adopted by the voters in 1944. The house vote on the proposal was sixty-seven for and twenty-four against the measure, a vote which was substantially greater than the three-fifths vote required to carry. However, the urban vote was divided sixteen for and fourteen against, while the rural vote was fifty-one for and ten opposed. On the basis of these figures it would be extremely difficult to draw the conclusion that the amendment would have failed to secure a three-fifths vote in the house if the urban areas had had a more equitable share of the seats, but in view of the band-wagon tendency in the house, some doubts can be raised. And it is especially interesting to note the rural preponderance in deciding an issue which has almost exclusive application in the urban areas.[39]

The specific instances which have been cited afford strong evidence to support the contention that the present apportionment of the Florida legislature has something of a chain-reaction effect on the substantive issues of Florida politics (and often on issues which go beyond the state's boundaries). Other broader and even more complicated examples drawn from such important policy areas as metropolitanism, constitutional revision, and the tax structure could be given. In brief and without exaggerating, the entire political process in Florida is beset with this problem.[40]

Chapter 4

Selection and Membership

THE people of the state of Florida elect 133 members of
the legislature—95 members of the house and 38 senators—to represent them for the purpose of passing the state's laws and otherwise
attending to its affairs. The method by which the selection of this
assembly is carried out and the type of people selected are, like the
system of apportionment, of considerable importance to the way in
which the legislature and the other instruments of state government
operate.[1]

Qualifications for voting in Florida generally follow the pattern
in the other states: the elector must be at least twenty-one years of
age, a citizen of the United States, and must have resided in the state
at least one year and in the county for six months. It is also necessary
to be registered with the county registrar of voters in order to be
carried on the voting rolls. In addition to these positive requirements,
there are certain grounds on which a voter may be disqualified; these
include persons under guardianship (such as people confined in
public prisons), persons *non compos mentis* or insane, persons convicted of a felony unless restored to civil rights, persons who have
been convicted of bribery, perjury, larceny or any infamous crime,
persons convicted of betting or wagering on the outcome of an election, and persons who have voted in another state or county within
the previous twelve months where residence in that state or county
is a requirement for voting there.

Voters so qualified select their representatives (and most of their
other state and county officials) at regularly scheduled state primary
and general elections. Florida's method of nominating candidates is

typical of the practice in the southern states: nomination takes place through direct primary elections in which only those electors who are registered as members of the party conducting the primary may participate. The state thus uses the closed primary; and in addition the law requires that the nominee poll a majority of the votes cast, with the result that if no candidate receives over half the vote in the first primary, a second, or run-off, primary is held to decide which of the two leading candidates in the first primary shall be the party's nominee at the ensuing general election. Through 1956, the first primary was held on the Tuesday after the first Monday in May of even-numbered years and the second primary followed three weeks later. In the 1957 session, however, a bill[2] was passed which moved the primaries to September—the first primary was to be held eight weeks prior to the general election and the second five weeks before the general election. In large measure this bill was an outgrowth of the increasing interparty competition in Florida and was designed to shorten the total period of campaigning. Since the general election falls on the Tuesday following the first Monday in November of even-numbered years, a candidate who had opposition in both the primary and general election under the former system was involved in a political campaign for virtually the entire year. As long as the Democratic party had little more than token opposition from the Republicans (and then often in only a few constituencies) this long period from nomination to final election did not impose a hardship on a candidate, but the increasing Republican strength in several counties in recent years has meant that a number of candidates must remain in the political race from April (or earlier) until well into November. Nevertheless, the 1959 legislature enacted legislation returning to the old system of May primaries.[3]

A few years ago the Kefauver Committee's investigations in Florida revealed some rather embarrassing connections between Florida politics and certain gambling interests, especially in the matter of campaign contributions. One of the outcomes of these investigations was the passage, in 1951, of a very strict and apparently effective campaign expense law known as the "Who Gave It—Who Got It" act.[4] Under the law every candidate (other than those for municipal offices) is required to designate a campaign treasurer, who maintains a strict record of all contributions and expenditures. All monies must be deposited within twenty-four hours of receipt in a separate campaign fund in a previously designated bank depository. Expenditures are closely confined to the amount of money on hand at a given time, and a comprehensive set of reports is required, in which all contributions and expenditures are separately listed. Candidates for the legislature, along with many other office-seekers, make these reports to the secretary of state. No person is permitted to contribute (either in a primary or a general election) anything in the way of money, time, or supplies with a total value in excess of one thousand dollars. Certain categories of people are prohibited from making contributions at all. These include persons holding a dog or horse racing permit, persons holding a license for the sale of intoxicating beverages, and persons operating or serving as officers or directors of a public utility which is subject to a grant of franchise or regulation by the state or any of its political subdivisions. Penalties for violation include denial of nomination or commission to office, revocation of charter or permit, citation for contempt, and the possibility of conviction on charges of misdemeanor or felony. This law has the advantage of bringing all expenditures into the open, allowing the respective candidates to observe closely the financing of their opponents' campaigns, and placing the responsibility for keeping within the law on contributors as well as on candidates. Most observers seem to feel that the funds reported are a reasonably accurate guide to the costs of campaigning in the state.

Legislative Elections in Florida

The members of the house of representatives in Florida are elected for two-year terms at each state general election, after having been nominated in their respective party primaries. Senators are elected for four-year terms, but the members of the senate are divided into two groups (on the basis of odd- and even-numbered districts) and half of them are elected every two years. In order to be eligible for a seat in either of the two houses, it is necessary only that the aspirant be a duly qualified elector of the district or county he represents. If a member moves out of the county or district from which he has been elected, he automatically vacates his seat, although there is no prohibition against a senator moving from one county to another if both are included in the same multicounty district. Any person holding a lucrative office under the state or federal government is also prohibited from holding a seat in the legislature.

In order to run for either the house or the senate, the individual must file his qualification papers with the secretary of state and pay his filing fee and party assessment not earlier than noon of the seventy-seventh day and not later than noon of the sixty-third day prior to the first primary. The candidate must take an oath or affirmation stating the party of which he is a member, that he voted for 90 per cent of the nominees of the party of which he is a member at the last general election and that he pledges himself to vote for 90 per cent of the nominees of his party at the next general election,[5] the title of the office for which he is a candidate, that he is a qualified elector of the state, that he is qualified to hold the office for which he wishes to run, that he has paid his party assessment, that he has not violated any of the state's election or registration laws, and that he has taken the oath of allegiance to the United States and the state of Florida. The filing fee is 3 per cent of the annual salary of the office sought, and the party executive committee may levy an additional assessment up to 2 per cent of the annual salary. For convenience the total 5 per cent (sixty dollars) may be filed with the secretary of state at the time of qualifying. If a recognized party elects at least three-fourths of its legally authorized number of members of the state executive committee and has 5 per cent of the total registered voters in the counties from which these committee members are elected,[6] the full 5 per cent goes to the state executive committee of the party to help defray its expenses.

In counties from which more than one member of the house is returned, the candidates file and run in groups and, although all seats are voted upon by the county at large, the voters can vote for only one candidate within each group. At first the group system applied only to primaries but was extended to the general election as a result of a controversy over a legislative election in Orange County in the legislative session of 1947. In the preceding general election, two Democrats and two Republicans were competing for Orange

County's two seats. A Democrat polled the most votes, a Republican was second, and the other Democrat third. The third-place Democrat contested the seating of the second-place Republican, contending that the Republican candidate was running solely against the leading Democrat and that, as victor over the fourth-place Republican he (the third-place Democrat) was entitled to the second seat. The house affirmed the right of the Republican to the seat under the law, but subsequently amended the statutes to provide that the group system be made part of the general election as well as the primaries.[7]

In some counties from which two or three representatives are elected, a rather interesting informal practice of allocating the seats to different portions of the county has sprung up. In Alachua County, for example, it used to be understood that the member from Group I would be from Gainesville and the member from Group II from "out in the county," i.e., from the rural area or one of the small towns. A perusal of the list of places of residence of members from counties with more than one representative indicates that this practice is widespread; in some cases a rural-urban division is manifested, in others the allocation is on the basis of electing one or two representatives from a large urban center and the second or third one from a smaller city in the county. The usage is so common and so completely accepted that some otherwise well-informed people have the idea that it is not only politically unwise to try to break the pattern, but that it is *legally* necessary to file in the groups which by tradition are assigned to these fictional districts. Here is an excellent illustration of extreme localism and of the demand for close adherence to direct representation, with perhaps some admixture of the functional concept of representation. On the whole the practice seems to narrow the outlook of some of the legislators even more than usual and to confine the possibility of choosing the best qualified men within a geographical and social framework even smaller than the county. Thus the arrangement of election by groups —which was a convenient way of avoiding the complexities of plural voting—became a device for extending the concept of extreme localism and in some cases accentuating the rural-urban split.

The rotation of the senatorial seat from county to county in several of the multicounty districts is a related practice. This method appears to be adhered to fairly closely in the fifth (Liberty, Wakulla, Franklin), twenty-fifth (Bay, Washington, Calhoun, Gulf), twenty-ninth (Clay, Baker), and thirty-eighth (Pasco, Sumter) districts. The first district (Santa Rosa, Okaloosa) was regarded in the past as a rotating district but Senator Newman Brackin was elected to consecutive terms in 1944 and 1948 (in the latter case he was president-designate of the senate for 1949) and returned to the senate in 1956 after an absence of only a single term. There is, therefore, a question about the extent of adherence to the ground rules in that district. On the whole the rotation of senate seats among the counties making up a district probably compounds the faults of the house system of breaking up the counties by insuring against continuity of membership.

In 1956 first and second primaries were held in many counties and districts, and general election contests followed to elect all the house members and one-half the senate. The following table contains information on the number of contests and contestants in these elections:

Table 3
Election Contests in 1956

	Seats at Stake	No. of Dem. 1st Prim. Held	No. of Rep. 1st Prim. Held	Total Dem. Cand.	Total Rep. Cand.	Dem. 2nd Prim. Held	Rep. 2nd Prim. Held	Gen. Election Contests	Ret. W/O Oppos. in Prim. or Gen. Elec.	Ret. W Oppos. in Gen. Elec. Only
House	95	68	6	225	27	28	1	20	20	5
Senate	20*	15	2	49	6	5	0	4	3	1

* A special primary was held in the fourteenth senatorial district to fill an unexpired term and is included in the figures.

It is noticeable that the Democratic party is still overwhelmingly the majority party in terms of participation in state legislative contests, although the Republicans are making a strong, concentrated bid for enlarging their numbers in the legislature. During two recent sessions (1955 and 1957) they held six seats in the house and one senate seat,[8] and in 1961 they added a seventh house seat. As late as 1949 there were no Republicans in either house (although there had been one in 1947), but three Republican house members made their appearance in 1951, and two additional house members and a senator were elected on the Republican ticket to serve in the 1953 session. The growth of presidential Republicanism in the last three elections has given a strong impetus to the desire to challenge Democratic dominance of state politics. In 1956, and again in 1960, a number of candidates ran on the Republican ticket for county offices in the more populous South Florida counties, and the party has gained control of both Pinellas and Sarasota counties.

Insofar as the legislative races are concerned the Republicans have husbanded their resources—both financial and personal—very well. They have spent little time in intraparty contests, except in Pinellas County, and have concentrated their efforts on the areas where there is some hope of early success. In contests for seats in the house of representatives in 1956 Republican candidates qualified for twenty races covering twelve counties; all but one of these counties (Escambia) was in South Florida. In every county in which the Republicans entered candidates except Escambia and Hillsborough they polled more than 40 per cent of the votes in the general election. Only in Pinellas and Sarasota, however, do the Republicans seem to have a really solid hold on their legislative seats. The accompanying table indicates the extent to which the Republicans have made inroads into state politics in the areas in which they ran candidates for the legislature.

Despite redoubled Republican efforts and the reasonable degree of success that these efforts have produced, there is not as yet a feeling of a real party "situation" in the state. The Republicans are much more reliant on organization and certainly have achieved a far greater degree of cohesion on state issues than the Democrats,[9] but the Democratic response has not been in the direction of tightening its own organization to meet this challenge in a unified fashion. The Democratic party (and particularly the legislative portion of it) has seemingly been more concerned with measures to prevent the

Table 4
Republican Efforts in House of Representatives Contests,* 1956

County	Registered Voters				Reg. Reps. Voting in the 1st Primary	% of Regis. Reps. Voting in 1st Primary	General Election			Presidential Vote		
	Primary		General				Total Vote for Legislature	Republican Vote for Legislature	Percentage of Total Vote which was Rep.	Total Presidential Vote	Eisenhower Vote	Percentage of Total Vote for Eisenhower
	Dem.	Rep.	Dem.	Rep.								
Brevard	16,013	2,684	17,776	4,212	no contest	—	12,676	6,583	51.9	13,932	10,004	71.8
Broward	50,722	15,063	58,306	20,770	4,771	31.7	52,596	25,201	47.9	60,113	43,552	72.5
Dade†	265,904	35,873	285,966	42,031	7,397	20.6	181,991	77,776	42.7	236,497	130,938	55.4
Escambia	53,131	967	54,991	1,521	no contest	—	28,293	4,748	16.8	35,547	13,227	37.2
Hillsborough	95,346	7,134	102,243	9,189	no contest	—	64,646	16,339	25.3	80,499	41,889	52.0
Manatee	18,310	3,348	19,725	4,283	no contest	—	16,167	7,209	44.6	17,298	11,904	68.8
Orange	45,244	8,841	51,677	12,212	no contest	—	44,012	21,389	48.6	52,014	37,482	72.1
Palm Beach	52,638	10,188	58,754	13,599	no contest	—	42,172	18,737	44.4	50,067	35,746	71.4
Pinellas	61,309	39,801	69,469	51,572	16,060	40.4	91,146	56,682	62.2	102,427	74,314	72.6
St. Lucie	10,247	998	10,841	1,212	no contest	—	7,216	2,992	41.5	8,166	5,435	66.6
Sarasota	8,922	7,252	11,526	10,030	3,574	49.3	17,622	8,973	50.9	18,989	13,937	73.4
Volusia	38,588	4,656	42,044	6,626	no contest	—	33,411	14,117	42.3	39,592	25,103	63.4

* Where there were contests in counties having more than one group, the highest figure in any group was used.

† In Dade County where there were three Republican first primaries, the highest figures from the three groups were taken showing at least that many Republican voters participated. In Group II, where there was a runoff election, 11.1 per cent of registered Republicans in the county took part in it.

growth of the Republican party in order to preserve Florida politics of the type described in Chapter 2 than with the creation of a strong organizational counterpoise to rising Republicanism.[10] In carrying out these maneuvers the Democrats have an advantage based on the system of apportionment because overrepresentation is in the communities where the symbolism of Democratic party membership is much stronger than any real sense of common purpose, with the result that these are the areas which the Republicans have not penetrated and are not likely soon to penetrate.

The ambivalence of Democratic party membership in Florida is illustrated by attitudes toward the claim that party makes on an individual. Just as Republican party affiliation is a symbol of propriety and respectability among the suburban middle class in many other sections of the country, so Democratic party adherence is an important means of establishing identity with the things that count in the South. There is considerable evidence to show that this symbolic hold of the party label is weakening among the younger generations, especially those in the urban areas. One former senator, who, though he was elected from South Florida and has amassed considerable wealth, still exhibits many traits of a North Florida background, pointed out that he had felt a definite responsibility to vote for Stevenson in 1952 while he was still in the legislature, but shifted to Eisenhower in 1956 when he was out of office. This man, along with many others of his type, exhibits a strong moral compulsion to support not only the local candidates of the party under whose label he sought office, but also the national candidates of that party as well, even though the party's stand on issues is completely opposed to that for which he (and his state and local party organization) stand. Among most of the newer Florida politicians there is no comparable sense of organizational affiliation which, even in its limited way, rises above differences on interests at all geographical levels. There is no apparent feeling of obligation on their part to support the party's presidential candidate simply because they have been elected to state office as members of that party. Although the label "Democrat" may long remain as a useful symbol for local purposes among such individuals, they are in a much better position than the older type of politician to seek their natural party alignment should it become expedient to do so in the face of an emerging two-party system. As a matter of fact, the prospects for two-party government in the near future rest to some extent on the degree of flexibility that these figures exhibit in terms of over-all party loyalty. In the meantime party differences do not play a predominant role in Florida legislative politics, either in elections or on the floors of the houses themselves.

In view of the remarks just made it is obvious that the Democratic primaries still loom large in legislative politics in Florida. Frequently five or six candidates will file for nomination to a seat, and as many as seven candidates contended for the 1956 Democratic primary in one senatorial district. The size of the district has less effect in determining the number of people who run than factors such as the real or presumed vulnerability of the incumbent or the fact that the former member is not contesting the election. In some cases the futility of running against the incumbent is apparent to most potential opponents and the man in office gets a free ride; fairly often persons who have been designated as speaker or speaker pro tem of the house or as president or president pro tem of the senate will not be opposed.

Although turnover in the Florida legislature appears to be fairly high when looked at from a standpoint of the number of new faces at each session, this state compares favorably with most others in terms of legislative tenure.[11] Thirty-eight members of the 1957 house (40 per cent) were not in the 1955 regular session. Of these, however, four had previous service in earlier regular sessions and four others had been elected in special elections to serve in the 1956 special session. Despite this apparently large turnover, the legislative experience of the house in 1957 was extensive: twenty-one members were serving their second terms, twenty-one others their third terms, nine their fourth terms, five their fifth terms, and the few remaining varied in experience from the seventh to the thirteenth term. In the senate there were ten new members (26 per cent), but two of these were returnees on the rotation system and four others had previously served in the house; therefore only four senators were without any previous experience in the legislature. Nine senators were serving their second session, seven their third, three their fourth, four their fifth, and the rest were scattered from their sixth to sixteenth sessions. Many of these men had had experience in the house, which together with their longer terms, accounts for the generally higher proportion of periods of service in the senate as compared to the house. Occasionally a rotating senator will even manage to win the house seat in his county between his periods as a senator.[12]

If we carry the analysis a step further it may be seen that a relatively few members in each house are the victims of electoral defeat. Of the thirty-eight new members of the house in 1957, only fourteen had defeated individuals who had served in the 1955 session. The remainder had died, retired voluntarily, or resigned to run for the senate. Of the ten new faces in the senate, five had defeated incumbents. In one of these cases—that of the seventh senatorial district (Polk County)—it is very likely that the incumbent would have been returned (since he was president-designate of the senate) but for the fact that a scandal occurred in which he was accused of offering a bribe to another candidate to get out of the race.[13] On the whole it may be said that in Florida, as in a great many other states, there is considerable advantage in being in office already in terms of potential success in a campaign.

An adequate treatment of legislative elections in Florida would require a close analysis of campaigns in each county and district over a long period of time. Such an election study, of course, goes beyond the bounds of the present book. On the basis of selective data, however, a few generalizations may be presented about campaign techniques and the sort of issues which may win or lose an election for a candidate.

In the first place there is a considerable difference between the types of campaigns waged in the smaller as compared with the larger counties. Candidates in both types of area are concerned, of course, with getting their names and qualifications before the public. In the smaller counties, the approach can be much more personal because of the smaller number of people, lack of possibilities for use of newspapers, radio, television and other mass-opinion media, and the greater homogeneity of population. The personal call, the school house or court house political rally, letters that are individually directed, and similar techniques are most in vogue in these areas.

If the people in such counties can be lured into talking to their friends about what the representative or senator has done for them as individuals or about his personal relations with them, the candidate may realize considerable political advantage (or disadvantage if the talk goes the other way) by way of the infectious nature of public sentiment. Although local issues are likely to be very important in large and small counties alike, it is much more likely that they will be the *only* issues in small counties. The strength of an incumbent may rest especially on his having obtained a public institution, a road, or some other project that wins favor in the area. In many respects, too, the relative lack of socio-economic differentiation among people in these areas may mean that the candidates will not have to placate opposing groups on questions involving larger issues of education, social welfare, and taxation. It is likely on the other hand that a single issue like teacher pay may be much more prominent in small than in large counties, possibly because of the greater prestige of public school teachers and their pressure organizations together with reliance on the state to equalize educational facilities in these areas. Both the evidence of recent campaigns and the differences in attitudes of small and large county representatives toward teacher pay in the 1957 session serve to bear out these observations.

Interest in the primary campaigns in the smaller counties is noticeably greater than in the larger ones, in part perhaps because of the closer personal knowledge of the candidates and the resultant greater intensity of feeling about the outcome of the election, but also because interest in politics in the larger areas seems to be focused on a broader set of problems. Eight counties[14] had a turnout of more than 80 per cent of the registered voters in the first primary in 1956. All of these are small counties and all but one (Martin) are in rural North Florida. On the other hand, the nine counties[15] in which less than 50 per cent of the registered vote turned out in the first primary included most of the larger counties of urban South Florida. By way of contrast nearly all of these latter areas had very high percentages of their registered voters participating in the presidential election; in fact, several of them recorded a presidential vote of more than 80 per cent of those qualified, and in most cases the proportionate quantity of voters paralleled closely the degree of participation in the first legislative primary in the smaller counties. It is also worth noting that in the nine counties in which the first primary participation was smallest (along with many other large counties), participation in the general legislative election fell considerably short of the vote cast in the presidential race which was, of course, held at the same time.[16] Because of these differences in the number of people participating, the candidates in the small counties and those in the large counties are faced with somewhat different campaign approaches in legislative primary races. It is imperative that the small county candidate actually win a physical majority of the people over to his side (since they are apparently going to vote anyway), while the large county candidate is faced with the possibility of losing the election because he cannot get a sufficient number of potential supporters out to vote at all.

In the larger counties the campaigns will usually be more diversified both in terms of techniques and in terms of types of appeal. Radio, television, and the newspapers are usually much more important than the personal touch, especially since it is difficult to build an organization large enough to do much effective personal canvassing. More account, too, has to be taken of the group basis of politics in these areas. A typical campaign in the larger counties may follow approximately the following pattern: the candidate will select a platform which makes individual concessions to each group that he feels is important enough to merit special attention, e.g., labor, small business, the old age pensioner, the farmer, etc. He will then make it his business to get into contact with members of these groups and emphasize their areas of special appeal in each instance. In addition, he will choose certain state-wide and local issues (the proportions varying in terms of any number of factors) which he feels will not alienate any substantial group and will use these as the strong points of his broadcasts, newspaper ads, throw-aways, and other material designed for county-wide dissemination.[17] In both large and small counties, if there is an incumbent it is probable that he will be attacked on either or both of two points—his voting record and his having used his influence to procure benefits for himself or groups with whom he is closely asso-

ciated. Some members get to be known as "special interests" representatives; references are frequently heard to "trading-stamp men,"
"race-track men," "small-loans men," and to any variety of others. On
the other hand the incumbent has, of course, the great advantage
of appealing to his experience and often to his expertness on a
legislative subject dear to the hearts of his constituents.

Newspaper support, or at least the lack of opposition by the
papers of wide circulation, is very important to a legislative candidate. Neutrality (or unobstrusive favortism) is the more frequent
response of the papers, but they may at times take a decided stand on
a legislative candidate. In some places newspapers seem to take the
attitude that their condemnation can lose the election for an individual; and, although it may be difficult to beat a man on a single issue
except for serious cases of scandal, the daily newspapers may wield
persuasive influence, particularly in relation to local issues of great
magnitude.[18] It is easy enough for a legislator to get into difficulties
with the papers even while intending to cater to them, because
several of the dailies are inclined to be very favorably disposed toward
certain economic doctrines and interests, yet they reverse their attitude without warning in cases in which a local public activity
comes into conflict with the erstwhile corporate favorite.

Campaign expenditures vary widely in Florida, but as might be
expected there is some positive correlation between the amount expended and the size of the constituency.[19] Some of the candidates in
the smaller counties spend very little more than their filing fees,
and it is rare to find a candidate whose expenditures reach a thousand
dollars in the smaller counties. In Dade County, on the other hand,
the winning candidate in Group I in 1956 spent more than fifteen
thousand dollars, and in several other instances (including senate
races) expenditures of more than ten thousand dollars were recorded. In cases like these, the use of a professional public relations
advisor and the purchase of television and radio time constitute the
more expensive items of a campaign which must reach large numbers of voters. On the basis of the reports, it may safely be said
that, in the larger counties (especially where there are daily newspapers and radio stations), a candidate should be prepared to lay
out anywhere from fifteen hundred to five thousand dollars, depend-

ing to some extent on whether there is a second primary and/or a general election contest.

In most cases the amounts expended by candidates for the same seat relate very closely to one another, especially if the election is a tight one. There does not, however, appear to be any special correlation between amounts spent and success, nor between the amount spent by challengers as compared to incumbents.

A great percentage of legislative campaigns are mainly self-financed, partly as a result of the proportion of campaigns that take place in small constituencies. In the counties where expenditures are very large, of course, the candidates usually depend on contributions; in a few instances the candidate may expend very little in the way of personal funds, but in most cases even in large counties the candidate and members of his family are the primary contributors. Although the limit on contributions is one thousand dollars for any individual, the percentage of individual contributions of more than one hundred dollars is very small.

The lion's share of the money is spent in the primaries. In the 1956 primary campaigns for the senate $111,334 was spent, while only $911 was laid out on the general election. Candidates in the house primaries spent a total of $210,588, while only $21,411 was expended in house general election contests. These differences are not merely products of the fewer general election campaigns; in many of the races in which both primaries and general elections were held, more money was laid out on the primaries. Only in the few instances in which the primaries were less hotly contested than the general election did the expenditures in the latter compare closely with or exceed those of the former. One noticeable factor in the 1956 campaign contributions of the parties which relates to their differing degrees of institutionalization was the fact that the Republican State Executive Committee contributed up to one hundred dollars to the general election funds of its candidates. In addition, several Republican candidates received contributions from local party organizations and from informally organized Republican party associations of various sorts. No campaign funds for legislative candidates were forthcoming from comparable Democratic party organizations.

The absence of a party situation, the nature and extent of the

use of the direct primary, and the significant differences in sociological composition of the various counties and senatorial districts in
Florida make for a great variation in the factors that influence a
legislative election and campaign expenditures from county to county.
Short of interviewing practically every voter in a county, it is sometimes difficult to understand the reasons why one individual is pre-
ferred over another in Florida. Henry Jones Ford apparently had
some difficulty in resolving this problem, too. At one point he
quotes John Stuart Mill, who said: "Unless a man is fit for the
gallows, he is thought to be almost as fit as other people for almost
anything for which he can offer himself as a candidate." To this
Jones adds: "If American experience suggests any modification of
this statement it would be that the one reservation made by Mill
is no longer called for by the facts of the case."[20] Although the
visitation of this judgment upon the members of the Florida legislature would be excessively harsh, it is possible that more can be
explained about the type of men that the people of Florida select
to serve in the legislature than about their reasons for putting
them there.

Characteristics and Influences

Even a cursory description of the origins and social backgrounds
of the members of the Florida legislature will reveal that the members are far from constituting an ordinary cross section of the Florida
population. In terms of education and success in other endeavors
they are above the average, and in most respects they appear to
have some claim on the positions of leadership and prestige which
they have achieved. Although there are very specific exceptions, the
public seems for the most part to have chosen legislators who do
not mirror their constituencies so much as they reflect what many
of the individuals in those constituencies would *like* to see when they
look in their mirrors—pictures of success, self-assurance, and just
enough of the qualities of the common man so that the belligerent
insistence on equality so characteristic of American life is not denied.
The legislator usually is a man quite pleased with himself, one whose
opinions count, whose contacts are important, and whose actions
have effect. A slightly pompous manner and an air of being a prac-

tical man of the world—an insider—are traits which can easily stim-
ulate among the constituents a feeling of personal pride in their
representative and a sense of identity with him, both of which are
very important elements of political success.

In 1957 the average age of the house member was forty-three
with a range from twenty-seven to sixty-eight; in the senate the
average was only slightly higher, forty-seven, with the youngest
being twenty-nine and the oldest seventy-six.[21] The senators are
usually men and there are few feminine members in the house, although several women have run very strongly in recent campaigns.

It might be assumed that the great influx of people from other
states into Florida would produce a legislature of widely diverse
origins in terms of places of birth and upbringing. That is not so,
however; heavy importance still seems to be placed on the "local
boy" aspect of state and county politics. This emphasis is not
surprising in the relatively stable sections of North and West
Florida, but even in the "gold coast" and other resort areas there
is a strong tendency to select a long-term resident, preferably one
whose family background is Floridian. In view of the social structure
of the resort counties it is somewhat surprising that so many legislators from these areas come from families with long-standing political connections in Florida, and often in the older sections of the
state. Time after time newspaper reports on gubernatorial possibilities among members of the legislature will report that, although
the individual comes from Dade (Miami) or Broward (Fort Lauder-
dale) or some other South Florida coastal county, he has lived or
has family connections in Madison or some similar county and understands the problems of the small rural county as well as those
of the urban areas. No less than sixty-one members of the 1957
house were born in Florida, and of the remainder sixteen were born
in Georgia or Alabama and in many cases were brought up in
Florida. Only thirteen of ninety-five members of the lower chamber
were born outside the southern or border states. The somewhat more
conservative senate demonstrated this characteristic even more clearly:
thirty of its thirty-eight members were native Floridians, and if Missouri and Cuba may each in its own way be considered border areas,
only one senator was a Yankee proper.

Although most members would (with justification) hasten to repudiate the stigma that attaches to being an intellectual, the Florida legislator is, on the average, very well educated in the formal sense. Fifty-six representatives were college graduates, twenty-four of these had more than one degree, and only twenty-three had never attended college. The University of Florida claimed the greatest share of those attending colleges or universities with forty-four; other Florida universities and colleges were attended by eighteen members, and the rest (including some who went to more than one school) were widely scattered, but included a respectable sampling of the exoticism of the Ivy League. Twenty-two senators were college graduates, three had more than one degree, and only six did not have any higher education. Twenty-three senators were enrolled at one time or another at the University of Florida and eight at other Florida colleges or universities.

Graduation from the state university is an important attribute of politicians in a great many states, both from a standpoint of local identity and the personal associations there, but we are not aware of any state in which the affiliation is as close as it is in Florida. Campus politics and student government at the University of Florida do not differ greatly from the practices in other states except that the connections made in them and the attitudes formed by them seem to persist strongly and carry over into state politics more than they do elsewhere. Campus politics is a frenetic affair, the meaning of which seems to be completely exhausted in the lining up of personal support and making of "deals" by which the aspirations of self-consciously ambitious young men can be realized through election to offices which seem to be valued far more than their intrinsic importance warrants. The posturing air of campus politicians, along with their apparent unconcern with substantive questions that politics might raise and help to settle, seems to remain as the dominant feature of state politics. There is even a certain organizational fostering of this tendency in the university leadership society known as Florida Blue Key. Membership in this organization is restricted and much coveted. New members are co-opted and honorary members are taken in from outside the student body; in this way successful politicians who did not previously belong can be admitted to this select circle. The organization furnishes a bond among its members which cuts across fraternity and other lines. The activities of Blue Key bring the campus political leaders into contact with successful state politicians and help younger office-seekers to make the jump from university to real politics, while furnishing the old campaigners a close continuing association with the university.

In the recent past the gubernatorial campaign ordinarily has begun on the university campus at the elaborate fall homecoming festivities prior to the spring primaries. These homecomings are attended by practically all of the leading political figures in the state and most of the hopefuls. Nearly all of them have some opportunity to speak or at least to be publicly recognized during this extended festive occasion. Blue Key activities form a very important part of the homecoming panorama; the organization holds its annual dinner at this time and sponsors the combined pep rally and spectacular open-air variety show known as the "Gator Growl," an event which draws more than forty thousand spectators.

The law school plays its own particular role in the homecoming drama, offering a special skit in which Florida politics and politicians are lampooned. The law is commonly regarded as a stepping stone to politics in Florida as elsewhere in the United States, and a great many of the state's lawyers are University of Florida law school graduates. Naturally the law school draws many campus politicians and among these are included a representative sampling of Blue Key, so that a further professional tie-in is apparent. Campus politics thus furnishes an entree into the political life of the state and in turn influences the manner in which that political life is carried on.

In terms of occupations, the lawyers form the dominant group in the legislature; in 1957 there were eighteen in the senate (excluding Senator Shands who had a law degree but had not practiced) and forty-two in the house. A number of lawyers listed business or agricultural pursuits in addition to the practice of law. Farmers also made a reputable showing in both houses; if the citrus growers, cattlemen, timber-growers, and general farmers are lumped together (as they may be for occupational if not for political purposes), approximately 25 per cent of each house was made up of members engaged exclusively in agriculture or with agricultural interests. Most of the legislators who fall outside these two categories

were engaged in a wide variety of occupations, but were for the
most part in some sort of business. Insurance and real estate agents
were included in farily sizeable numbers and there were a few bankers, manufacturers, motel operators, contractors, merchants, and
druggists. The house contained three teachers, a student, a commercial fisherman and, most unusual of all, an alligator farm operator
(not included in the agricultural computation). It is noticeable that
only three or four men listed occupations that would enable them
to be classified as laborers or workers, although a few others listed
former occupations of this type and no doubt there are still others
who have in the past been wage-earners. Since the 1957 figures
are typical, it may be said that the Florida legislature is composed
overwhelmingly of professional people, businessmen, and well-to-do
farmers. In part these occupational characteristics may be related
to the desire of the public to see these types in public office, but it
is also true that such occupations offer the advantage of permitting
those in them to take off the time necessary to perform legislative
duties for which there is no full-time compensation. From the actions
of a great many of the legislators it may also be inferred that they
consider it advantageous to be in the legislature from the standpoint
of business "good will."

A great many members of each house normally are former
office-holders. In 1957, forty-three members of the house of representatives and twenty-five senators had held (and some still held)
appointive or elective political offices, mainly in their cities or
counties. These offices ranged in importance from service on relatively minor local boards and commissions to responsible legal or
judicial positions and to municipal or county executive offices of
considerable authority. A few legislators had held or still held offices
in their parties or seats on various executive committees of the
parties. The political experience of the Florida legislators adds up to
an impressive total which is most noteworthy for the extent to
which it fits the legislator into the political picture in his particular
constituency, despite the fact that a few of the activities range far
more widely.

The personal life of the legislator is likely to be an external
model of American domesticity and public spiritedness. An over-

whelming proportion of the members are married and have children. Nearly all of them indicate formal religious affiliations and a large number are very active in church work. Church memberships tended in 1957 to be predominantly in the evangelical churches—Baptist, Methodist, and Presbyterian, in that order—which are usually associated with the Anglo-Saxon South. Episcopalians followed closely (in the senate they outnumbered the Presbyterians, five to three), to provide a respectable representation for this symbol of the finer elements of the old South. The cosmopolitanism of the state was reflected in the fact that there were several Roman Catholics in the legislature along with at least two members of the Jewish faith and a fairly broad scattering of members of some of the smaller Christian congregations.[22]

The average state legislator in Florida is a joiner, a facet of his personality which seems to emerge from (and serves) a combination of economic, social, and political ambitions. Membership in service clubs—mainly Rotary, Lions, and Kiwanis—normally includes well over half of the house and almost two thirds of the senate. In addition a great many legislators belong to the Elks and Moose clubs, over one-third of the house members and a considerably larger proportion of senators are Masons, and the veterans' organizations are very heavily represented. Many members naturally are affiliated with their local Chambers of Commerce. Although a variety of trade associations and agricultural organizations which have an economic interest orientation claim Florida legislators as active members and supporters, there is a noticeable lack of membership in labor organizations.

The Florida legislator is very much a product of his background and associations, even though these may be considerably narrower than the social characteristics reflected by the constituency as a whole. The fact that the Florida legislature is composed largely of the respectable middle class does not mean, however, that the individual member is subject only to influences generally associated with a prototypical suburban or semisophisticated rural background. Although the characteristics of this type of individual are very prevalent in the makeup of the legislature, many other factors enter into the political outlook and actions of the representatives and senators, not least of which are those incalculable attributes of individual personality such as moral fiber, propensity toward rational calculation, powers of self analysis, and personal role assumption. If we try to relate these factors to issue orientations, we come up with a fairly broad range of types. Before setting out a sort of loose typology, however, it might be well to recall some of the more obvious influences on the thinking of legislators, several of which have already been indicated.

In the broader sense, it is very noticeable that the attitudes taken by the general run of the legislators toward the issues with which they are confronted are not very reflective, if by reflective we mean the ability to see an individual decision as part of a more complex whole. In part this nonreflective characteristic is due to the type of man who is elected to office. A man whose private affairs are controlled by practical (and often ingenious) responses to single and rather simple sources of motivation and whose underlying premises are largely compounded of ready-made doctrines which he absorbs completely and unquestioningly through association with his own kind is unlikely to venerate the abstract qualities of reflection. Such consistency as he displays in his thinking on social problems is often the result of his conditioned response to certain stimuli (such as labor, public education, taxes, etc.) rather than the product of deliberative mental processes. To be sure, the average legislator dignifies these responses with the title "my philosophy of government," but any attempt to elicit logical justification for his presuppositions probably will be met with a cliché or an even more uncommunicative reaction of suspicion.

In some respects the unwillingness (or unawareness of the need) to think through the broader implications of the decisions involved in legislation is bolstered by the conditions under which the legislator works. The multitude of complex issues thrust upon the legislature for settlement in a very short time practically forces the legislator to react rather than cogitate and the legislature as a whole to develop techniques of decision-making that do not involve all the members in that most difficult of all tasks—clear, hard thinking. One member (himself a man whose depth of perception was far greater than the average in the Florida house) remarked of a colleague that "the trouble with old Henry is that he is always thinking; when you go to a man with a little bill that doesn't mean a thing to him you don't want him to tell you he'll think it over, you want his vote." Naturally, there are few cases in which a legislator can use Bentham's felicific calculus as the sole basis for his vote on a bill; it is extremely doubtful that any man could at any time foresee all the implications of the simplest measure even if he could be expected to free himself from subjective influences so that the pure light of intellect might play upon the legislation before him. But the legislative reality falls far short of the working ideal when practically all attempt at this type of analysis is abandoned.

It is perfectly true that, where the legislator does mirror his constituency to some extent, the type of response described above can sometimes produce a close correspondence between the popular will and the legislation passed. In this way some of the requirements of direct democracy can be fulfilled. The Florida legislator seems to conform to this expectation fairly closely because a great deal of sociological relativity is apparent in his actions. Thus it is that some of the older politicians among the members, who are reputed to have been liberals in the past (especially during the New Deal period), are now in the vanguard of what in more sophisticated circles would be called the New Conservatism; that is, they are so completely at harmony with the era of prosperity and "progressive moderation" that they apparently no longer feel an urge toward that type of reform which they advocated at a time when a majority of the public found social welfare legislation so agreeable.

The extent of local influence on the individual legislator and his decisions has already been mentioned several times and will recur at later periods, but some examples of the pervasiveness of this control of the members' thinking and behavior may illustrate the extent to which it penetrates to the very core of the legislative process. If he has not already learned this lesson (and he probably would not be in the Florida legislature if he had failed to learn it), the freshman legislator is soon made aware that his actions will have to be taken with one eye on the folks back home. Not only is this concern with local attitudes related to the popular demand for direct representation, but part of the *modus operandi* of the two houses themselves

is built around this expectation. The speaker of the house warned
the freshman legislators in the presession school for new members
prior to the 1957 session that "we always have a few missing faces
in the Legislature, and it's largely due to mistakes made on local
legislation."[23] It is not on local legislation alone that this attitude
looms so importantly. Perhaps the clearest statement of the prevailing
sentiment in this respect was made by Representative Tom Beasley,
at the time speaker-designate for 1959, a possible gubernatorial
candidate, and a dominant figure in the legislature. Beasley said:
"As a representative, my duty is first to the people who elected me
and secondly to the people of the state as a whole. Therefore, as a
member of the legislature, I could never conscientiously vote for
legislation that would be good for the state as a whole yet injurious
to the people of my county."[24] The combination of moral sentiment
and reasons of practical politics which is usually apparent in a member's explanation of his vote frequently relates to this tendency to
place local considerations uppermost.

Another direct influence on the legislator's attitude and behavior
is the tone of the chamber in which he serves. A number of factors
enter into the compulsive orientation of the member of the assembly.
Mention has been made earlier of the effect which the lack of party
or factional organization has on the legislature of Florida. An elaborate façade of unity is built up, behind which the many divisions and
cross currents are partly hidden and bartering and trading for votes
on various types of measures goes on. In such circumstances a man
may find it extremely difficult to stand aloof and be a real independent, which is the role in which most Florida legislators like to envisage themselves. In the first place, the rather forced air of unity
causes many legislators to be unwilling to be recorded as voting
against a measure which carries by a wide margin; consequently there
is a bandwagon atmosphere on many bills which might otherwise
be opposed in strength. In the second place, the combination of
localism and a relatively unorganized legislature means that most
members are very vulnerable on certain issues. If a county contains
a state educational institution, hospital, or other important installa-
tion, it is difficult for the member from the area to resist the organized
pressures which threaten to "vote against your appropriation unless

you go along with us on this bill." The only saving factor in the situation is that most of the other members are equally vulnerable and the use of such pressures is automatically limited. On some subjects it is also considered unwise to vote opposite to the vote recorded by the recognized "expert" on that particular question.

Despite the general absence of acknowledged groups in the legislature, occasionally such a group will be formed. In the 1957 session (and in some earlier ones as well) the small county representatives held several caucuses. The motivation for this display of unity does not appear to have been a desire to decide collectively which way these counties should go on certain measures—this was predictable in most cases—but to tighten up the sense of common purpose and to bring the small county leaders into closer association with the rank and file, who might otherwise be lured away by blandishments from the big city. It was noticeable, too, that a number of social functions were organized along these lines. The extent of the success of this organizational move is measurable by the solidity of the small county delegations on many crucial issues and by statements which indicated the degree of cohesiveness that had been effected. One representative remarked, for example, that "the little counties are fighting for their lives."

A member is usually affected to some extent by the other members of the legislative delegation from his area. Because local legislation is passed automatically if it receives the unanimous support of the legislators whose area is affected, it is necessary to secure co-operation if the local bills are to go through. In most cases area delegations make a show of harmony and in some instances a natural leader will appear upon whom his colleagues will depend for guidance. Sometimes, however, differences may arise from the fact that two representatives from the same county or a representative and a senator from the same area are supported by different local factions or have conflicting ambitions. In quite a few instances delegates from the same county vote differently on important measures and little notice is taken of the differences, but where the break is open and known it receives considerable publicity. This is especially true when there is a breakdown in the local legislation process. A number of these delegation splits occurred in the 1957 session. The Tampa *Tribune*, for example, reported that "the most pronounced split in delegations to the 1957 legislature probably is in the Escambia County delegation." In this case the break was between one of Escambia's representatives, J. B. Hopkins, and Senator Philip D. Beall. The effect of the division was that local bills which had passed through the house were put on the "invisible" calendar in the senate where they wait upon the pleasure of the local senator, and its cause apparently was a considerable difference in opinion on general issues, combined with the possibility that Hopkins might run for the senate.[25] A second split which received some attention at the hands of the press was between the two representatives from Monroe (Key West), J. Y. Porter and Bernie Papy, who were old political rivals. Papy, whose political influence in Key West is long-standing, was also faced with senatorial opposition.[26] Many other temporary splits were reported throughout the session, but most of them were of less intrinsic interest because the divisions were not related to broader political differences.

The political ambitions of a legislator may also influence his manner of looking at issues. It is probably unfair to attribute votes on specific issues or a change in the pattern of a man's votes solely to his aspirations for higher office and thereby deny him the charity of assuming a change in conscience. Nevertheless, there are instances of marked changes in an individual's stand on issues which appear to be traceable to his desire to run for state-wide office. The rural-urban division in Florida means that a small county man who wants to run for governor will need to have a broader outlook than most delegates from these areas manifest in their votes. The courtship of the large urban areas by supporting and voting favorably on legislation designed to aid these areas or to reflect their opinions (especially where these votes do no violence to the interests or views of his constituency) appears to be a fairly common practice of the ambitious small county man. As one urban member, who had ample reason to be cynical, put it, "I wish we could get all of them to run for governor—they start acting like statesmen then."

Since turnover is fairly heavy in the Florida legislature, the role of the new member requires some stress. A man serving his first term is treated very much as a neophyte who must prove himself before he is allowed to become a full-fledged member. All legislative bodies seem to have a sort of tribal rite of initiation which serves the dual purpose of humbling the new braves and making sure that they are completely permeated by the system before they achieve full brotherhood. It is expected that a new member will not be seen or heard from the floor too much, that he will be very careful to make himself agreeable to experienced members, especially those who are recognized leaders, and that he will not push himself too much in his first term. Usually he can best satisfy these conditions if he places himself under the wing of a senior member who can advise and direct him through the bewildering maze. By failing to adapt to the behavior expected of him the beginner may forfeit his chances for real influence in the legislature and may even be defeated at the polls if his fellow members set out to make him look bad enough. If, for example, a new member should, through gaucherie, sponsor a bill of any importance without having previously lined up his support behind the scenes he probably would find himself in a very embarrassing position in terms of the number of votes that he could muster. A very few mistakes of this sort are sufficient to peg a man as a poor candidate for leadership and possibly even as one whose proposals do not deserve serious consideration. The practices with regard to the new member are much more noticeable in the house than in the senate, probably because the senate is so much smaller and more staid in its conduct, and a substantial proportion of its new members have had previous experience in the house. In 1957 (and again in 1959) the new house members formed a sort of caucus of their own, which they called the "57" club. A few individuals expressed the hope that some of the new members in 1957 might prove to be insurgents who would rebel against the dominance of the small-county men and small-county attitudes, which was built in part on the loss of experienced members from the urban areas. Although some freshmen had very promising starts in this session, there was no apparent open violation of the doctrine of restraint by these men. It can be safely said that a member will find it difficult to accomplish what he wishes in either house unless he learns to conform to certain accepted practices which do not appear in the printed rules.

From what has been said thus far, it might be expected that the variety of influences is so great and the organizational controls so weak in the Florida legislature that almost any man's vote would likely be open to random choice. Some members allege this to be the case and insist that they can make no sense of the way in which individuals vote on different pieces of legislation. To some extent this is true, and the mere search for a pattern of voting might yield few results and almost certainly would tell very little unless the issues were selected so that the crucial differences in outlook among the various members were revealed rather than obscured. This choice involves a knowledge of many influencing factors and how they are related to one another. A member might, for example, be adamantly opposed to a bill and try without success to amend it, but vote for it on final passage for any of several reasons. A vote on an amendment, then, might reveal far more of the divisions in the legislature than the vote on final passage. Because of these complicating factors, more knowledge may be forthcoming by approaching the man before trying to categorize his vote. A considerable attempt was made by the writers to learn all they could about the way that the members of the house and senate looked at social issues and governmental problems. By talking to a great many people in and out of the legislature (both biased and unbiased), by cross-checking impressions against one another, by following the newspapers closely, and by observing the members on and off the floor, we reached the conclusion that it is possible to group the members into general types in terms of liberal-conservative orientation. It is only necessary to add that these are *general* types and that even when an individual fits into a category very neatly (and most of them spill over from one into another), other influences may cause a shift on one or a number of issues. Like the economists we are forced to fall back on the omnipresent qualifying clause, "other things being equal . . . ."

A Florida Legislative Typology

The overwhelming majority of Florida legislators seem subject to classification into one of the following types: (1) the rural conservative who, if the connotation had not become so perverted, might be called the rural reactionary, (2) the rural populist, (3) the urban business conservative, (4) the rural-urban combination, and (5) the independent.

The rural conservative type is very prominent in the Florida legislature because of the strength of the small counties in the assembly. He is usually an extreme segregationist, a strong believer in interpersonal relations as the proper approach to decision-making, an opponent of governmental reorganization (especially when it strengthens the governor's powers or interferes with the spoils system), a believer in decentralization to the point of promoting a governmental system rooted in isolated units of personal power, and he is likely to show an almost complete disregard for the welfare of the metropolitan areas. His method of operation in the legislature is horse-trading, and he is very well satisfied with the practice of enacting hundreds of local bills at each session because it preserves his local political ties and caters to his desires to settle even state-wide matters on the basis of laws of local application passed through the courtesy of intercounty reciprocity. It almost goes without saying that he is the hard core of the opposition to reapportionment.

A sharp distinction should be drawn between the leaders and followers in this group. The leaders are likely to be drawn from the "county-seat elite." They are very shrewd and usually have an excellent grasp of the legal system as well as the fundamentals of the existing method of politics. Although they jealously guard the financial resources of the state against distribution on the basis of overall needs (in order to secure economic advantages for their local areas), they are by no means supporters of a rural as opposed to an industrial society. In fact, most of them have an economic stake in the world of industry and commerce, and they are prone to be as staunchly opposed to government regulation of business, progressive taxation, and laws beneficial to labor as the most ardent capitalist. In the senate, these leaders and their followers have come to be known as the "pork chop gang," although by no means all of the porkchoppers are exclusively small county. The rural follower, on the other hand, is likely to be a "good old country boy," one who is more a mirror of his constituents than the leaders are. His moral and political outlook is similar to that of the rural leader class, but he is more the manipulated than the manipulator. He recognizes in the representative drawn from the county seat elite the type of man that he is accustomed to respect, and the rural leaders are able to play on his feelings of identity and pride in being a fellow legislator to bring him into line.[27] Although the small county follower is less likely to have economic interests outside his local area than the leader, he is also very susceptible to pressures from the business world and can often be won by a display of deference to the eminence of his position as a legislator.

The second type—the rural populist—is not present in great numbers and is mostly to be found in a somewhat watered-down version in the contemporary legislature. The term "populist" is used here in a loose fashion to indicate a leaning toward some of the things that populism stood for in certain rural areas of North Florida at the turn of the century. The present day legislator of this type displays some of the characteristics of agrarian individualism, moderated by a feeling of personal sympathy with the unfortunate and some recognition of the necessity for governmental intervention to redress the balance of economic forces. He shows signs of being a "conscience Democrat" on the race question and will vote against the more extreme anti-integrationist legislation. He is, in most cases, a former supporter of Claude Pepper and was a New Dealer in the thirties; in consequence he is usually favorably disposed toward social welfare legislation and in a few instances may display some antipathy toward private financial or industrial interests. On many measures (such as reapportionment, tax distribution, and milder forms of anti-integration legislation) he is, of course, compelled to vote in conformity with the local will, but in other respects his rural liberalism may take him pretty far from his more conservative colleagues.

The urban business conservative is to be found mainly among the younger lawyers and business men from the more populous counties, although a fair number of older men would also be included in the category. He is usually urbane and capable of using the mass media of communications very effectively in his campaigns. He is a promoter and may best be classified as the Junior Chamber of Commerce type. In a few instances such a man may be pointed out as a representative of special business interests, but there is no need, in most cases, for these interests to set out deliberately to win him over—he is already theirs by natural inclination. He conforms very much to the new type of politician portrayed so brilliantly in Edwin O'Connor's novel, *The Last Hurrah*. In many respects this politician is representative of the new trend in state-wide politics; he comes much closer to a manifestation of the economic and social spirit of the times than does the stump-speaking cracker-barrel wit of the piney flats.

The urban business conservative is usually a governmental reformer; honest government conducted by means of textbook governmental machinery is something of a substitute for a more liberal social and economic policy. On racial questions he leans toward moderation but may occasionally move to extremes. The chances are very much in favor of his being economy-minded and disposed toward consumption taxes for the support of governmental functions, but he does understand the needs of the cities and is willing to take steps to relieve their plight. He is consistently a promoter of business. While making a fetish of the doctrine of free competitive enterprise, he is usually favorable to governmental programs which are designed to aid business at the public expense, and in a good many cases he will go along with legislation which actually restricts competition in order to ensure advantages to existing members of the guild. This type of representative usually supports reapportionment.

The combination rural-urban type is mainly a product of the middle-sized counties and partakes of the more conservative qualities of both rural and urban groups. The urbanization of the state has been so rapid that even in some counties with sizeable cities and a large urban population the social lag succeeds in turning up a rural type, but sometimes the type now being described will succeed in being elected as an intermediary. He usually displays the poise and sophistication of the younger business conservative, but in most other respects he reflects a rural conservative outlook. In some instances this may be due to his ambitions; if he thinks that the small-county bloc is firmly in control, he may find that championing its interest is the way to achieve personal power. It is more difficult to fathom his motives than any of the other types, and especially is it difficult to credit him with sincerity. Some members who seem cut from this pattern appear to be vindictive, and their air of charm repels even while it attracts. The few individuals in the legislature who are of this type are strong segregationists, antiadministration, opponents of governmental reorganization, proponents of governmental economy in all but a few pet cases, and advocates of the small-county plans of apportionment and distribution of tax resources.

The independent may come from either an urban or rural constituency, although the type is somewhat more common among the representatives and senators from urban areas. Usually the independence characteristic of such a man is a result of the acceptance by his county or district of his unimpeachable integrity. Although the rural independent may have much in common with the rural populist, he is less a product of the conception of direct democracy than the populist and so is considerably freer to "vote his conscience" on matters that may be at cross purposes with the immediate views of the local populace. Although the independent may be conservative in much of his thinking, he is not bound to any docrtinal view and can usually be convinced by the facts. This does not mean that he is a pragmatist pure and simple; to the contrary, the strength of his position lies in his acceptance of the general welfare as the moral end toward which he is working and his refusal to compromise that end by overemphasis on any given means to its achievement. At the same time the independent is practical enough to work within the framework of the existing legislative structure, so he can be quite effective at times.

On major issues the independent's voting record usually looks quite liberal in comparison with those of his colleagues who were previously described, especially in terms of racial legislation, governmental reorganization, and bills promoting economic interests. He is very often a thorn in the flesh of the special interests and their legislative friends because he insists upon looking behind the surface of legislation to its intent. Some of his fellow-members, in fact, are a little in awe of his moral qualities. This type of man ordinarily will stand high in the esteem of the reporters who follow legislative activities closely, and independents usually are very prominent among those voted on or elected as recipients of awards such as those the St. Petersburg *Times* makes to a senator and a representative for the best legislative service in each session.[28] Ordinarily, however, independents do not come out nearly so well in polls taken among the legislators themselves to decide upon the most valuable members. The house has a greater proportion of independents than the senate, but because of their fewer numbers the senate independents may be given more prominent places in the news.

Although we have spoken of the distinctions outlined above as indicating a liberal-conservative range, it is very noticeable that there is a heavy conservative dominance in the typology offered and that the liberal per se is not even included in a separate category. As far as groups go, the rural populist and the independent serve in some respects as the liberal element in the Florida assembly. As a matter of fact, however, only one man who has served in the Florida legislature recently—Representative John Orr of Miami—seems to be an integrated social and economic liberal.[29] Orr was the only man in the 1956 special session to vote against all five bills designed to preserve segregation in Florida. His moving speech on a point of personal privilege at the close of that session, in which he explained his stand, was very coldly received in the legislature. Later he was presented the Fund for the Republic's Heritage award for his refusal to compromise on principle in the face of great obstacles. Although Orr is an economic liberal as well as a civil libertarian, having been a strong Pepper supporter, favoring most forms of social legislation, and depending for a great measure of his support on minority and labor groups, the primacy of the race question and the fact that he is not quite so isolated on social welfare legislation have made his views on integration more widely known.

Orr was by no means uninfluential in the legislature. He is a very effective speaker, quite good in face-to-face relationships, and very adept at playing the game of Florida politics according to the ground rules in cases in which he does not have to capitulate to forces completely at odds with his views. Most of the independents and quite a few other members regarded him as a friend and valuable colleague, although they were a little apprehensive about his doctrines. He was very careful, on the other hand, to avoid compromising some of his fellow-members in their constituencies; he went out of his way, for instance, not to identify a man too closely with himself or his position on issues if he felt that it might harm the other member. A few of the conservative members were not willing to accept him very gracefully and might have been willing to send him to Coventry if they had thought that most of the legislature would have gone along with them. One rather prominent member maintained that Orr stood alone in the face of all the other members and that he had no counterpart among the conservatives; that is, nobody on the right varied so much from the legislative norm as he did. This seems to us a palpably false judgment; although the Florida legislature is very conservative on the whole, there are certainly members on the conservative side who are less restrained (and much less astute and practical) in their stand on issues than the legislature's one former "liberal intellectual."

Legislative Profiles

In order to illustrate the complexity of some of the types in a more specific manner, the following anonymous profiles of members of the Florida legislature are offered. Most of the men treated are or were leaders in the sense that they have had some degree of influence (in some cases it may be with a minority) and have demonstrated a capacity to handle themselves very well in the legislative arena. Some have by now left the legislature. No special attempt has been made to choose according to the types listed above; as was previously suggested, it is rarely possibly to find a man who fits neatly into a category. Nevertheless, the reasons for the classification used should become fairly obvious as a result of this more specific appraisal of individuals.

House of Representatives, Profile I. This man is very young (he is still in his twenties) for the legislative prominence that he has achieved, but he gives the impression of a maturity beyond his years, and in other ways he is ideally adapted to the type of politics apparently dominant in Florida. He comes from a rural background and was elected from a rural county, but he has also been successful in a small way in business. He is warm and outgoing and appears genuinely interested in people; he is anxious not to do anything that would upset people or create personal situations that would make it difficult to work with any single member of the legislature. It seems quite likely that his desire not to offend and his capacity for compromise are important ingredients in his rather remarkable success in the house. At any rate, the system as he understands it seems to call for these qualities. In some cases (if the magistrate were harsh) his attitude might be judged to be hypocritical, but it seems almost certain that he himself is sufficiently convinced of the general usefulness of this method of operation to preclude the application of so categorical a term to his actions. His practice in this connection seems to be this: when he disagrees with another member, it is most important to placate that member by assurances that "our philosophy is the same, but on this particular point we have to go our separate ways." Thus the door is left open for working together in the future, and it is apparently not unusual for him to make amends by an almost immediate direct overture to the man he has been opposing. Surface harmony and even unanimity seem to play a great role in legislative politics as he envisages it. Divisions on questions of principle he apparently regards as dangerous—possibly because they might lead to the creation of factional majorities and minorities and to the presentation state-wide of legislative programs based on these divisions. If such a thing happened, popular and party or factional control might replace personal influence and the politics of exclusive intimacy.

This representative is not known especially for his ability to perform on his feet; he rarely speaks, and when he does he is brief and to the point. He has certain connections with the influential agricultural groups in the state which have stood him in good stead and made him strong with the rural element in the house. If he has a strong tie-in with any interest, it is with the dairy lobby.

His vote is mostly quite conservative, except on farmers' bills, and occasionally he may "take a walk" and not vote when a particularly hot issue comes up. He trusts the small county men and adheres closely to their conception of governmental programs and organization, although he would strongly insist on his fairness in giving a hearing to the large county representatives. He did not like the impersonal approach to legislative leadership characteristic of the recent governor and may have been covertly antiadministration, but he was not prepared to make an open break. He works quietly and unobtrusively to entrench and stabilize the power position of the small-county bloc, while eschewing the application of the term "power" to any aspect of politics in which he is engaged.

Senate Profile I. This veteran senator has certain deceptive qualities of physique and physiognomy. In newspaper photographs and seen at a distance in the senate chamber he appears somewhat small, meek of demeanor, and slightly dour in expression. In face to face contact he is rather larger than one would expect, he reveals exceptional qualities of mental and physical vigor, has a strong face, and is outgoing and rather charming. He looks a great deal younger than his age—he is in his late sixties. He has amassed a sizeable fortune and has interests in almost all of the major types of enterprises in Florida.

In an interview the man was willing to talk and appeared to enjoy it, although it was doubtful that he fully appreciated our aims or method, possibly because he is not capable of sufficient detachment to generalize on the type of politics in which he is engaged. He is very much an involved man—when one introduces a subject and attempts to give a local illustration, his entire treatment immediately shifts to the specific local situation and steers him away from the attempt to generalize, theorize, or categorize.

Despite his emphasis on practicality, he makes numerous references to his "philosophy of government." In essence this philosophy is a compound of certain vague doctrines (particularly the separation of powers), neutralized by overriding considerations of self-interest and an outlook derived from his experience as a business manipulator. He places strong emphasis on the need for studying a problem before taking action on it and deplores studies with a built-in bias, yet he has no difficulty adopting the results of a study with an obvious slant when it accords with his preconceptions and even in making up his mind on a measure without any study when it happens to touch upon his self-interest or any one of a number of fixed attitudes. He opposes severance taxes without benefit of ex-

tensive study, noting that the phosphate "boys" (of which he is one)
would come down heavily against them and the pulp interests are
already contributing greatly to the state through reforestation. He was
willing to go to great lengths, on the other hand, to support the
idea (arising in part from his opposition to homestead exemption)
that everybody should be a taxpayer, by personally financing a survey
which demonstrated that in his county 80 per cent of the property
owners with children in school do not pay ad valorem taxes.

He has strong feelings on the matter of public service; he is always
careful to measure his activities by the standard of promoting the
general welfare. Governmentally he is a negativist, holding firmly to
the conviction that "the state has never been hurt by anything that
the legislature failed to pass." He renders lip-service, however, to
the idea of adequate support for the governmental services which
the state has undertaken.

He appears to have no great regard for the vast majority of his
fellow legislators. He feels that many of them "come to Tallahassee
and just sit there without getting anything for their districts or
thinking much about the business of the state." They tend to vote for
every appropriation and against every tax—a fact which he rightly
recognizes as a form of weakness and the worst type of pandering
to an ill-informed public. In part at least his feeling about those
legislators is connected with the fact that they apparently do not
have his puritanical rigidity of character. But it may also arise in
part from his unarticulated recognition that the American respect
for wealth for its own sake enables him to speak with authority on
unpopular measures without an extensive sacrifice of prestige, especially among his peers, many of whom got to the legislature by
reflecting the symbols of American success without possessing them
in quite so tangible a form as he does.

In contradiction to what one might expect, he does not view
the movement of political power to higher levels of government
with alarm. He thinks that the school system not only will increasingly be run by the state, but that it is desirable that it should
be. And this conviction extends to other services and activities.
If this willingness to accept a greater degree of centralization con-
trasts with what might be expected by an outside observer, it is not

inconsistent with the senator's broader political outlook. His lack of respect for lower levels of government, his personal participation at the state level, and the hint of an attitude that government probably improves as it moves further from the people all contribute to this conception.

He is a staunch defender of the political system in Florida as it works in practice. He is very much at home with the technique of the "inside clique" settlement of issues and with the exercise of personal influence built on individual power that comes from having a close tie-in with all the prestige-carrying groups. He apparently does not believe that great numbers can participate in political decisions, and definitely thinks that they *should* not do so. His opposition to reapportionment probably derives less from the fear of big-city dominance than from the possibility that a greater reflection of the mass vote in terms of legislative power will depersonalize and institutionalize Florida politics and make great blocs of economic interests (rather than small groups of the ante bellum political elite) dominant. He is certainly not adverse to the influence of certain great private corporate blocs on the state's politics, but he wants to act in the capacity of interlocking director to represent their interests and to tie a complex of such groups together personally. In many respects his "stake in society" conception makes him a twentieth-century Federalist, but his southern rural personalism works in another way by curbing his federalist tendencies toward rationalizing the political processes. In politics he is a curious mixture of Puritan capitalist leader and southern hedonist boss. He has rigid scruples and a strong tendency to self-righteousness and self-justification in one direction and an equally obvious enjoyment of personal political manipulation in the other.

He openly admits and tacitly approves the trading of votes, and obviously prefers the private working out of a "compromise" among those who collectively have the power to push a decision through to the creation of a party or factional system which would compromise and clarify issues and set up divisions on them prior to their appearance in the legislature.

House Profile II. This representative is elected from one of the larger cities of the state and exhibits many of the traits of the urban member. He comes from a family which is prominent in his home county, and he had an outstanding activity record on the campus of the University of Florida as well as a distinguished war record. He is a very successful lawyer. Superficially he may bear some of the marks of the urban Junior Chamber of Commerce type, but he is too straightforward, too little susceptible to the superficial appeal of a slogan as the explanation of a complex social phenomenon, and too much a thinker to conform to that pattern.

On most legislative matters this man is extremely well informed and he makes a very able presentation on the floor or before a committee. He has in the past been a valued proponent of the bills of the governor, but his strong stand on reapportionment and other issues caused him to be looked on with suspicion by the small county group in the 1957 session. Despite the fact that he was out of favor with the most powerful element in the house, his talents could not be easily overlooked; consequently some important committee posts came his way and he was in the thick of many of the more significant legislative battles throughout the 1957 session. Once again he pushed a number of the governor's bills, and while he was not always successful in getting them through unscathed, he consistently made a good showing in terms of diligence in preparing the groundwork and in effectiveness of presentation.

The policy stand of this representative is somewhat conservative when he discusses the role of government in the abstract, but he is very much open to conviction by the facts of a particular situation. He has for a long time been a supporter of the constitutional amendment and legislation necessary to enable Florida cities to acquire federal funds for undertaking slum clearance projects. He is consistently opposed to special interest legislation and has a firm grasp of the needs and methods of governmental reorganization. On racial questions he is moderate; although he seems to dislike the idea of integration, he recognizes the futility of the more aggressive legal enactments to preserve segregation.

This man is very outspoken, and he may be somewhat handicapped in his effectiveness by a tendency to react too brusquely to opposition, particularly if the opposition is ill-informed or is acting on the basis of motives which are suspect. He is very quick in grasping the main

features of a piece of legislation and the arguments on it and cannot
easily abide obtuseness in others. For these reasons a few members
have indicated that they think he is inclined to be too "personal" in
his attacks. On the other hand, he often displays a sincere quality
of geniality; despite some fairly bitter exchanges, he gives the
impression of having learned to conform to legislative expectancy
by bearing no obvious grudges.

He places great emphasis on independence in politics and affirms
that if party control ever developed to any appreciable extent he
would leave the legislature. In some ways this is a contradiction because he could probably work very well in a moderately liberal Democratic party organization and almost certainly would be more
effective in a legislature characterized by strong party divisions than
in the present one. In the contemporary Florida legislature, however,
he certainly fulfills his desires to be independent.

Senate Profile II. This man is one of the younger members of
the senate and has been extensively referred to as a gubernatorial
prospect. He is from a multicounty district which is located in the
south-central part of the state and is rural, except for a few small
towns. His family has been very prominent in Florida politics for
a long time and has its roots planted deeply in the area that he
represents. He is engaged in agricultural pursuits and appears to be
quite prosperous.

He is a modest and most unpretentious man. He takes a very
active interest in church work, and his whole personality seems
suffused with the high personal moral standards that he has set
for himself, standards that are not paraded externally, but are
evident in his actions and are attested to by those who know him
well. Although he is by conviction opposed to social drinking and
apparently is not particularly interested in the social whirl attendant upon a legislative session, he is far from being a prude and
is accepted as a man's man. He was an athlete of some note and
retains an active interest in sports and the outdoor life. He has the
rugged angular frame, the weather-beaten demeanor, and the bearing and manner of the southern Anglo-Saxon farmer, but his smart-
ness of dress indicates a far more sophisticated side. Sometimes he
gives the impression of being phlegmatic, but upon further contact

this apparent characteristic may be ascribed more to self-control than to lack of intense convictions and feelings.

This senator is more than usually reflective and, while at times he may appear to be somewhat slow in arriving at a judgment, he rarely speaks without having a fund of supporting information at hand. Even though he may be out of step with the majority of senators on many questions, he commands a great amount of respect, and he usually occupies some important committee posts. He works extremely hard at being a member of the legislature. His vote is a very independent one and is in many cases—such as on racial legislation—a conscience vote. Although he is no racial integrationist, he is morally opposed to the extreme measures taken by his colleagues and is convinced of their political impracticality. On legislation designed to further certain local areas at the expense of the state or to give aid and comfort to vested interests he joins with one or two other members, who also regard their mandates very broadly, to harass the proponents by calling attention to their proper representative functions. In some respects he and his kind provide a useful core of permanent opposition to the worst forms of horse-trading localism and special interest representation.

The independence shown by this senator is a product of the relation he bears to his constituents. A person close to him indicated that in the eyes of the people of his district he can do no wrong. His forthright manner, combined with an unassuming and unself-conscious common touch, makes it possible for him to act both in the face of his constituency and on the floor of the legislature within a very desirable framework of rationality and consistency. Interwoven with these traits is a quality of *noblesse oblige,* which is the more impressive for never having been articulated. In all likelihood it has never been formulated consciously even by him. Needless to say it would be extremely difficult to beat him in an election.

House Profile III. This young representative is from a middle-sized central Florida county which is in a somewhat transitional position in that it has sociological characteristics of both the old and the new Florida. On the one hand the county enjoys the benefits of a sizeable tourist trade and contains a small but quite urbane city, and on the other it is still heavily agricultural. Although the agriculture in the area is diversified, the county lies within the section of the state penetrated by slavery and still bears some marks of an ante bellum experience. Since legislators from this area have achieved prominent positions in both houses in the past, there is some pressure on its delegates to live up to previous performances. It should be noted that the legislators who have been elected from this county have not uniformly conformed to any particular type and that at any given time there may be a considerable difference among the individuals who represent the constituency.

The representative under discussion has not had a long period of service, but he has already managed to achieve for himself a position of potential, if not yet actual, leadership. He is very strongly entrenched in his county and appears to be one of those men of good family and reputation who may be hard to unseat even in the face of a dubious legislative performance. He is a handsome man, cast very much in the Junior Chamber of Commerce mold and has a great amount of surface charm and sophistication. He was of some prominence on the campus of the University of Florida as an undergraduate and law school student, and now practices law.

This man has adopted the small county conservative position almost completely, if indeed he has not improved upon it by extension. He is an extremist on the race question, absolutely closed against accepting any idea of reapportionment, a firm adherent of the status quo on matters of governmental reorganization and political practices, a proponent of regressive forms of taxation and tax distribution, and a sure affirmative vote on questions involving governmental assistance to business. The only apparent explanation for the seeming contradiction between the impression he gives as a person and his actions as a legislator is that he sees in the small-county bloc the source of support which may enable him to achieve personal prominence and a measure of political power. If the balance of power shifted, it is quite conceivable that he could accommodate himself rapidly and without embarrassment to the new order.

His technique is one of exaggeration; he has gone all out to be more small county than the small county boys themselves. He has a real flair for bombastic speech and uses it at every opportunity.

He is on his feet as often as any man in the house, and most of his argument is destructive. He is usually heard either in direct opposition to some major piece of legislation or in support of an amendment designed to cripple or kill a bill. He is an unremitting foe of the governor's office and all of its legislative proposals, and the writers have observed cases in which he shifted the grounds of his arguments so completely as to refute his own reasoning within a period of a few minutes, when he saw that one oppositional approach to an executive bill was failing and a different appeal had to be made. Although he can at times be vindictive, this trait has not brought him the opprobrium that milder forms of personal attack can bring to some of the less even-tempered large county men. This man belongs to the category of combined rural-urban conservative as nearly as any man fits one of the legislative types we have set out earlier in this chapter.

Chapter 5

The Organization
of the Florida Legislature

No legislative body can function without a formal organizational structure. In part, such a structure is needed simply to make it possible for a group of thirty-eight (or ninety-five) men to work together toward the single goal of accomplishing the tasks of the legislature. But, in addition, these tasks have in recent times become so voluminous and burdensome that organization, like procedural rules, plays an essential role in determining how well the legislature can perform. One cannot judge legislative performance solely on the basis of the product, which is legislation: such a judgment is necessarily partial and subjective. A secondary criterion is, how well does the legislature organize itself for its job? Is it, for instance, able to give a proper amount of time and careful consideration to the matters confronting it, or is it hasty, slipshod, and haphazard? Does it have adequate facilities for obtaining factual and technical information? Is it able to carry out the will of its own majorities? The answers to these and similar questions will have a great bearing on any overall judgment of the quality of a legislative body, even though one's final verdict must inevitably rest on his opinion of whether the assembly passed legislation which is both good and responsive to the needs of the state. It is the aim of this and the following chapters to submit the Florida legislature to a test based on questions such as the foregoing.

Frequency and Duration of Sessions

Like many state constitutions, that of Florida strictly confines the legislature to a biennial session meeting in odd-numbered years. Further, the date of opening is specified in the constitution: the first Tuesday following the first Monday in April. The session lasts, according to constitutional edict, not more than sixty calendar days, but the basic law also permits the legislature by three-fifths vote to hold itself in "extended" session for not more than thirty days before the September first following the regular session.[1]

In a state as large and heterogeneous as Florida—a state, moreover, which is growing and changing rapidly—the need for legislation (good legislation) is probably too great to be satisfied by the short biennial session, which actually amounts to only about forty-four or forty-five legislative days—shorter than most other states. In each recent session an average of well over three thousand bills has been introduced, which amounts to more than sixty bills for each legislative day. Conceding that many of these are not worth a second look, even from the standpoint of bills passed the load is tremendous; a conservative estimate is that the 1957 legislature actually *passed* at least one thousand pieces of legislation, or twenty a day. The uncalled-for burden of local legislation accounts for a large proportion of this, but even one important general statute a day would present a difficult task for a legislative assembly.

In fact, one study has condemned the limited biennial session strongly, pointing out that it intensifies "all evils associated with legislative halls."[2] It does not allow proper study and consideration of bills either in committee meetings or on the floor; it opens the door to excessive pressure group influences; it gives excessive power to minorities able to use delaying tactics; and it makes real debate all but impossible, especially in the larger house of representatives.

In Florida, as in other states, one of the pronounced effects of the short biennial session is the rush of bills reaching the floor toward the end of the session because the committee stage takes up the early weeks. This rush is signified by the placing of the calendar under the control of the rules committees in about the fifth week of the session; from then on these committees really run the session. And the daily sessions get longer and longer. To a leisurely 10:00 A.M. to 1:00 P.M. session in the early weeks, an afternoon session of from 2:00 to 5:00 is added; and later often an evening session as well, and even Saturday sessions. As the sessions take up more and more of the day it becomes almost impossible to schedule committee meetings around them except at extremely difficult hours in the late evening and early morning.

The session, always physically tiring, thus becomes exhausting in the late stages, when even the social lobby finds it difficult to operate. It is hard to conceive that any legislator working under such conditions can, even with the best of will, talent, and physique, do an optimum job.

Yet though these difficulties are obvious to all observers of the legislative process, the legislators themselves show a strange obtuseness on the subject; it is difficult to find one who is not attached to the sixty-day biennial session. Such a session is part of the status quo, but this in itself would not seem adequate to explain completely the legislative attitude. It seems possible that (at least subconsciously) their position as part-time politicians influences the ideas of lawmakers.

Legislative Salaries

The average member of the legislature does not make a living out of politics. Indeed, the $1200 a year earned by legislators, plus a $15 a day allowance during sessions, will not easily cover his out-of-pocket expenses in the session and in his campaigns, let alone contribute to his family income. He is consequently under a good deal of economic pressure to minimize the time spent on legislative affairs in order to maximize his income from his full-time occupation. One senator (J.B. Rodgers of Orlando) resigned in 1957, claiming that the regular and special sessions of 1955 and 1957 were too much for him to carry financially. A longer session held annually would impose a serious economic strain on many members, especially those whose businesses suffer during their absence.

At the same time, American political habits include a rather pronounced attachment to the ideal of the amateur in legislative politics. To increase the pay of legislators to a point at which they could live on it would be automatically to professionalize them. While this may not be a serious theoretical handicap, it seems to have some practical significance.

Opponents of the unlimited session also make much of the cost of the legislature to the taxpayers. Years ago such an argument may have had some validity, but today the expenses directly attributable to the legislature are an insignificant share of the state's budget. The necessity for frequent extra sessions in a state with an excessively brief session may balance out the extra expense of an annual unlimited session. In any case, Florida's legislative costs in 1957 were only about 0.2 per cent of the state's expenditures.[3]

Special Sessions

The Florida Constitution permits five different types of special sessions. These are (1) the extended session, (2) the special session called by the legislature itself, (3) the special session called by the governor, (4) the reapportionment session, and (5) the impeachment session.

The extended sessions mentioned above are permitted by a constitutional amendment adopted in 1954, which was first used in the 1957 session.[4] There is no reason to suppose that its use will be rare; on the contrary it may well become customary in view of the number and complexity of the issues facing the Florida legislature in the present day world. Even this extended session is limited to thirty days, and these must come between the adjournment of the regular session and September 1; consequently at a maximum this adds thirty days to the session every two years. One other limitation on the extended session is that new bills may be introduced only with a two-thirds vote of the members of the relevant house,[5] a measure designed to preserve the extension as a means of clearing up legislation which could not be completed during the regular session.

More recently, in 1956, an amendment gave the legislature power to convene *itself* in extra session.[6] The mechanics of doing so are rather complex. They have not yet been used, and (judging from the experience of other states having similar provisions) they are not likely to be used frequently, if at all. The amendment was adopted, apparently, in a seizure of legislative pique directed against the governor, rather than because of any real need.

The governor may also call extra sessions,[7] which he may adjourn at will, and in which he may dictate the subjects to be considered. The legislature may, however, by a two-thirds vote of each house, take up other matters. Special sessions thus convoked are limited to twenty days, although there seems to be nothing which would prevent the calling of immediately successive sessions totaling more than this limit. Extra sessions are comparatively rare in Florida and there seems to be no discernible trend toward an increase. Political considerations usually prevent the governor from calling them except under relatively grave circumstances or when the subject is of such great importance that it could not be given sufficient consideration during regular session. Such conditions were presented by the extra 1956 session to consider the proposals of the Fabisinski Commission on how to avert school integration and by the session called in 1957 to take up the constitutional revision proposals of the Sturgis Commission.

The governor is commanded also to call a special session in case the legislature fails to reapportion itself at the appointed time.[8] Since apportionment (see Chapter 3) presents such great political problems, it is seldom accomplished during regular sessions so that reapportionment sessions are a regular decennial feature of the Florida political landscape. Such sessions must be called (though they need not actually convene) within thirty days after the end of the regular session; they may consider no subject other than reapportionment, and they are constitutionally bound to remain in session until the job is completed. The 1955 reapportionment session thus extended (with long recesses) into the fall of 1956 and was finally adjourned—unconstitutionally, it must be assumed—with its job only half completed, for it had not even then succeeded in reapportioning the senate. Governor Collins obviously felt that his obligation to call reapportionment sessions was a continuing one as long as reapportionment is not accomplished, for he called another one for the fall of 1957.

A fifth type of extra session—rarely used—is the impeachment session of the senate.[9] Impeachment proceedings may be held at any time within six months of the date on which the house prefers the Articles of Impeachment. Conviction can be secured only upon a two-thirds vote of those senators present. The most recent use of an impeachment session came in the summer of 1957, with the trial of Judge George E. Holt of the Dade County Circuit Court.

The importance of the special session to the Florida legislature was dramatically underscored in connection with the 1955 and 1957 legislatures. These legislatures met in two extra sessions, one extended session and an impeachment trial. Perhaps the members of the Florida legislature already have a full-time occupation!

The Presiding Officers

An interesting and significant aspect of the power structure of any organization is reached by a study of its institutionalized leadership. This will tell only part of the story, for there are likely to be hidden sources of power which will not be so easily disclosed. Even so, we may learn something of value from investigating the leaders of the Florida legislature and their functions.

The presiding officers in the Florida legislature occupy formal positions very similar to those held in most states, although their actual powers seem to be somewhat greater and, in the senate, selection is slightly unusual. Since the selection in 1951 of C. Farris Bryant as speaker of the house for 1953, the house has always nominated its speaker in a Democratic caucus held early in the session preceding the one in which the nominee will serve. Thus, Tom Beasley was nominated to preside over the 1959 session on the second day of the 1957 legislature. Nomination by the Democratic caucus is, of course, tantamount to election since there is no Republican candidate.

The speakership apparently falls to those who pursue it. Almost anyone who can stay in the house three terms or longer is regarded as a potential speaker. If he wants the job he will begin campaigning for it at least four years in advance, in order to get pledges lined up before anyone else approaches them. The strategy is to get so many pledges that no one else will enter the race. While one former speaker says he was drafted, this (according to other legislators) is never strictly true. What may happen is that some other legislator may remark that "you would make a fine speaker," and in 1955 and 1957 the small-county men had a pronounced tendency to concentrate their support behind one man so as to make sure the speaker chosen would be one of them, after their "difficulties" with "Ted" David—a Collins man—during the 1955 session. But even such a candidate must line up some votes from medium or large counties. This requires trades, pledges, promises. Rumor has it that the 1957 speaker had a deal with a prominent legislator for his support, in return for which the future speaker was to keep the same man as chairman of the appropriations committee. It is also said that the Dade delegation supported Beasley for the 1959 speakership in return for his promise to give them good committee assignments in that session. Such stories are, of course, unverifiable, but something of the sort is certain to happen.

The small counties seem to control the selection of the senate president more completely than in the house; this seems to be due to the mode of election. The president is elected by the nineteen holdover members—that is, those who need not run for re-election for the session over which the next president will preside. He normally is selected from among the other nineteen who are running for re-election. This means that ten votes will elect the president. At almost any time ten or close to it of the holdover members will be small-county men, so that they can put in almost anyone they choose. This is indicated by the fact that in the postwar legislatures—1947 to 1961—all eight senate presidents have been small- or medium-county men, a characteristic which has been true of only slightly over half of the speakers of the house.[10] Contrary to past custom, the 1959 president was not chosen during the 1957 session; speculation was that a contest between two senators held up the choice. He was eventually chosen after the November, 1958, general elections, and this now appears to have become the custom.[11] In general it does not appear that senators run for the post as actively as do the representatives.

The powers of the two presiding officers are quite similar formally, although the president apparently wields greater—if less obvious—influence. The bases of power are their ability to interpret the rules,[12] recognize claimants for the floor, appoint committees, and refer bills to the committees of their choice.

The interpretation of the rules is a matter of some importance since it will make it possible at times to favor one side over another. Although a good deal is made of the necessity for "fairness" on the part of a presiding officer, this term is construed within a rather special legislative framework of meaning. Interpreting rules to favor one side is generally not regarded as unfair except perhaps by the losing side. Presiding officers are rather expected to act as agents of the majority party or faction. The rulings of the speaker and president are seldom challenged and apparently never overruled from the floor.[13] Perhaps this means merely that speakers do try to be fair, or that at least they have avoided the more egregious forms of favoritism.

Much the same may be said of the power of recognition. There is no specific house or senate rule covering this matter. The practice that if two members rise at the same time the speaker shall choose who is to speak obviously lends itself to partiality in application. And the small county people complained of the speaker's unfairness in this regard during the 1955 session. However, it is difficult to tell whether the complaints were justified or proceeded merely from the fact that the speaker and house leadership were dominated by Collins men in that session. Small county people were heard to vow openly that no big county representative would again be allowed to become speaker; so far, they have succeeded in making the threat good.

Both houses allow their presiding officers to appoint all committees.[14] The importance of this duty is great, and extends beyond Robert Luce's rather offhand comment that "this lets him put his friends in the desirable positions, and through a continuance of friendly relations lets him exert influence over legislation."[15] For it is rather obvious that friendship as such plays little role in committee assignments. Rather, the attempt is to stack the important committees with majorities which the speaker hopes will share his general political viewpoints so that no overt influence during the session need arise. The key is identity of interest and viewpoint rather than friendship.

All American legislative committees are subject to the possibility of stacking, but not always is this as flagrantly the case as in Florida. For instance, one may compare the Agriculture Committees of the United States Congress with the Forestry and Citrus committees of the Florida legislature. All of these are effectively stacked, but in Congress the stacking is in greater degree automatic and nondeliberate: it results in part from the large element of free choice of committee assignments by members of Congress. In Florida the control of committee assignments by the presiding officers is complete (subject, of course, to the normal necessities of politics, such as in the case of W. C. Herrell to be mentioned shortly); consequently stacking can only be a deliberate choice based on some sort of political calculation.

It is almost axiomatic in Florida that committees will be stacked, that is, over and above the inequities resulting from malapportionment. Two reasons appear predominant: the presiding officers hope to control the legislative output by stacking committees in the direction of their personal political policies (which are usually bloc-oriented), and for certain committees dealing with economic interests it is felt to be both "proper" and "wise" to make sure the committee represents the particular interest concerned, to the practical exclusion of the *public* interest.

Committees coming under the first of the above-mentioned criteria, that of importance, have been carefully selected. They handle, in an average session, more bills—and more *important* bills—than the rest. Positions on such committees are thus indices of personal position in the legislature and control of them is a matter of prime political significance. If there is, as we have indicated, a rural-urban contest for legislative dominance, it should show up most clearly in the selection of members of these key committees. If the presiding officer is an urban man (as was Speaker "Ted" David in 1955) this fact should be reflected in urban control of these committees; while if he is a rural man (as is commonly the case), rural men should control them.

The speakership of "Ted" David can be viewed in several ways as a bench mark in the evolution of the rural-urban cleavage in the house. Prior to 1955 the conflict had been present, but muted and transformed by the character of legislative politics elaborated above. But David's role as the governor's leader led to his more or less open identification as a "big-county man." The speaker thus served, perhaps for the first time in Florida, as a partisan symbol of the desires of the urban population for certain types of governmental action and for more equitable representation. At the same time, David's fulfillment of this role brought about a sharp reaction on the part of the rural representatives, who felt that their exclusion from the positions of control constituted unfair treatment. Two factors seem to account for the open eruption in 1955 of the tension between the "ins" and the "outs" which we have identified as following a rather complicated geographical split along North-South and rural-urban lines. The first was the increasing awareness of the governor's role as a representative of the "new" urban (primarily southern) Florida. The second was the bitterness of the reapportionment fight in the 1955 session, which greatly sharpened the lines of cleavage in the house membership. Thus prior to 1955 it was possible, though rare even then, for a personable man such as David, who played the legislative game of interpersonal relations extremely well, to get himself elected speaker even though his constituency was in urban South Florida. However, David's identification with Collins' programs for institutionalizing administrative practices, for changing the bases of allocating highway construction projects and other policies that affected the rural-urban split, and, above all, for reapportioning the legislature, solidified the ranks of rural members in opposition to the chief executive, his legislative lieutenants (including Speaker David), and the urban house bloc which supported the governor and his legislative leaders.

The formal organization of the small-county bloc was a result of the reaction to these conditions, and the small-county men vowed openly never again to allow an urban legislator to become speaker. Since they have made good their threat (into the 1961 session), it is probable that the sessions after 1955, the wound having been laid open, reveal the rural-urban cleavage to be both deeper and

broader than most observers had imagined. Committee assignment
has thus probably become more significant than it was before 1955.
Tables 5 and 6, based on the membership of the key committees
in both houses in three recent sessions, indicate clearly that for
important committees the presiding officer sees to it that the groups
he represents—rural except for the house in 1955—are heavily overrepresented.

But several other considerations should be kept in mind. In
the first place, a legislator must be viewed as a person as well as a

Table 5

Committee Stacking in
Key Committees of Florida House of Representatives, 1955-1959*

Committee	1955			1957			1959		
	Rural	Mixed	Urban	Rural	Mixed	Urban	Rural	Mixed	Urban
Finance & Taxation	8	8	8	12	4	5	11	3	7
Rules & Calendar	6	11	10	11	7	7	13	3	5
Constitutional Amend.	3	6	7	12	5	4	8	6	7
General Legislation†	—	—	—	—	—	—	2	5	2
Apportionment	4	5	8	7	2	2	7	0	2
Public Schools	12	2	3	11	3	7	7	3	11
Appropriations	11	6	6	10	4	7	10	6	5
"Doghouse" Committee:‡ Aeronautics (1955, 1957), State Advertising (1959)	4	0	3	0	2	5	3	3	7
Total Seats in House	45	23	27	45	23	27	45	23	27

*Counties are classified as rural, urban, or mixed on the basis of census data
as to percentage of urban population, modified by the authors' personal
evaluation (based on fairly thorough acquaintance with each county) of
the type of population which dominates each county. Also, due to the rapid
growth of many counties, some may no longer be in the status implied by
1950 census figures. An instance of the procedure used may be helpful:
Polk County has no large urban centers and would classify, according to
1950 census data, as a nonurban county. However, we reclassified it as
"mixed" because we felt that the contiguity of a number of smaller cities,
containing a high proportion of retired people and having a tourist-oriented
type of commercial development, deprive it of real rural dominance. Space
precludes a breakdown of the detailed characteristics on which similar ad-
justments were made for other counties.
†Set up in 1959 to handle race discrimination legislation.
‡Two members of this committee were Republican in each session.

Table 6
Committee Stacking
in Key Committees of Florida Senate, 1955-1959*

Committee	1955			1957			1959		
	Rural	Mixed	Urban	Rural	Mixed	Urban	Rural	Mixed	Urban
Finance & Taxation	6	4	3	9	3	1	9	3	1
Rules & Calendar	10	2	1	10	1	2	9	1	3
Constitutional Amend.	8	1	2	10	0	3	8	2	3
General Legislation†	—	—	—	—	—	—	11	1	1
Education	4	2	5	2	3	6	5	4	2
Appropriations	8	4	1	5	2	2	10	2	3
Minor Committee:‡									
Veterans, Aviation, Radio & Television	3	3	1	—	—	—	1	4	2
Total Seats in Senate	18	9	11	18	9	11	18	9	11

*See explanatory note to Table 1.
†Set up in 1959 to handle race discrimination legislation.
‡Included for comparison only; this is apparently not a real "doghouse" committee such as the house uses.

representative (especially in a system in which so much emphasis is placed on independence of organizational ties) so that his actual attitudes and voting record do not necessarily reflect the type of district from which he comes. In the second place, many quantitatively urban districts, such as Pensacola, are experiencing a cultural lag; they have grown so fast that their objective urbanization has not yet been accompanied by the growth of urban attitudes. Thirdly, some urban districts (especially those in the "Old South" areas of northern Florida) show typical rural attitudes on race issues.

These factors mean that the actual rural predominance on committees is likely to be considerably greater than the figures given in Tables 5 and 6 suggest. Presiding officers know these facts, and often their appointment of one or another urban legislator to positions on key committees is made in the knowledge that their commitee work will satisfy rural desires. When W. C. Herrell of Dade County (Miami), for instance, was chosen chairman of the House Appropriations Committee in 1959 by the rural speaker (Tom Beasley of Walton County), one may suspect that Beasley believed Herrell's

ideas on appropriations matters were suitable and that a concession
to urban demands for influence could be made without greatly dis-
turbing the substantive policies followed by the committee. It was
also rumored in the 1957 session, when Beasley was "designated" as
1959 speaker that he (though a rural man) had secured the support
of the Dade County delegation in return for a promise of good
committee posts for them in 1959. If so, Herrell alone reaped the
payoff, for in addition to the chairmanship of the Appropriations
Committee, he served on two of the six other "key" committees in
1959. This shows, incidentally, one way in which the rural counties

Table 7

Committee Stacking in Key Committees of
Florida House of Representatives, 1957 Session Only, Adjusted*

Committee	Rural	Mixed	Urban
Finance & Taxation	14	3	4
Rules & Calendar	16	4	5
Constitutional Amendments	16	2	3
Apportionment	7	2	2
Public Schools	14	2	5
Appropriations	14	2	5
"Doghouse" Committee:			
Aeronautics	1	1	5
Total Seats			
in House (Unadjusted)	45	23	27

*For this table the writers compiled a "dossier" on every legislator, consult-
ing experienced political observers, other legislators past and present, and
particularly the voting records on key issues during the session. Each committee member was then classified as to whether or not he stood with the
rural bloc, regardless of the type of district he represented. The rural bloc
is sufficiently well-defined to justify the assimilation of urban members to
this bloc on the basis of the voting records of the latter on key issues relating to the attitudes which define the coalescence of the dominant rural
group. Florida political observers commonly make statements such as the
following: "He's from Pensacola, but he's really a porkchopper." With the
power structure in rural hands, some urban members clearly join them in
order to get ahead in the legislature. That this tendency to join the rural
bloc *generally* manifests itself among members who are from geographical
sectors which are rural-urban transitional (mixed) or are in North Florida,
was shown up most clearly when we scaled the legislators' responses to
major issues.

Table 8

Committee Stacking in Key Committees of Florida Senate, 1957 Session Only, Adjusted*

Committee	Rural	Mixed	Urban
Finance & Taxation	10	3	1
Rules & Calendar	12	0	1
Constitutional Amendments	10	0	3
Education	4	1	6
Appropriations	7	0	2
Total Seats in Senate (Unadjusted)	18	9	11

*See explanatory note to Table 7.

maintain their slim control of the house: they manage by such favors or promises of favors to keep the urban counties from solidifying as a bloc. It may also be significant that in 1959 Beasley was "running" for governor and needed to do something to try to gain urban support.

Such facts make a reliance on the quantitative method somewhat unsatisfactory unless it is complemented by close knowledge and used with some sophistication. Accordingly, we have attempted to correct the bias in the figures by making a much closer study of the 1957 legislature and presenting adjusted data (Tables 7 and 8) which have taken into account the factors adduced above. The authors have prepared (Figure 11) a scale showing the "conservative" rank-order of members of the 1957 Florida House of Representatives, based on six key issues on which social attitudes could be readily identified. The pattern was remarkably clear: of the thirteen members who were identified as "least conservative," all were from urban counties and all but one were from South Florida. Of the twenty-one "most conservative" members, only two were from an urban county, and the county from which they were elected is in the transitional area of recently urbanized counties on the periphery of North Florida. The scale as a whole shows a strong tendency toward "conservatism" in the North Florida rural areas, a fairly heavy conservative bias in rural South Florida, a slightly less pronounced conservatism in the urbanized areas of North Florida and the transitional areas, and a pronounced nonconservative bias in the urban

South Florida vote. The issues concerned ranged from bills dealing with racial legislation to matters directly affecting the real or presumed urban-rural division, such as the distribution of funds for the purchase of highway rights of way. The same kind of study could doubtless be made for any rural-dominated session with much the same results. To a large extent our adjustment of the tables to reflect the personal attitudes of legislators regardless of the type of county from which they were elected is based on information of the type yielded by such studies of the voting patterns of the members.

Tables 5 through 8, then, indicate that (except for the 1955 house) the rural bloc dominates both houses of the Florida legislature. This dominance is obviously maintained through the selection of sympathetic presiding officers who will use their considerable powers to bolster rural power. The pattern is more obvious and more secure in the senate than in the house, since malapportionment is more extreme in the former. In the house, members from urban or mixed counties actually hold a majority, but many of them (as noted above) do not always in reality represent urban interests, or at least they represent a combination of the rural and business-conservative elements in their respective counties. An additional factor is that in some mixed counties such as Alachua it seems to be more or less customary to "give" one seat (in attitude if not physically) to the out-county rural population. Even so, rural dominance of the house is rather shaky, depending as it does on rural-minded urban men to tip the balance. In the senate, on the other hand, as the tables show, the rural districts have a clear margin of control. The rural bloc is usually said to contain twenty-one or possibly twenty-two members of the total of thirty-eight (in 1959); on many issues it is much larger. In view of these figures, it is apparent that the extent of the predominance of rural interests shown in Tables 5 through 8 cannot be explained by reference solely to malapportionment. The role played by the speaker and the president in making committee assignments is also of key importance.

It is also clear from the tables that rural interests consider some committees more important to control than others. The education committees especially (and to a lesser extent the appropriations committees) have included a high proportion of big-county legislators.

In the case of the education committees, this seems to be due to the fact that all counties, regardless of size, have a major and similar interest in the welfare of schools. The situation as to the appropriations committees is more obscure; it seems possible, however, that considerations like those mentioned above in the appointment of Representative Herrell may explain the matter. Since the big counties supply most of the state's revenues, it would be most unfair to discriminate against them as grossly as is the case with other committees, and with proper care they can be given the appearance of influence without its substance. Then again, since fiscal conservatism (at least in Florida) seems as common among urban representatives as among their rural colleagues, (as in Herrell's case) there is little to fear from allowing them substantial influence on this particular committee.[16] The "economy bloc" cuts across other cleavage lines. The committees handling rules, taxation, constitutional amendment, apportionment, and racial matters are, on the other hand, prime examples of areas in which rural dominance must be maintained because it makes so much difference to the whole political power structure and to the economic and social patterns of rural Florida.

The "doghouse" committee is of interest mainly because it shows the extent to which rural-urban rivalry can go on occasion. Its usefulness is largely symbolic: it indicates the determination of one side or the other to maintain its control. This shows up most clearly when the control of the chamber changes, as from 1955 to 1957 in the house. Since the "porkchoppers" always control the senate no doghouse is needed there. Although it is obvious from Table 5 that the House Aeronautics Committee was "reverse stacked" both in 1955 and 1957, the figures do not tell the whole story. The 1957 speaker, Doyle Conner (a rural legislator from Bradford County), languished in the 1955 doghouse, while such 1955 urban movers-and-shakers as Henry Land (Orange County) and John Orr (Dade County) were relegated to the doghouse for the 1957 session.[17] It is also noteworthy that this committee serves as a repository for Republicans.

Table 9 reveals the extent of "interest packing" which can exist because of the influence over committee selection of the presiding officer, custom, and (to a certain degree) political beliefs. It is obvious

Table 9

Committee Stacking in Selected "Interest" Committees, Florida House of Representatives and Senate, 1955-1959*

Committee	1955 Interest	1955 Non-Interest	1957 Interest	1957 Non-Interest	1959 Interest	1959 Non-Interest
House-Citrus	—	—	13	0	12	1
House-Forestry	—	—	11	0	8	(1?)
Senate-Citrus	13	0	—	—	13	0
Senate-Forestry & Parks*	7	4	—	—	8	3

*Evidently some of the members of the Senate Forestry and Parks Committee are selected to represent the "recreational interest" as distinct from the "forestry interest"; they are shown in the table as "noninterest." Obviously citrus and forestry interests are primarily rural, so there is a direct tie-in between interest stacking (at least on these two committees) and the predominance of rural interests.

that there is a conscious effort to keep anyone off such committees as citrus and forestry who might conceivably represent consumer interests or even the interests of the state as a whole, as distinct from those of the clientele group served (literally) by the committee. Legislators with personal[18] or representative stakes in the interest with which the committee deals make up all or almost all of its membership.

This type of stacking by interest is publicly acknowledged in Florida and is so taken for granted that even those who might suffer from it seldom think to question it; no one, then, need bother to defend it. An incident in the 1957 session illustrates the confident acceptance of this practice. The Senate Committee on Forestry and Parks had before it a bill to impose a severance tax on pulpwood. When the bill came up for hearing, the lobbyists for the important paper industry were present to testify against it, but its legislative sponsor was unable to appear. As is customary, the hearings were postponed until the absent legislator could be present.

The pulpwood spokesmen were understandably not overanxious to make the trip to Tallahassee again and were thus somewhat put out by the postponement. In order to placate them one senator pointed out that their presence was really not necessary anyway: "I think," he said, "if you will look at the membership of this

Table 10
Continuity of Leadership in the Florida Senate, 1955-1959*

Senator	Type of District	Number of Key Committee Assignments		
		1955	1957	1959
Johns	Rural North	3	1	5
Pearce	Rural South	2	3	2
Connor	Rural South	3	2	4
Clarke	Rural North	4	4	4
Johnson	Rural North	3	2	Senate President
Hodges	Rural North	2	2	4
Stratton	Rural North	2	2	3
Edwards	Mixed South	2	3	3
Bronson	Rural South	1	2	4
Carraway	Mixed North	1	2	3
Davis	Rural North	Senate President	3	5
Rawls	Rural North	1	3	5
Shands	Mixed South	2	Senate President	—
Adams	Rural North	—	2	3
Beall	Urban North	—	2	4
Brackin	Rural North	—	2	2
Totals:	Rural, 12 North, 11			
	Mixed, 3 South, 5			
	Urban, 1			

*All senators serving in two of the three sessions and holding multiple assignments in two sessions are included.

committee you will realize you can all go home without saying anything." The committee chairman added, "I don't think you have anything to worry about," and the pulpwood lobby went home.[19] Thus, regardless of the state's urgent need of new revenue sources and the (admittedly arguable) objective merits of the severance tax, the membership base of the committee made impossible the consideration of the proposal from any viewpoint other than that of the woodpulp industry itself. The incident underscores the danger to the public inherent in the practice of "interest stacking" of legislative committees.

One would expect, in view of the discussion thus far, that there would be a high degree of continuity in legislative leadership. Table

10 indicates that this is the case, at least in the senate: to a large extent the same men have held the positions of power for the last three sessions. It shows, in addition, that almost all of them are from rural districts, mostly in North Florida. Even the exceptions are more apparent than real, for Senator Beall of Escambia County (Pensacola) is widely regarded as a "porkchopper," which probably accounts for his success in obtaining influential positions in the senate. Continuity of leadership has not been as pronounced in the house, partly due to the "urban breakthrough" of 1955. But even in the house, taking the two more recent sessions, a high degree of continuity exists, and again it is largely rural. Doyle Connor, 1957 speaker, was Rules Committee chairman in 1959; Tom Beasley, Rules Committee chairman in 1957, was speaker in 1959; and Bill Chappell, who was speaker for 1961, served on three key committees in 1957 (chairing one) and on four in 1959.

It is also noteworthy that the key committee posts form a sort of interlocking directorate in each house, with the same men appearing on several such committees. There is thus a high degree of concentration in the leadership which, while not formally organized as a caucus or a party organization, nevertheless seems to function effectively to ensure rural control. The extent to which this is true is partially indicated by Tables 11 and 12, which show that Speaker Beasley and President Dewey Johnson used their committee appointment powers to construct or merely to recognize highly cohesive and homogeneous leadership groups. The pattern is much more extreme in the senate, largely due to factors already mentioned. In the house, in addition to factors already cited, it should be repeated that Speaker Beasley's ambitions to become governor required him to seek urban support, and thus he was perhaps constrained to make a public show of fairness to the urban areas in committee assignments. Yet, as Table 5 indicated, he was careful enough to ensure that the small counties retained numerical control where it was deemed essential. Obviously some "porkchoppers" are more able and experienced than others; all of them may not be considered as legislative leaders. The important thing to note about Tables 11 and 12 is the almost complete absence of representatives from the large urban centers, particularly in the senate.

It might be said, then, that each chamber is dominated by a rural-oriented oligarchy. This group is more readily identifiable, more cohesive and more secure in the senate than in the house, but it exists in both.

The power to refer bills to committee is also an important element in the influential role of the presiding officer, particularly in the senate. The house rules on bill reference are rather strict: no bill may be referred to more than one committee by the speaker unless it involves taxes or appropriations, in which cases double reference

Table 11

**Interlocking Directorates
on Key Committees of Florida House of Representatives, 1959***

Name	Type of County	1	2	3	4	5	6	7
			Combination of Committee Posts†					
Crews	Rural North		X	X			X	
Conner	Rural North		CH		X			
Herrell	Urban South		X				X	CH
Mathews	Urban South	X		X	X		X	
Inman	Rural North	X				X		X
G. W. Williams	Rural South		X			CH	X	
Livingston	Rural South	X	X	X				
Mann	Urban South	X	X	X				
Drummond	Rural North	X		X			X	
Shipp	Rural North		X				CH	X
Horne‡	Mixed North			CH	X			X
Mitchell‡	Mixed North	X	X				X	
Chappell‡	Mixed South	X	X	X	X			
Stewart	Rural North	X	X	X	X			
J. J. Griffin	Rural South		X			X		X
B. H. Griffin‡	Mixed South				CH			X
Cleveland‡	Mixed South	X	X	X	X			
Sweeny‡	Urban South	CH	X					
Totals:	Rural, 9 North, 8							
	Mixed, 5 South, 10							
	Urban, 4							

*All representatives serving on more than two of these committees, and their chairmen (CH), are included.
†1, Finance & Taxation; 2, Rules & Calendar; 3, Constitutional Amendments; 4, General Legislation; 5, Apportionment; 6, Public Schools; 7, Appropriations.
‡Designates men from mixed or urban counties but who were largely rural in attitude.

is permitted.[20] Multiple reference is possible only on a majority vote of the house. Local bills do not go to committee at all. Within such limits the speaker is free to refer as he sees fit, subject to overruling by a two-thirds vote. This may at times enable him to steer a bill to passage or to death, since the house's fifty-odd committees allow for a good deal of the kind of overlapping which permits discretionary reference.

The senate rules permit the president to make multiple reference of any bill, and this power is used to kill bills which the president opposes strongly enough to be willing to run the risk of public and chamber criticism. At least three bills in the 1957 session were referred to five committees, and since only one committee at a time considers the bill, such reference prevents the bill from reaching the floor before the end of the session.[21]

Table 12
**Interlocking Directorates
on Key Committees of Florida Senate, 1959***

Name	Type of District	Combination of Committee Posts†					
		1	2	3*	4	5	6
Carraway‡	Mixed North	CH		X	X		
Rawls	Rural North	X	CH	X	X		
Hodges	Rural North	X	X		X		X
Adams	Rural North	X		X	CH		
Connor	Rural South	X	X		X		X
Johns	Rural North	X	X		X	X	X
Davis	Rural North		X	X	X	X	CH
Stratton	Rural North	X				X	X
Clarke	Rural North	X	X			X	X
Bronson	Rural South		X	X	X	X	X
Edwards‡	Mixed South			CH		X	X
Beall‡	Urban North		X		X	X	X
Pearce	Rural South				X	CH	
Totals:	Rural, 10 North, 9						
	Mixed, 2 South, 4						
	Urban, 1						

*All senators serving on at least three of these committees, or holding the chairmanship (CH) of one, are included.
†1, Appropriations; 2, Constitutional Amendments; 3, Education; 4, Finance & Taxation; 5, General Legislation; 6, Rules and Calendar.
‡Designates men from mixed or urban districts but who were largely rural in attitude.

It can thus be seen that the presiding officers wield great power. These formal powers are abetted, especially in the senate, by the existence of a fairly well-defined bloc which, while it is not formally organized and is not unanimous on all issues, nevertheless is basically rural in nature and stands united behind the president in order to protect its position of dominance.

The Rules Committee

The committees on rules and calendar are perhaps second only to the presiding officers in importance. Their members are chosen by these leaders, however, so that as indicated in Figures 5 and 6 above, they commonly reflect the political viewpoints of the presiding officers. The influence of these committees stems largely from the short busy session which as mentioned above, forces each house to put the bill calendar under their control in the latter stages of the session. In the house, the rules committee may take over the calendar in the last thirty days of the session;[22] it then makes up a daily special order calendar, and no other bills may be considered unless perchance the special order calendar is completed before the day's session ends. In the senate the same procedure is permitted in the last ten days of the session.[23]

The rules committees also have general responsibility for framing the set of rules for acceptance by the members of each chamber. Much of this is, of course, merely the carrying over of the rules from the previous session, but at times serious issues arise. For instance, in 1957, the rules committees recommended, and both houses adopted, a rule requiring a two-thirds vote before bills could be submitted to Committee of the Whole. In earlier sessions only a majority had been required, but the small-county people (particularly in the house) were afraid that the device could be used to override reference to unfavorable committees; apparently the governor's bill to abolish the Florida Milk Commission—a rural county sacred cow—was especially in mind.[24]

In addition, in 1957 the House Rules Committee took over the duty of advising the speaker on matters of parliamentary procedure (a function which had previously been delegated to a separate committee and which is at times of some political importance).[25]

Committee Chairmanships

In view of the important place occupied by standing committees in Florida's legislative process, it can be assumed that the chairmen at least of the more important committees are men of significant influence. The exact committees which are of importance will vary somewhat depending on the issues confronting the legislature. The rules, appropriations, and finance and taxation committees are always of primary importance, and certain others like constitutional amendments and apportionment are periodically important under present Florida conditions. If one were to look for the men holding influential positions the chairmen and members of these five would be the place to start. Chairmen assume particular importance, for while the committees do much of the real work of the legislature, their heads have much to do with the nature of that work. Chairmen are not selected under any form of seniority rule; the heads of the more important committees will be men of experience, but this is largely because their political attitudes are better known to the speaker so that it is easier to choose from among them men who will fit the speaker's preconceptions. In the senate with its thirty-eight members and thirty-nine committees, even freshman members become chairmen of minor committees; in the house, almost everyone *except* a freshman does.

This selection process makes for a certain degree of unity in the leadership of both chambers. Woodrow Wilson probably correctly assessed the influence of chairmen when he wrote (of Congress) that

> . . . the House has as many leaders as there are subjects of legislation; for there are as many standing committees as there are leading classes of legislation, and in the consideration of every topic of business the House is guided by a special leader in the person of the chairman of the [relevant] standing committee . . . .[26]

Wilson, however, was speaking of a system in which the chairmanship was based on seniority; perhaps the Florida chairmanship is even more significant because of the presiding officer's freedom of selection, which makes chairmanships a device for tying together the house leadership.

At the same time, however, Florida committee heads cannot control the subject matter to be taken up, for both houses require all bills to be reported out: in fourteen days in the house and ten in the senate.[27] This means that a hostile chairman cannot prevent a bill from reaching a vote in committee. Despite this limitation, chairmen are quite important; at times they are regarded as the leading experts on the subjects that come before their committes, in which case their attitudes may dominate the committee. If their reputations are great enough they may even survive great changes in the political control of the house. Representative James Moody, for instance (a universally respected man), was chairman of the House Appropriations Committee in both the 1955 and 1957 sessions, despite the control shift from the urban to the rural counties.

Party Organization

Little need be said of the role of party in legislative leadership. At the present time and for years past the dominance of the Democrats has been so complete that there has been no pressure on them to organize and function in the legislature as a party. And conversely, the Republicans have not been numerous enough for organization to aid them. It is true that in 1957 they made some slight attempt to organize in the house and even to stand for a specific program.[28] But their numbers were too few for this to have any perceptible impact on the house.

Other Influences

Legislative influence cannot always be measured in terms of official position. Often it will appear through the number of important committees a legislator serves on. In 1955, for instance, Representative Henry Land was on four of the six key house committees surveyed in Table 5 above; and in 1957 Representatives John S. Shipp, Roy Surles, and W. C. Herrell were on four. And Senator B. C. Pearce was appointed to four of the five key committees in 1957. Influence may also appear through floor leadership and debate, as it did for Representative (now Governor) Farris Bryant in 1955 and Representatives John Crews and "Bill" Chappell in 1957.

Some legislators gain significance as minority leaders, especially when they combine with ability the integrity which gains them the respect of fellow members. They may, in some degree, serve as the "legislative conscience." Senator Verle Pope has filled such a role in recent sessions.

Leadership is, after all, a somewhat intangible thing which may or may not be correlated with official position. Every legislature will have in it men whose influence is far greater than their positions would suggest. They may be the expert compromisers working behind the scenes, the effective committee workers, or the floor performers who dominate debate. It is impossible to list such men with accuracy, nor would it mean much to do so since the list would change from session to session and even from day to day.

Legislative Officers and Employees

The duties of the officers and employees of the legislature are generally routine. Aside from the persistent practice of nepotism (many legislators' wives and children—apparently employed in violation of the child labor laws—hold positions as secretaries, clerks, or pages) there is little to engage our attention. It is of some importance that the house has made its chief clerk a permanent officer with a staff functioning between sessions. This development may lead to some really effective staff work for interim studies and committees, although it does not appear to have been extensively used so far.[29]

The house is seriously deficient in office space; only the speaker and the oldest member in point of service have offices. Some larger delegations have rooms, and their counties will perhaps supply clerical personnel, but most members must use the rather inadequate stenographic pool. Some use their wives as general assistants. The senate is more generous: every member has fairly adequate office space, alloted by seniority, and each is entitled to at least two attachés.

There are in addition many clerks, typists, pages (usually school children), proofreaders, payroll office personnel, doorkeepers (apparently selected from among the political hangers-on who appear at any session almost like magic), and other miscellaneous personnel.

It appears that the legislative staff is reasonably efficient; the principal difficulty lies in the lack of staff reasearch agencies attached to committees. Such groups could do valuable work and to some extent perhaps reduce the legislators' tendency to turn to private sources of information; they would be of particular value in the conduct of interim studies.

The Committee System

It is generally agreed that "the most important work of the state legislature, like that of Congress, is conducted by standing and special committees."[30] This is because, in general, the real study and detailed discussion of bills goes on in committee or nowhere. The mere volume of work, combined with the short session, make floor debate largely ineffective in shaping legislation or in changing votes. Increasingly, floor action partakes of the nature of ratification of committee action, with infrequent rejection. Robert Luce, indeed, concluded that "rarely does a measure become law against the advice of a committee."[31]

Unfortunately, committees are not always adequate to the task. In Florida especially they lack both the time and the staff assistance which would be needed for good committee work. Perhaps it is these defects more than anything else which accounts for the very large number of committees; for committees allow work to be divided— *ergo*, the more work the more committees. In legislation, however, the answer is not that simple, for the limited membership of the legislature forces multiple committee assignments. You may split up the work among committees but you cannot avoid using the same men on them. The 1957 legislature was neither better nor worse than usual in this respect. The house of representatives had fifty-three standing committees, the total membership of which was 576— an average of six assignments per member. With such multiple assignments—and the more influential members were on the busier committees—elaborate plans have become necessary to schedule meetings so that members do not have to be in two or three simultaneously. Speaker David in 1955 developed a group system which was continued in 1957 by Speaker Conner. The fifty-three committees were divided into nine groups, each of which was assigned a different meeting time during the first month of the session. Care must be taken to assign members to committees in different groups. The Rules Committee schedules meetings in the last month of the session.[32] While such systems may successfully avoid schedule conflicts, they cannot make more time available for committee deliberations. And although they lend themselves to a rather elaborate façade of fairness, they do nothing to eliminate committee stacking.

The 1957 senate had thirty-nine committees, but no such complex arrangements were made public, despite the fact that each senator served on even more committees than did the representatives. The committees totalled 373 seats for an average of ten per senator.[33]

The size of committees in the house runs from five to twenty-five, and size seems to be a rough guide to the importance of the committee (or at least to the volume of business it handles). Almost all house committees consist of uneven numbers, as do all senate committees, which vary in size only from seven to thirteen. Other things being equal the size does not seem an important consideration. While the larger house committees appear cumbersome, they are often split into subcommittees to divide the workload still further; the appropriations committees especially do this.

Aside from the excessive number of committees (a feature which, incidentally, gives the presiding officer an unusual discretion in referring bills) the principal defects of the Florida system seem to be due to the short session, the large volume of work, the lack of staff assistance, and the practice of stacking committees. And since most committee assignments are not made in advance, little committee study can be undertaken before the session begins.

Other Types of Committees

Several other types of committees are used in Florida legislative practice. Both houses, for instance, may resolve themselves into Committee of the Whole (since 1957 by two-thirds vote) and proceed to handle a bill in the same manner as would a standing committee. The device is intended to enable the majority to have its way against the house leadership and the committee to which the bill would otherwise be referred. Since the small counties jammed through the two-thirds rule the device is seldom used. The house majority, led by Farris Bryant, used it in the 1956 special segregation session to bring an interposition resolution to the floor; this maneuver was forestalled only by timely adjournment of the session by Governor Collins.[34]

To reconcile the inevitable differences between the two houses in the final version of legislation, Florida (like other states) uses a conference committee. Such a committee is set up by resolution. Selected members from each house make up the committee, which sits only to settle the differences on the one bill for which it is appointed. Each presiding officer has freedom to choose the conferees from his chamber, but by custom they are chosen from the standing committees responsible for the bill. By exercising due care in the selection of the conferees, the presiding officer can dictate in advance the attitudes represented by the members from his chamber. There is apparently no rule which would prevent the conference committee from making considerable substantive changes in a bill, except the risk that either house might refuse to accept the changes. Bills as reported from conference ordinarily pass: occasionally, however, several conferences are needed, and once in a great while a bill will be killed because of the inability of the conference to find a satisfactory compromise.

Apparently the Florida legislature never uses joint committees except on an interim basis, though there is some evidence that at times senate and house groups will meet together to save time and avoid duplication of effort.[35] In such a case the two committees would not, of course, vote as a unit.

Interim Activities and Legislative Aids

One of the keys to the proper functioning of a legislature—particularly where a biennial session is in use—is the kind and quality of preparatory work that goes on before the session. Florida has a typical variety of interim activities and in fact is much better off than many states in this regard. Yet its preparation for the session is inadequate and leaves too much of the spadework to be done during the session itself. The necessity for presession work is universally admitted, but the legislature has been slow to respond to it. Belle Zeller's study points out that "research and discussion in advance of a legislative session are fundamentally as much a part of the legislative process as the actual session" and that "the legislatures need fact-finding agencies and expert assistance of their own creation which will be free from the bias of special pleaders from the outside, whether they be public or private."[36]

One way to go about this is to appoint and convene regular standing committees in advance of the session. Since 1951 it has been customary for this to be done in the case of the appropriations committees of both houses. These meet with the State Budget Commission before the session; joint subcommittees are set up to study particular aspects of the budget.[37] This practice has enabled the appropriations process to be completed much earlier than before: in pre-1951 sessions the bill did not reach the governor until almost the end of the session, which allowed little time for consideration of vetoed items or for adapting tax measures to the final level of appropriations. Present procedure is a vast improvement in this respect. But apparently no other advance committee work is done.

Another means of accomplishing intersession spadework is the employment of interim legislative committees. These may be either joint or confined to a single house. A joint committee created by the 1956 special session and continued by the 1957 session studied the difficulties created by the integration problem; it presented the 1957 session with a set of bills designed to curb the activities of the NAACP. The 1955 session also set up interim committees to study policies relating to game and fresh water fish and to select and install an amplifying system in the house chamber. The senate in the same session authorized interim studies in five areas.[38] For the most part such committees employ little in the way of a research staff, and this is possibly one of their chief defects. Not only does it reduce the effectiveness of the study, but it makes reports inadequate. Interim committee reports often do not reach legislators in advance of the session; consequently there is no time to digest them properly. Yet they do provide opportunity for fuller study than can be accomplished during a session. Interim committees are not used quite as much now as they were before 1949, when the present

Legislative Council was established, although even now they are often used as substitutes for Legislative Council studies.

Occasionally interim work will be authorized by a committee composed not only of legislators but of private citizens as well. The most recent example of this was the Constitution Revision (Sturgis) Commission, created in 1955 to study and propose a revised state constitution. It was required to report back to the 1957 legislature. The commission was composed of thirty-seven members, including the eighteen legislators who were members of the legislative council, eight private citizens appointed by the governor, five by the chief justice, and five by the state bar association and the attorney general. It had a $100,000 budget and a staff for research studies. However, it was handicapped by its members' legislative orientation (three-fourths were legislators or former legislators) and the fact that any changes proposed would have to be approved by the legislature before going to the public on a referendum. Constitutional revision was thus made not a constituent but a legislative process, no doubt mainly in order to prevent substantial modification in directions not approved by the rural counties—particularly apportionment.

The Legislative Council and the Reference Bureau are exceedingly important aids to the legislature both in and between sessions. These closely related agencies were created in 1949 to provide vitally needed research and fact-gathering services for the legislature. The council is a permanent joint legislative committee composed of a senator and a representative from each of the eight Congressional districts existing in 1950, plus, ex officio, the two presiding officers. Membership is by appointment of the presiding officers, and members serve "at the pleasure" of the house they represent, which means permanent membership since neither house has ever removed a member.[39] Vacancies are filled by the speaker or president, unless they occur after a general election, in which case they are filled by the other members. In effect the council is a continuing body which has the advantages accruing from experience with its work and stability of policy.

In connection with the council, a Legislative Reference Bureau was set up which conducts research studies as directed by the council. The council uses committees to consult with the bureau on its studies. The council thus acts as a screening agency so that the bureau is not overly burdened with requests for work from individual legislators or standing committees.

Upon completion of a study the Reference Bureau presents a written report to the proper committee of the council, which then passes the report on to the full council with its recommendations. The reports are distributed to all members of the legislature. If the council approves a recommendation for action, it is framed as a bill by the Reference Bureau and submitted to the legislature. House rules permit introduction as a Legislative Council bill and provide that even an unfavorable report by a house standing committee will not table the bill.[40] In the senate, council bills must be sponsored by the members of the council.

Due to the indefinite tenure of council members it is relatively difficult for any presiding officer to "pack" the council. It is reasonable to assume, however, that the agency would generally reflect the rural control of the legislature. In 1955 the council membership included five rural and four urban senators, while there were three rural, one mixed and five urban representatives—which probably reflected the speakership of "Ted" David to some extent.

The Legislative Council and Reference Bureau supply legislators with periodic bill summaries during sessions and perform various other services, including the organization of a presession school for new members of the house of representatives. They have proved to be valuable aids to the legislative process in providing for careful and at least relatively unbiased study of many problems confronting the legislature. The council is in essence a "super interim committee with an area of action as wide as that of the legislature itself."[41] Through the provision of a research staff it has at least partially corrected one of the outstanding defects of the formal legislative process in Florida. It nevertheless appears to be true that the legislature does not get full value from this agency. The Reference Bureau has not eliminated the use of interim committees. It has been poorly staffed and financed, and there is a feeling among scholars interested in the legislature that its personnel has not been wisely chosen. For instance, the staff has rarely contained more than a single trained social scientist. The quality of the bureau's studies compares unfavorably with those of states which have well-established bureaus. The liaison between council and bureau is probably not conducive to good bureau work, since it places bureau personnel too close to political influences. In sum, the existence of the Legislative Council and Reference Bureau bears some of the markings of a "cover-up" for doing business the same old way.

The Zeller study has pointed out the great benefits to a legislature that may accrue from the use of a council and reference bureau. They may aid "in informing the public on imminent problems and issues," a significant informational function; they may foster better relations between the two houses, since the council is a joint agency; and they may provide some degree of internal legislative research independent of the governor or other executives.[42] It does not appear, however, that the Florida legislature has made the most of its opportunities in this regard.

Another legislative aid of some significance is the Bill-Drafting Service of the attorney general's Statutory Revision Department. This service was created in 1943 but for some years was not widely used.[43] It has more recently become a well-accepted facility, however, and drafts over half of the bills introduced, in addition to many amendments to pending legislation. It has gained a reputation for impartiality in carrying out the wishes of a bill's sponsor which goes far to explain its popularity. And since drafting is a highly technical operation requiring particular skills and training, such a service can greatly improve the quality of legislation, considered from the purely technical standpoint.[44] In addition to these services, which are available to all members of the legislature and of the executive branch, the Bill-Drafting Service publishes a manual for the guidance of the individual who still wishes to write his own bill.

The Statutory Revision Department is also responsible for the important tasks of indexing the laws, publishing the Florida Statutes biennially, and (even more important to the legislature) preparing and submitting to the legislature "reviser's bills" which are intended to clarify the law by the "amendment, consolidation, revision, repeal or other alteration" in the existing statutes. The aim of this revising procedure, according to the enabling statute, is to reduce the number and bulk of the laws, remove inconsistencies, redundancies, and unnecessary repetitions.[45] These are important functions, and Florida compares very favorably with the other states in making provision for them.

Legislative Investigations

One type of committee which was deliberately not discussed in the foregoing analysis is the legislative investigating committee. All committees, of course, conduct investigations of topics within their subject-matter areas. Particularly the interim committees are charged with investigatory functions and perhaps partake largely of the character of Congressional special investigating panels similar to those recent notorious ones headed by Senators Kefauver and McCarthy. Perhaps as good criteria as any for distinguishing them are whether the committee has the power to subpoena witnesses to appear before it and whether it is a special committee created for the specific purpose of investigating one particular problem area. If it satisfies both of these standards it may probably be called an investigating committee. It does not particularly matter whether it is in operation during or between sessions of the legislature. On the basis of available information it is impossible to tell how often such investigating units are used by the Florida legislature. The major example known to the authors is the joint committee set up in 1956 to investigate ways and means of achieving the peaceful maintenance of segregation. This committee was headed at first by Representative Land of Orange County—a moderate on this question chosen under the Collins-dominated speakership of "Ted" David; after the rural-controlled 1957 session decided to continue the committee, Senator Charley Johns, an irreconcilable, replaced Land as the chairman. The committee has been fairly active; it has called a good many witnesses, including John Kasper, who instigated the Clinton (Tennessee) race riots; and it has at least discussed the possibility of citing a Miami newspaperman for contempt of the legislature. It also submitted to the 1957 legislature a set of bills designed to curb the activities of the National Association for the Advancement of Colored People (NAACP). These bills passed the senate but failed in the house.[46] In 1958 and 1959 the committee turned its attention to the investigation of the desegregation-minded University of Florida faculty. The result was a Keystone cops tragi-comedy, ending in an investigation of homosexuality; the university was nationally smeared, and the reputations and careers of several faculty members destroyed.

It is possible that the special committee set up by the house to investigate whether to bring articles of impeachment against Judge Holt might be considered an investigative committee.[47] On the whole, however, the Florida legislature appears to make relatively little use of the formal investigation.

Impeachment

The case of Judge Holt also provides an illustration of the use by the Florida legislature of impeachment proceedings as a means of removing a public official from office. The use of this method is apparently quite rare; there seems to be no previous case of an impeachment proceeding under the 1885 constitution. For this reason the Holt case was unprecedented and the senate, which sits as court of impeachment under the chairmanship of the state's chief justice, had to make its own rules of procedure, following the practices of the U.S. Senate where possible.[48]

Under the state constitution, articles of impeachment are brought by the house of representatives on a two-thirds vote, and the senate sits *en banc* to try the case.[49] The house selected a sort of committee to act as a prosecuting team, while Judge Holt had his own lawyers to defend him.

Although impeachment is a dramatic event, its use in Florida as in the national government is so rare as to make it of only slight significance. Potentially a technique for legislative control of administrative or executive officials as well as judges, it has never been used for that purpose. Its importance is therefore minimal.

Senate-House Relations

A few words may be added concerning the formal and informal relations subsisting between the two houses of the legislature. It is first of all true that the general characteristics of the chambers vary in some respects. The senate's longer term may mean somewhat looser contact between the legislator and his constituency; senators also seem to have a greater life expectancy in office, and as a result the senate is an older, more experienced, and more dignified body. We have earlier stated our belief that the senate is more nearly controlled by an oligarchy than is the house; it appears therefore to be more disciplined because of the oligarchy's usual control of the seats of power.

As a result of such differences there exists, contrary to what an outsider might expect, some distrust and dislike between the houses. Senators often regard the antics of the house with mixed amusement, paternalism, and disrespect. If nowhere else, this is expressed in the idea that the senate has no obligation to take up house bills promptly but expects the house to do so for senate bills. In fact, some house members claim that some senators will use their committee standing to "sit on" house bills until they are sure of getting favorable treatment of their own bills in the house. It may be that part of the senate's attitude stems from the rather common fear that one or more of the representatives is preparing to challenge the senator for his seat. This was publicly noted as a reason for discord in the Escambia County delegation in 1957.

For its part, the house seems to resent the airs of the senate, but at the same time house members are proud of their individuality and are fond of pointing out that no oligarch controls them. The house in practice, while less disciplined, pays somewhat more attention to the ethical nature of its operations, as its prohibition of proxy voting in committee and its lobby-registration rule indicate. In addition, house members seem to believe that the public utilities' retainers' fees are less common in the house.

It is doubtful, however, whether such intangible pulling and hauling between the two houses has any substantial effect on the overall effectiveness of the legislative process. It may possibly inhibit to some degree the development of co-operative arrangements such as joint committees, but otherwise it seems to have little effect.

Chapter 6

Transaction of Legislative Business

THE actual process of passing legislation is one which does not easily lend itself to description. The formal procedures are carried out under such a complicated system of rules that the narrator is unlikely to be able to do justice to these important matters and at the same time catch the subleties of the adaptation of this framework to the human element which works within it. Without any intention of prejudging the case it may be said that the formal conditions which legislation must meet prior to becoming law in Florida certainly seem to provide every reasonable protection against the possibility of hasty or ill-contrived action. As one former member put it, "It's hard to get a bill passed because you have to win at every stage of the game, but the opposition really only has to beat you once and you're finished on that one." Regardless of the difficulties, however, the ingenuity of the skilled politician will not be easily thwarted by formal processes, and good procedure is no guarantee against bad legislation.

Opening Day

The opening day of the Florida legislature is largely a festive panorama, with a few items of formal business woven into the gala activities. In some respects it might be compared to a Mardi Gras celebration: it falls on a Tuesday, it is very colorful and high-spirited, it precedes a long and arduous effort and it passes from frivolity to deadly seriousness at a specific time—in this case at the moment the governor begins to deliver his message. The comparison ends

here, however, for the observer of the forty-four or forty-five legislative days which succeed the opening day may see many evidences
of piety among the members, but he will rarely have an opportunity
to witness a true act of penance, and he will certainly not find the
arduous work of the legislators during the session accompanied by
personal abstemiousness. Indeed one of the prime qualifications for
service seems to be the possession of a physical constitution that is
capable of standing up under the dual strain of long hours of
work and an almost equally unremitting round of wearying social
activities.

On opening day the legislature goes through the formal motions
of setting up an organization which has been finally determined
well in advance of the session. It carries out this organization in a
setting that is lavish and exciting. Ordinarily more visitors turn up
on this day than on any other. The halls are crowded, thousands
of hands are shaken, some maneuvers for political influence are
begun, while many others (which were previously carried out in
the counties) are resumed in the capitol corridors or offices. Hundreds of people mill about the corridors; some look awed and
somewhat lost, others appear hungry for any crumb of recognition
from the mighty, and some few are obviously there merely for the
sport. The members move confidently through the crowd, many of
them sporting a large carnation or rose in the lapel of a new suit.
They nod to acquaintances and in many cases to persons they do
not know (especially if one looks them straight in the eye) for
fear they may fail to recognize someone who should be greeted.
The legislative employees, especially the temporary ones, are usually
slightly frantic; no matter how carefully they have prepared for it,
opening day always finds them overtaxed and lacking in the smooth-
ness of manner and operation into which they will settle after a
week or ten days.

The houses themselves are gaudy with flowers; every member's
desk is covered with several bouquets. The quantity of flowers is
supposed to be related to the prestige of the member; therefore it
is often said that deficiencies are made up by the legislators themselves. It has been alleged that some of the shorter members are
unable to follow the proceedings and must rely on information

from their neighbors because their vision is entirely cut off by these floral tributes.

Many of the families of the members are in attendance, and in the house of representatives they sit in chairs interspersed among the desks. When a member is elected to an office such as speaker, his wife is also escorted to the rostrum and introduced. If she is not intimidated by the pomp, she may even say a few words of thanks to the assembly. A touch of domesticity can be very useful in reassuring the onlooking voter of the stability of the legislature in terms of the more homey virtues.

The oratory on opening day is as lush as the setting. Nominating speeches can best be described as overripe rather than fresh. Although there has been a noticeable decline in references to Roman senators in the nominating and seconding speeches, there still is a superabundance of log cabins, self-education, integrity, fairness, and statesmanship. A considerable amount of really execrable poetry is quoted and the superlatives increase as speaker follows speaker.

Despite their insistence on simplicity and their tendency to spurn tradition and ritual, Americans seem secretly to adore formalism of all kinds. It is likely, however, that there are some guilty feelings about this love of pomp and circumstance, because most Americans seem to compensate for their indulgence in these things by carrying out their ritualistic performances very badly. In the Florida legislature the cut and dried opening decisions are taken with a flourish which frequently fails to produce the desired effect. Committees appointed to escort distinguished guests or newly elected leaders to the stand often appear hesitant and awkward, and since they usually have to carry out their escorting duties through aisles that are in a state of virtual melee, dignity gives way to self-consciousness and even embarrassment. Occasionally an actor will forget his part and have to be prompted. Although it occurred in a house Democratic caucus on the second day of a recent session, the following incident is a good illustration: at one point in the meeting the chairman of the caucus put the usual question, "For what purpose does the gentleman rise?" before the man had risen. One of his colleagues then called the forgetful member's attention to the speaker's actions by jabbing him with a forefinger. By the time the man struggled to his feet, however, the chairman had already carried out his job for him by stating, "the gentleman moves that a committee be appointed to escort the speaker *pro tem* designate and his 'lovely lady' [no reference to a lady is ever made which omits the prefix lovely] to the rostrum." Looking slightly dazed, the member whose motion had been made without his having uttered a word sat down again.

Despite the apparent superfluity of opening day ceremonies, certain very useful purposes are served by these activities. The pervading spirit of bonhommie is typically American in its artificiality, in its forced conviviality, and in the fact that the façade of uninhibited good humor covers the deadly seriousness with which Americans seem to approach all activities, not excluding their recreation. If the British House of Commons is the most exclusive club in the world, the American state legislature is the world's most effective composite of the Rotary, Lion's, and Kiwanis clubs. Opening day may not have been designed for the purpose, but it has been turned into an opportunity to demonstrate to the state's citizens that the legislature is united, that its members trust one another's motives implicitly, and that each member is convinced of every other member's unfailing devotion to the welfare of the state as a whole.

Under this façade of complete unity and co-operativeness, however, the perceptive observer can detect evidences of divisions and personal tensions that will later manifest themselves in legislative deliberations. Some of the early speeches are quite clearly designed to patch up differences and to restore the member who is speaking to favor with one group or another. Others are concessions of defeat by those who have failed in their bids for leadership posts, and these remarks may occasionally offer evidence that the rejected member recognizes that he will have to occupy a subordinate role in the coming session. A few orators become more than usually flamboyant in their addresses because their stars are rising, while others have difficulty concealing their cynicism behind hearty praise for some member whom they will oppose on almost every important issue.

These factors were especially noticeable in the house of representatives in the 1957 session because of a particular concatenation of political circumstances. As has already been mentioned, the 1955 session had been presided over by a large county speaker who was very close to the governor. As a result, the patterns of influence and the individuals who made the most effective showing in the house during that session were members who came from large counties and were most devoted to the support of the governor's program. In some quarters it was suggested that in 1955 the "big counties" could get anything they wanted through the house, and it is undoubtedly true that the success of the governor's program in the house was largely due to the fact that his supporters occupied the most advantageous positions from which to carry out maneuvers designed to win legislative victories for his proposals. This development alarmed the small counties, however, and caused them to unite more effectively than ever in an attempt to regain control of the house. Their efforts in this direction were aided by the fact that several of the prominent large county leaders of the 1955 session were no longer in the house. One of these men went to the senate; another died; a third, who was not from a large county but was an able parliamentarian and supporter of the governor's program, ran for governor; and one or two others did not run again. Their replacements may have had great potential, but being new they did not as yet have sufficient standing to act with the boldness necessary to retain some measure of control over a house of representatives in which small- and medium-sized county representatives predominate. The preponderance of legislative leadership, then, fell to the small-county members.

This change-over in influence, although obviously more subtle than a party or factional majority change, could nonetheless be detected quite clearly in the behavior of the members during the opening formalities. At one point, for example, a member of the Dade County delegation was participating in a prearranged bit of sheer horseplay, but he interrupted his remarks to congratulate a member from another urban county, who had played a prominent role in the 1955 session, on his appointment to the chairmanship of the committee on aeronautics. He described the responsibilities of this chairmanship (which he related to the importance of the committee's activities) in glowing terms. The tone of the remark was heavily ironic, however, because the committee is completely insignificant, and, as the member from Dade cleverly insinuated, the appointment was a method of relegating not only an individual, but an entire group to a less prominent place in the conducting of house business. The byplay did not stop with this acknowledgment by the large county members of a new pattern of small county dominance. A prominent small county legislator quickly rose and asked whether this was not the same committee over which he had had the honor to preside in the previous session. The answer came back that it was not—the questioner had been chairman of the aviation committee, which was far less important than the aeronautics committee. "In fact," said the member from Dade, "the aeronautics committee is really the aviation committee cleaned up."

The actual opening day process of organizing for the transaction of business is routinized. The two houses meet in their respective chambers at the appointed hours, usually 12:00 M for the senate and 11:00 A.M. for the house of representatives. The presiding officer from the previous session is in the chair if he is still in the legislature. The roll is called[1] and the newly elected members are sworn in. Following a prayer, the houses proceed formally to elect their presiding officers, deputy presiding officers, chief clerk or secretary, and sergeant-at-arms. A resolution is then passed in each house providing that the rules of the previous session apply until the committee on rules and calendar has an opportunity to report on the rules for the coming session. After these steps have been taken each house appoints committees to inform the governor and the other house that it is organized and ready to proceed with business. A few more items of business (such as resolutions providing for details of house management) may be passed before the chambers recess until time for the governor's message.

The climax of the day's events occurs in the middle of the afternoon when the governor, having previously expressed his desire to address a joint session at a certain time, is escorted to the speaker's rostrum in the house of representatives, where he delivers his message to the two houses. Accompanying the governor, in addition to the family retinue, are the members of the cabinet and the supreme court, who take seats at the clerk's desk in front of the speaker's stand. Although the contents of the speech—or at least the major legislative program embodied in it—are well known to most of the legislators already, the formal presentation is a high point in the day's proceedings and constitutes an announcement to the public of the major asking points that the governor is putting before the legislature for the particular session. The galleries are packed and there is an overflow into the corridors. In form the speech is ritualistic; the governor nearly always begins each major topic with an explanation of the progress that has been made in the particular field and then proceeds to make his recommendations for further improvements. The suggested legislation provides excellent material for reporters to dangle before the legislators for comment, and the members are thereby afforded an opportunity for putting themselves on record as being sympathetic to these requests but cautious in asserting the necessity for "looking into each proposal with the greatest care." Following the address, the senate returns to its own chamber and the houses usually adjourn shortly thereafter until the following day.

Legislative Procedure

Once the opening day ceremonies and organizing processes are out of the way, the two houses very quickly get down to business. Meetings are scheduled in the house of representatives on Monday through Friday, from 10:00 A.M. until 1:00 P.M. during the first thirty calendar days of the session, and thereafter as determined by resolution originating in the committee on rules and calendar.[2] Senate rules provide that meetings shall be held except on Sundays from 11:00 A.M. until 1:00 P.M., and if afternoon meetings are decided upon, they are held from 3:00 to 5:00 P.M.[3] In practice these time restrictions are not closely adhered to since the rules can be waived to provide for different meeting times. The senate, for example, does not meet on Saturdays unless pressed to do so near the end of the session, and the house may have to resort to extra meetings earlier in the session than the time prescribed by the rules. In the opening days business may be handled in a short space of time, but it gradually piles up as the weeks go by so that special arrangements have to be made to complete the legislative work.

A quorum in each house consists of a majority of the erected members, although a lesser number may meet and adjourn to compel the attendance of others. All meetings of the house are open to the public, but the senate may use an executive or closed session, usually for the purpose of considering nominations for appointments by the governor. From time to time protests against executive sessions are heard, but the senate continues to use them whenever it appears necessary to do so.

Each house has a prescribed daily order of business[4] by which it proceeds to consider pending matters. In considering measures in the order specified each house works from a daily calendar. In the house the calendar is divided into three parts: house general bills and joint resolutions, senate general bills, and house and senate local bills. The senate uses four divisions in its calendar: senate general bills, house general bills, senate local bills, and house local bills. Each of these calendars is further divided to show the stage of the bills which are contained on it, that is, whether they are on second or third reading. Although the rules specify that matters shall be taken up in the order in which they appear on the calendar, when the time arrives for the applicable order of the day, exceptions are provided for and there is much deviation in practice. In the senate the adherence to the calendar is usually closer than in the house. House rules provide that any committee or individual member may apply to the committee on rules and calendar to take up a bill ahead of its regular place on the calendar if it has been reported out of committee favorably. The rules committee may grant such requests by two-thirds vote and may also on its own discretion submit a special order of business to be considered on a specific legislative day or part of a day. During the last thirty calendar days in the house and the last ten days in the senate, the respective rules committees of the two houses are allowed to submit daily special order calendars, and business included on them takes first priority.[5] Bills can be removed from or placed upon the special order calendar only by two-thirds vote of the house or the senate. The special order calendar is, of course, a means of assuring that the more important pending measures receive consideration before the close of the session. In some cases the order of business on the regular calendar may never be reached after the rules committee takes over the arrangement of the calendar;

therefore the only way to obtain consideration for bills is to get them on the special order calendar. Another way in which the order of business may be changed is by motion to suspend or waive the rules. Such a motion needs a two-thirds vote for approval in either house, except for a few rules which may be suspended only with unanimous consent.

The Florida legislature acts through the passage of five types of measures. By far the most numerous and probably the most important of these is the bill. A bill is a proposal which, when finally approved, becomes part of the ordinary law of the state. A second type of enactment is the joint resolution, which is used in proposing amendments to the constitution. Joint resolutions go through the same procedures as bills, except that they require a three-fifths majority in each house and are not subject to the governor's veto. Concurrent resolutions are measures proposed by one house and concurred in by the other; usually these resolutions deal with some matter of internal concern to the two houses. A concurrent resolution may be passed, for example, to provide for a joint interim committee to study a subject on which legislation may be contemplated. A house or senate resolution is much the same as a concurrent resolution except that it is enacted by and applicable to one rather than both of the houses. A resolution may be passed to express a sentiment of the house or to regulate some matter concerning the house or its members which does not require a law. The final (and probably least used) form of enactment is the memorial. Memorials are passed to petition congress on some matter deemed of interest to the state. The rules of the two houses do not require the latter three types of measure to go through all the steps prescribed for bills and joint resolutions.

Since the bill is the form given to potential statutes during the course of passage, the formal process of legislation is fairly well subsumed by describing the course of a bill through the two houses. In the first place, the constitution requires that certain basic procedures be used in handling bills.[6] Each law enacted must be confined to but one subject, and this subject must be briefly expressed in the title of the bill, but no law can be revised by reference to its title only. Every law must also carry an enacting clause which reads as follows: "Be it enacted by the legislature of the State of Florida."

Laws are frequently found by the courts to be defective because they
have not adequately fulfilled such requirements as these. Every bill
is required to be given three readings on three separate days in each
house, although the constitution itself specifies that the house in
which the bill is pending may dispense with this rule by two-thirds
vote. Suspension or waiver of the rules and final passage of a bill
immediately after its second reading is so common a practice in
Florida today as to constitute the rule as much as the exception. Each
house is required to keep and publish a *Journal* of its own proceedings, and the votes of the members on final passage of all bills and
joint resolutions must be entered in the journal.

A bill begins its course by introduction in either of the two
houses. There is no limitation in Florida, as there is in a number of
states, on the number of bills that a single member may introduce
or on the time during which bills may be placed in the hopper.[7]
Bills continue to make their appearance until the closing days of
the session. Although only members can introduce bills (except
Legislative Council bills in the house),[8] the drafting of proposed
legislation may have been carried out by a member of the executive
branch or by an expert selected by the governor to draft his
legislation, by a private individual, by a legislative committee, or,
most frequently, by the bill-drafting service of the attorney general's
office. Sometimes a member may find it difficult to refuse to introduce
a bill despite his objection to its substance and may enter the words
"by request" on the bill's cover; the senate has even adopted a rule
requiring that these words be entered in the journal when a bill is
introduced on request.[9]

To introduce a bill, the sponsor turns an original and five
exact copies of the bill over to the clerk of the house or the
secretary of the senate.[10] Senate rules spell out the use to which each
copy of the bill shall be put: the original and one copy are kept
in separate files by the secretary, the third copy is for the use
of the press, the fourth goes to the sergeant-at-arms who keeps it
on file in his office for the use of the public, the fifth copy is delivered to the legislative reference bureau for use in preparing the
daily summary, and the final copy goes to the house for its use.[11]
The original of the bill is the "working copy," while the second

one is the senate (or house) copy which is held for the use of the members. Until recently neither house required that bills be printed, but in 1955 the house of representatives adopted a rule providing for the printing of general bills following their introduction. Although there is no senate rule requiring the printing of bills, both houses now make a practice of doing so.[12]

As bills are turned over to the chief clerk or the secretary, they are numbered serially in the order that they are received, without differentiation as to the type of measure. That is, the first measure introduced may be a house or senate resolution, which becomes H.R. 1 or S.R. 1, whereas the next measure may be a bill, in which case it becomes H.B. 2 or S.B. 2. When a bill makes its first appearance before the house in which it is being introduced it is read by title only, unless one-third of the members desire it read by sections— a contingency which is so remote as to be practically nonexistent. At this time the speaker of the house or the president of the senate refers the bill to a standing committee. The practices in this respect differ in the two houses. In the house of representatives the speaker is not permitted to refer a bill to more than one committee on his own discretion, except for bills carrying appropriations or dealing with tax matters. In the latter cases, the speaker must refer such bills to the committee on appropriations or the committee on finance and taxation and may refer the bill to one other standing committee. In the senate, on the other hand, there is no prohibition against multiple reference by the president, and the rule even provides that consideration of such a bill shall be carried out separately by the committees in the order in which the multiple reference was made, rather than simultaneously.[13] In the house of representatives it is possible, by majority vote, to refer a bill to a second committee at the time of its introduction; and it is also possible, again by majority vote, on the day of introduction (or on the succeeding day no later than the order of business of "Motions Relating to Committee Reference"), to withdraw the bill from the committee to which it was referred by the speaker and refer it to another committee. This rule does not apply, however, to bills or joint resolutions referred to the appropriations, finance and taxation, or constitutional amendments committees. In addition, any committee of the house of representatives claiming jurisdiction over a bill may at any time raise the question of proper reference, and the issue will be decided by a majority vote.[14] In all other cases, a two-thirds vote is required to withdraw a bill from committee in order to refer it to another committee or place it on the calendar. In the senate, the rules do not provide a method for floor reference or withdrawal for re-reference short of the ability to muster a two-thirds vote, a fact which greatly enhances the power of the senate president to condemn a bill to death by multiple or unfavorable reference. In both houses, multiple reference (except in the case of reference to appropriations or finance and taxation) is regarded as an expression of disapproval of a bill and almost invariably means defeat.

The committee stage of a bill is a most important part of the legislative proceedings, for it is then that a bill supposedly receives its most detailed consideration by a small group specialized according to subject matter. It is during these committee hearings, too, that interested outsiders have an opportunity to express themselves on legislation. Since the organization and effects of the standing committee arrangement in Florida were discussed in an earlier chapter, it only remains to indicate some of the ways in which Florida committees go about their work. The number and length of meetings of a committee are naturally determined by the amount of work that it has to do. Usually, the chairmen of committees adjust their meetings to the legislation which is pending before them. No committee except the rules commitee is permitted to meet while the house from which it is drawn is in session. Committees meet in rooms assigned to them by the sergeant-at-arms, and forms are available on which written notice is supposed to be given to committee members by the chairman prior to each meeting. In addition to this notice, the times and places of committee meetings are posted on boards outside the chambers.

The work of the standing committees of the Florida legislature varies in quality almost as much as in amount, but a somewhat uniform method is used in handling matters in committee. One of the most noteworthy features of legislative procedure in Florida is the care that is taken to assure that the sponsor of a bill shall have full opportunity to guide his bill through the intricate processes and be fully in touch with the measure at all stages. The house of representatives has gone to the extent of adopting a rule requiring committee chairmen to give written notice of hearings to a bill's sponsor at least two hours in advance of the committee meeting, and their failure to comply can result in recommittal on a point of order if the bill is reported out of committee unfavorably.[15] The sponsor of a bill is thus usually allowed to make the initial explanation of the bill's substance and intended effect at the hearing, and the success or failure of the bill may depend to no small extent upon the skill with which the sponsor handles the committee and upon the fund of knowledge with which he is equipped to answer questions.

In the high pressure conditions under which most legislative business is transacted in a sixty day session, the best approach of a sponsor usually is one which combines firmness with sufficient deference to avoid leaving the impression of overconfidence or patronization. An appearance of uncertainty about the facts of the bill or about the results it is designed to produce may cause the questioning to become hostile and create an atmosphere which is prejudicial to the piece of legislation. Since committees in Florida usually work without regular professional staff assistance, more often than not their decisions are reached without benefit of technical analysis of the bills. The observer is frequently struck with the extent to which crucial matters are discussed and settled solely off the tops of the heads of those on the committee. This Jacksonian method and the extreme time limitations under which the committees work mean that an earlier approach to the individual members, a correct appraisal of the committee mood, and a careful attempt to get around the known prejudices of the members may be even more important means of influencing action than the amount of data presented.

All committee meetings are public, and interested persons are normally allowed to speak if they desire to be heard. On the more important bills especially, the chairmen will usually call for presentation by opponents or proponents of the bill after testimony has been given by all those who have previously indicated that they wish to be heard and before the committee begins its final deliberations. Most lobbyists make a point of putting in an appearance and offering testimony at committee hearings on bills affecting the interests they represent even when their groundwork has been well laid in person-to-person contact. It is useful to make a public showing of strength on the one occasion when private persons have access to the floor. The rule of thumb for successful lobbyists is similar to that for bill sponsors; it is worth remembering that most of the individual minds are probably made up already and the greatest hope for further solidification or slight changes in attitude lies in an appeal to whatever collective factors may enter into the particular committee's deliberations. Only rarely it is possible to stampede a committee.

Under prevailing rules, committees are not permitted to pigeonhole legislation; the house requires that all bills must be reported back in fourteen days, while the senate allows only ten days from the date of reference until a report is due. In the house this time limit does not apply to reports of the appropriations, finance and taxation, and constitutional amendments committees during the first thirty days; in the senate it is not applicable to the appropriations committee at all. Committees often request extensions of time, either on single bills or blocks of bills, and the extra time is usually given. Although most bills are reported out of committee, it is still possible to postpone action on some bills either by repeated requests for extension or by not working on a bill introduced very late in the session; consequently a good many bills die in committee at the end of the session despite the time limits.

Committees in both houses may report bills favorably, unfavorably, with amendments, or with committee substitute. In addition senate committees may report bills without recommendation. Although some sort of stenographic record is kept on all committee hearings, the house of representatives (in addition to recording the committee vote on the report) requires that its committee file with each report a form entitled "Committee Information Record." This form shows the time and place of the meeting at which action was taken, the name and address of each person addressing the committee (together with the interest represented if the person is a lobbyist), and the vote of each member on all motions except procedural ones. The house has thus done more than the senate to formalize committee proceedings and reports and to do away with some of the more obvious committee abuses.

In the preceding chapter some of the political influences that enter into the organization and selection of standing committees were indicated. It is worth re-emphasizing that certain committees are in a position to exercise considerable power and that the influential members of each house solidify their positions in most cases either by the committee posts they hold or by the relations in which they stand to the leaders of the more important committees. One indication of the prominent place of committees is the fact that any suggested change of procedure (whether permanent or temporary) which touches upon any aspect of committee practice will always evoke opposition charges that "this is a threat to the integrity of our committee system." Not the least of the powers that committees hold is the ability to put a bill practically beyond the reach of legislative action by reporting it unfavorably. In both houses unfavorably reported bills are automatically tabled and can be taken up and placed on the calendar only by two-thirds vote. An unfavorable report of any one committee has the same effect in cases of multiple reference.

Favorably reported bills (including those with amendments and with substitutes recommended for passage) are placed upon the calendar and are taken up for second reading when their place in the order of business has been reached. The second reading of a bill must be in full unless the rules are waived and it is read by title only, which is more often than not the case. Second reading is the stage at which amendments may be offered from the floor,[16] and it is at this time that the main floor discussion of a bill takes place.

Debate is carefully restricted. In the house of representatives no member may speak longer than fifteen minutes during the first thirty days and ten minutes during the last thirty days on any question, except that the member introducing the measure (or someone designated by him) is allowed to open and close the debate and the sponsor may have five minutes to close even if he has used his allotted ten or fifteen minutes in opening.[17] This rule also applies to members who have sponsored amendments to the bill, but if the effect of the amendment would be to kill the bill, the member who introduced the bill is entitled to speak last. No senator is allowed to speak more than once on a question, to the prevention of any other senator who wishes to speak, and no one may speak more than twice without obtaining leave from the senate. Senate speeches are limited to thirty minutes unless majority consent to speak longer is obtained.

It is, of course, to the tactical advantage of the opposition to attempt first to kill the bill outright and, failing that, to amend it so that it will achieve as little of its purpose as possible. One of the favorite methods for testing the strength of the support for a bill without impairing the right to further opposition is to move an amendment to the bill which would strike out the enacting clause. If this motion carries, the bill is in effect dead, but if it does not pass there is still opportunity to delay or amend the bill with the idea of drawing its teeth. A motion to postpone indefinitely is another way of attempting to beat a bill without bringing about a vote on the main question. Unless used fairly cautiously, however, motions such as the latter two may hasten the bill's passage by revealing the strength behind it and encouraging the sponsor to try immediately for a vote on the main question.

During the course of debate the presiding officer is usually careful to give a fair hearing by recognizing proponents and opponents of the motion before the house alternately. Members who wish to speak rise in their places and address the chair as "Mr. Speaker" or "Mr. President." The chair will then say, "for what purpose does the gentleman from such and such a county (or district) rise?" Upon being informed of the purpose, and if the action is in order, the chair will grant the floor. In many cases the chair will have been informed in advance by those desiring to speak. Although the presiding officer has the power of recognition and often has to decide the order in which members will be recognized, it is the practice not to curb debate until every member who wishes to speak has had the opportunity to do so. Frequently the chair will recognize one man and at the same time indicate that he will later recognize others in a certain order. No member who has the floor may be interrupted by another member without giving his consent, except that any member may rise at any time to raise a point of order. The usual form of interruption is an inquiry directed toward the member who has the floor, "Will the gentleman yield for a question?" If the member who is speaking yields, a question is in order, and it may be followed up until the presiding officer thinks the give and take has gone far enough and bangs his gavel. Positive statements by a questioner may be ruled out as being a "speech," but one means of putting a direct point in the form of a question has become very common in the house of representatives in Florida; in debate after debate questioners rise to put a statement to the man who has the floor by saying, "Mr. [Brown] would you believe me if I were to tell you. . .?" Usually this is a friendly question designed to reinforce a point or to enable the member who has the floor to reply with fervent conviction, "I would believe you, Mr. [Green] because I know that . . . ." In some instances this type of affirmative question may be hostile and the member to whom it was directed may be forced to reply, "If you said it, Mr. [White], I would believe you, but . . . ." Repeated sufficiently in the course of a single speech, as it often is, this tactical ploy can become ludicrous.[18]

The house of representatives has installed a public address system with a microphone at each desk and speeches may be made "in place." However, many debators prefer the dramatic effect of facing the full audience when they speak, and they come to the "well" in front of the rostrum to speak. Senate speeches are usually less strident than those delivered in the house, and the intimacy of the chamber makes it easy for any senator to be heard even when speaking in moderated tones from his desk without the benefit of sound boosters.

Most of the debates in both houses are conducted in an atmosphere of good humor. In fact the quality of many of the spontaneous quips is higher than the philosophical content of the speeches. Sometimes, however, a heated situation will develop and accusatory points will be made against other members or groups. Rarely does the debate reach high levels of philosophical sophistication; the man who comes to the house or senate expecting to hear specific legislation discussed in terms of the broadest principles will be very disappointed. A good case may still be made for the idea that the function of a legislative body in plenary session is to take a bill whose details have been ironed out in committee and inquire into its general applicability in terms of a certain set of conditions, governmental philosophy, and constitutional framework. Measured by this criterion, debate in the Florida legislature, as perhaps in all state legislatures, falls far short of expectations. Even in terms of the literary quality of debate, there seems to have been a decline in the twentieth century from the standards set in the nineteenth by people who were still able to cap arguments with a biblical or classical quotation and to make subtle allusions to the better quality literature. Despite the more prosaic tone of contemporary debate, however, in which the ascriptive words "this is a good bill" or "this is a bad bill" may be substituted for a logical explanation of why it is a good or bad bill, there is still a watch-dog atmosphere in the Florida legislature which nearly always results in attention being called to the more obvious aberrations from high legislative standards. But calling attention to these undesirable features by no means produces the assurance that the offending measures will be purged.

Although motions for the previous question (which if approved brings the question under debate to a vote), for adjournment, for recess, or to lay on the table may be made at almost any point in the debate and are not themselves debatable (except for the five minutes allowed the sponsor of the motion under debate), it is not usual to close debate abruptly if members are waiting to be heard.

Despite the closure rules, it is possible to adopt delaying tactics that may be quite successful. Although a filibuster may not be undertaken very easily by a single member, one can occasionally be arranged by a group of members who may rise to speak in turn and have previously planned interrupting questions. In addition the use of delaying motions may be very effective because of the availability of such a wide variety of them. Since a formal vote can be demanded by a show of five hands, calling for votes even on minor motions can further hold up action. A member requesting permission to speak on a point of personal privilege also has a high priority, and the member may occupy the floor for some time and even speak to some points on the bill before the presiding officer calls him to order. It is not always easy to detect the point at which delaying tactics are aimed, because they may be used during the course of debate on one measure in order to delay or prevent consideration of some bill further down the calendar.

After all pending amendments have been adopted or rejected and debate has been completed, the vote is taken on the bill itself. As soon as the bill has made its way this far, it is the usual practice for the sponsor to move that the rules be waived and the bill be read a third time in full and placed on its final passage. If two-thirds of the members agree the bill is usually read and passed immediately. Although the third reading is formally required to be in full, the actual reading is usually very perfunctory—a few unintelligible words of benediction are muttered over the bill by the clerk, and the journal (as the official record of proceedings) subsequently declares that it was read in full.

Up to this point all votes may have been taken by voice (especially if the bill has little opposition), but as previously indicated the vote of the members on final passage must be recorded.[19] Record votes in the house are taken by electric voting machine, but in the senate the roll still is called orally. In both houses each member present must vote when a question is put, unless excused by the chamber or unless he has a direct interest in the legislation.[20] The speaker of the house does not have to vote, however, except to break a tie. In the senate a member may change his vote before the result is announced at the end of the roll call. In the house a member may request that he be allowed to vote or to change his vote after the machine has been locked but before the vote is announced, and the action will be recorded in the journal. The time between locking the machine and announcing the vote is so short, however, that this is seldom done. After the roll call has been announced a change in a vote can take place only with unanimous consent. Members are not allowed to explain their votes orally but may submit written explanations (limited in the house of representatives to 200 words) to the clerk or the secretary for recording in the journals of the respective houses.

Upon the passage or failure of any motion or main question it is in order (on the same or the succeeding legislative day) for a member who voted with the majority to move to reconsider the vote by which the motion was passed or failed. During the last seven days in the house and the last five days in the senate, such a motion is decided upon immediately. The uses to which the two houses put motions to reconsider are different. In the house of representatives the motion is usually made for the purpose of closing the question for the duration of the session: motions are made to reconsider and to lay the motion for reconsideration on the table.[21] If the motion is tabled the matter is dispensed with finally, since only one motion for reconsideration is in order except with unanimous consent. In the senate, reconsideration is mainly used to delay the passage of a measure. Since the oral roll call in the senate permits a member to keep an accurate account of the vote as it is being taken, a senator who sides with the minority may change his vote at the end of the roll call in order to be eligible to move for reconsideration. In the senate motions to reconsider lay over until the succeeding legislative day, when they become a special and continuing order of business. The delay is for one day only, however; if the matter is not disposed of on the second day it is considered abandoned, and if it is disposed of no further motion to reconsider is possible except by unanimous consent.[22]

Bills which have been amended must be engrossed, which is the term applied to the retyping of the bill to incorporate all changes so that it shows the final form in which the house approved the bill.[23] Except for a bill which is finally passed immediately after second reading, engrossment takes place between the second and third readings. A bill is placed on the calendar of bills on third reading after it has been engrossed. It will then be brought up for final reading when its place has been reached. If a bill is engrossed after third reading, naturally it does not have to go back to the calendar.

After a bill has passed through the house in which it originated, it is signed by the presiding officer and sent to the other chamber. There it repeats the processes of first reading, committee reference, second reading, engrossment, and third reading. The practice of introducing "companion bills" has become very common in Florida as a means of saving time. Companion bills are identical bills which are introduced about the same time in the two houses, worked on simultaneously, and merged at an advanced stage in their consideration. If, for example, a bill is on the house calendar and its companion has been passed through the senate, the senate bill may be put on the calendar in place of the house bill without reference to committees. From that point the bill will be treated as though it had originated solely in the senate and is passing through all the house phases as a senate bill.

All bills must be passed by both houses in identical form before being sent to the governor for consideration. If a bill previously passed by one house is amended in the other chamber, it then goes back to the place of origin for concurrence on the amendments. As was indicated in the preceding chapter, in some cases the originating house does not concur in an amendment adopted by the other chamber, and in this event a conference committee will be appointed to smooth out the differences. The conference committee members report the results of their deliberations to their respective houses and these reports ordinarily are acted upon favorably without further ado. It was also mentioned earlier that additional conferences may have to be held, and, more rarely, a piece of legislation will die in conference.

A bill which has been passed in identical form through both houses is enrolled and sent forward for the governor's consideration. Enrollment is the process of copying a bill on permanent record paper and having it signed by the chief clerk and speaker of the house and the secretary and president of the senate. The governor may sign the bill, in which case the process is complete, and the bill is ready to become an act of law. Unless otherwise specified in the act, bills which have passed become law sixty days after the session's adjournment.

If the governor decides to veto a bill, he has only five days, Sundays excepted, to return the bill to the house of origin, together with a statement of his objections. If a bill is held longer it becomes law without the governor's signature. However, if the legislature adjourns before the five days are up the governor is allowed twenty days from the time of adjournment before a bill becomes law without his signature. In the latter case the governor may still veto the bill and file it and his objections with the secretary of state so that the legislature may consider the matter at the next session. A bill can be passed over the governor's veto by a two-thirds vote of the members present in each house. In appropriations bills the governor is allowed to veto specific items of appropriations while approving the bill as a whole. The procedures for using the item veto and for passage by the legislature over the governor's veto are the same as those provided for the general veto power.

The laws passed by the legislature are separately published after each session. In recent years they have been printed in three volumes —a volume of general acts, a volume of general acts of special appli-

cation (such as population laws), and a volume of special acts.
Other forms of publication of Florida statute law were mentioned in
the previous chapter.

Special Acts

Most of the preceding discussion was concerned with the passage
of general acts, that is, with acts applicable to the state at large.
But there is another category of legislation which is of great importance in Florida—the special act. There are really two types of
special acts, the special act proper and the local bill.

Of the former little need be said. The special act is designed to
deal with some matter that is not applicable to the state as a whole,
but is nonetheless an obligation of the state which cannot be fulfilled
without passing a law. Special acts cover a wide variety of subjects
including such matters as pensions, road designations, and many
other similar things. Also included in this category are claims bills,
which are bills passed to make restitution to an individual who has
been injured in person or property by an agency of the state. In many
cases of special acts, especially claims bills, it would appear easy
enough to devise some administrative or judicial remedy so that the
legislature's time could be freed from demands made on it by these
details. Attempts have been made to do this, but they have not met
with success thus far. One might have every sympathy with the
necessity for the individual to have access to the legislative remedy
in the face of misfortune or arbitrary treatment at the hands of an
administrative agency, but it is questionable whether this access
should take the form of individual legislation.

A far more serious problem is the amount of special local legislation handled by the legislature. Local bills are bills that have
application only to a particular area of the state such as a city,
county, or special district which is within a single county. In recent
years local bills have constituted about half of all legislation introduced in the two houses and two-thirds or more of those passed.
Despite the special procedures that have been introduced to speed
up the process, a considerable amount of time in the two houses (and
an even greater proportion of the members' legislative time outside)
is devoted to work on local legislation.

Excessive local legislation is an outcome of the unwillingness to provide the legal flexibility necessary for local units (cities especially) to solve their problems locally. A recent study has shown that, of 345 local laws relating to cities, passed in the 1951 session, 105 of the bills applied to general city government (including changes in powers and duties and compensation), 75 concerned charter amendments and adoptions, 29 made changes in the tax structure of cities, 20 related to city elections, 47 to various aspects of employee relations, 27 to boundaries, 20 to direct legislation, and the remainder to a variety of other local matters.[24] Nearly all of these types of problems could be solved without legislative action if an adequate system of home rule were developed for the state. In many other instances local bills affecting counties could also be avoided if more effective general laws were adopted for the counties as a whole and they were granted more police powers.

The situation with regard to local legislation in Florida is somewhat peculiar because some attempts have been made to break the pattern of special legislation in this field. Although parts of the general law of the state relating to municipalities badly need reworking to allow the cities more flexibility in adapting to local needs, there are general laws on the statute books which cover most matters of concern to the cities, and procedures for local adoption and amendment of the charters are available.[25] For a variety of reasons, however, the practice of special legislation is so firmly entrenched that the general laws are not often used even when they would cover the needs of the municipality concerned. Usage (combined with the absence of any effective ban on the enactment of local legislation) causes the city fathers to turn to the legislature when they want to adopt a charter, and once enacted as a special act, it takes a special act to amend the charter. There is even a certain legal sanction behind the preference for the special act: in cases of conflict a general act will have to yield to a special act (whether enacted before or after the general law) unless a later general act specifically repeals the special law or indicates in clear terms an intent to regulate all Florida municipalities uniformly relative to the particular matter at hand.[26]

In 1933 an attempt was made to curb special legislation constitutionally. A constitutional amendment was proposed (adopted in

1934) which required the legislature to classify cities and towns according to population and provide by general law for their incorporation, government, jurisdiction, powers, duties, and privileges under these classifications. It was further provided that no special law respecting any of these aspects of municipal government was to be passed.[27] When the legislature sought to implement this amendment, however, it found the system too rigid; "consequently this provision of the Florida constitution has remained a dead letter, and the system of statutory home rule and local bills remains in force."[28] The constitution continues to prohibit special or local laws on a considerable range of subjects, but few of them are matters that affect city government.[29]

As has been intimated, the procedure used by the legislature to pass local bills differs from that followed for general acts. In the first place the constitution requires either that notice of intention shall be published at least thirty days prior to the introduction of a local bill or that the local law shall contain a provision to the effect that the bill shall not become operative until approved by a local referendum.[30] A standard affidavit to the effect that the bill has been advertised as prescribed must accompany the introduction of local bills which do not contain the referendum provision, and the house even uses a separate bill form for the introduction of advertised local bills.

The passing of local bills ordinarily is a formality. Sometimes they are passed on introduction; otherwise they skip the committee stage and go directly to the local calendar. If the delegation from the county to which the bill applies (or the senator from that district) favors the measure there is no problem. When the bill comes up the member (or members) simply raise their hands to indicate acquiescence, and usually the entire day's calendar of local bills is disposed of by a single roll call. The journals show that all the conditions imposed on the passage of bills were met. If a local bill is in dispute, the house normally will decide the issue on the basis of the votes of two of the three delegates (if there are three from the county) or will support the more popular of a two-man delegation. On the other hand, if the split is over the question of whether or not to hold a referendum on the bill, the chamber is likely to allow the referendum to take place rather than pass the bill on advertisement. If there is disagreement between the delegates from the two houses, the chances are that the bill will be killed unless an agreement can be reached.

A variation of the local bill which enables the legislature to circumvent the advertisement and referendum requirements (especially after it is too late to meet the advertisement deadline) is the general bill of local application, or population bill. These are bills which provide that their application shall be solely to cities or counties within a specified population range, as determined by the preceding census. In both houses such bills are referred to a committee whose only function relative to these measures is to determine whether or not the population bracket is confined to the single city or county for which the act is intended. If this is the case, the committee will report the bill favorably and it is then handled in much the same manner as a local bill. Should the population bracket include areas other than the one designed for inclusion, the units unintentionally embraced will have to be amended out. And, of course, after every census all the existing population laws must be revised to keep them from applying to new areas.

In view of previous discussions, any attempt to spell out the way in which this process of local legislation contributes to the prevailing local political orientation of legislators and caters to the desire for local instruction would belabor the obvious. The system is patently a part of the more general method of conducting legislative politics in Florida. From time to time suggestions have been made that Republican delegations be denied the courtesy of automatic passage of local bills, but even the new threat of party government is insufficient to endanger the local legislation system.

One indication of the extent of the involvement is the fact that in about half of the counties local legislative delegations hold pre-session "legislative clinics." These clinics are regularly scheduled hearings set up for the purpose of allowing interested parties to discuss pending legislation. There is naturally a great variation in the way in which these clinics are organized; some of them are long and involved and may be held in several localities in the county, while others are very perfunctory. Although many clinics permit discussion of general as well as local legislation, local matters are plainly dominant in these meetings.

Given the system of local legislation, the clinic idea may be a useful and necessary device for obtaining the sense of the community on legislative matters that will affect the local area. But it is also subject, as some members point out, to the abuses of domination by small, vocal cliques whose interests are often centered on trivial matters or on legislation which might adversely affect the community. Over and above this fault, however, is the fact that meetings of this type are symptomatic of the failure to develop sound methods of local self-government. At best the clinic idea is an unsatisfactory substitute for the local settlement of local issues and is utilized in the attempt to satisfy the demand for local deliberation on these matters, a demand which could probably be better satisfied within a narrower political framework.

On the whole most county officials, many city officials, and a majority of the legislature appear to favor the local bill system, and they do not seem aware of any conflict between their professed adherence to the idea of keeping control over government as close to the people concerned as possible and the practice of making the more important decisions relating to local units at the state capitol. Perhaps the reconciliation of the problem rests on the assumption that many legislators see all legislative problems solely from the vantage point of their own front porches—even when they go to Tallahassee some members never leave home.

In 1955 the legislature passed an amendment to the constitution providing for home rule in Dade County.[31] This amendment was adopted by the voters at the general election of 1956, and the residents of the Miami area subsequently ratified the locally drafted home rule charter, which went into effect in July, 1957. The charter was a very comprehensive one; it embraced a considerable degree of unification of the county government and the twenty-odd municipal corporations, a county-manager plan of government, and a sweeping prohibition against special acts. As a result of the new charter, the Dade County legislative delegation refused to introduce some 200 local bills in the 1957 session, a large proportion of which would formerly have been introduced and passed.

The tremendous growth of the metropolitan areas of the state may result in the development of a pattern similar to that in Dade County. That is, home rule may gradually be extended by constitutional amendments embracing one county at a time. Although this procedure would do violence to the structure of the state constitution, it may be the only way to provide some measure of relief to the areas which do not look so favorably upon the special act system as a whole.

Conclusion

From the first call to order at the beginning of a session until the last day when a legislative employee stands in the center of the capitol corridor in view of both chambers and drops a handkerchief so that the presiding officers may rap their gavels simultaneously to signify adjournment sine die, the legislature gives the impression of frenzied and often directionless activity. To the uninitiated it may appear that the legislature spends its entire time on a rapidly turning treadmill. Despite these appearances, the legislature does get things done—a fact which is attested to by the following table of matters handled at a recent (and typical) regular session.

The volume of work accomplished cannot always be carried out well in the time that the legislature has available, and naturally many things are left undone that should be done. Far too much legislation is passed in unseemly haste at the very last hour. Since most of this last minute legislation consists of matters which *must* be acted on, much otherwise good legislation never even has an opportunity to be considered. Many complaints are heard, for example, about acts that are introduced in an attempt to clarify an existing statute in order to make it fully operative, but are never brought to a vote. Neglect through haste probably kills more bills than cupidity.

Many criticisms could be directed against the legislative procedure used in Florida. The weaknesses of the committee system and the local bill evil have already been pointed out, but there are also serious deficiencies in such areas as the deliberative function of the legislature and in some of the rules. Despite the absence of the direct use of the guillotine in debate, the tight schedule on which the legislature

Table 13
1955 Legislative Statistics*

	House	Senate	Total
Length of Session in Days	60	60	
Days in Formal Session	44	43	
All Legislation Introduced	1945	1434	3379
Average Introductions Per Day of Actual Session	44	33	77
Bills Passed			
General Bills	160	299	459
Local Bills	766	518	1284
Relief Acts	25	27	52
Joint Resolutions	2	9	11
Concurrent Resolutions	12	9	21
Memorials	6	3	9
1953 Bills Passed Over Veto	1	1	2
Bills Vetoed by Governor	11	13	24

*Legislative Council and Reference Bureau, *Laws of General Interest Enacted in 1955 Regular Session of Florida Legislature*, Tallahassee, 1955, following p. 34.

works precludes the conditions of leisureliness necessary to draw out the best type of parliamentary debate and lessens the members' incentives to prepare themselves to the fullest degree for their individual and group roles in debate. Some of the rules, too, are outmoded, otherwise they would not be so easily and so often suspended. In some cases the rules are not very clear, or are incomplete, or are not organized in a manner which makes it easy to move from one logical step in their arrangement to another. The Florida legislature badly needs to take a look at its rules and procedures with a view to making them serve their purposes more effectively. Unfortunately, however, a large proportion of the legislature continues to cling to the ideas—so obviously antiquated by the very volume of business handled by the legislature—that the major aspects of state policy can be handled adequately in the highly artificial atmosphere of a sixty calendar day session and that the state never suffers from what the legislature does not do. As long as such conceptions are dominant there does not seem to be much chance that the legislature will take a long, unbiased look at itself and its activities.

Chapter 7

Legislative-Executive Relations

DESPITE the system of the separation of powers, American elected executives have always played a prominent role in the legislative process. If this role was largely negative during the nineteenth century, it is in the twentieth a powerful positive factor; and if the nation's presidency has led the way in this enlargement of executive functions, no level of American government has been unaffected. It is doubtful that de Tocqueville would write today, as he did in the 1830's, that "the struggle between the President and legislature must always be an unequal one, since the latter is certain of bearing down all resistance by persevering in its plans."[1] For whatever may be said of American executives today, few remain who regard them as mere executors of the will of the legislature. The governor of Florida is no exception.

Today the governor is an independent executive, for no longer does the assembly select him as was formerly done in some states. His term of office is now four years, which enables governors to develop effective programs with some hope of success in seeing them enacted during their tenures of office. And the governor has the veto power, in fact, having proceeded even beyond the federal constitution by gaining an item veto on appropriations measures. These powers, abetted by circumstances, have given contemporary Florida governors significant weapons with which to act as legislative leaders.

Why have these changes come about? There have undoubtedly been many causes, of which only the more significant may be mentioned here. The growth of party organizations was certainly a major factor in many other states. In a functioning two-party system, the governor would normally be regarded as the leader of his party, a position which, if vigorously and effectively used, could give him significant influence with the legislators who belong to his party. The growth of such two-party systems has, however, been anything but uniform; probably less than half of the states have such a condition. But even in normally one-party states governors may be effective party leaders if the dominant party has achieved and maintained a relatively high level of organization and cohesion so that the leader has something to lead. In Florida the disintegrated nature of the dominant party prevents the governor from assuming such a position; but even so, governors are typically more powerful legislative leaders than formerly. Party is not, obviously, the only cause of such a situation.

The growth of the governor's appointment power, coupled with the typical nineteenth-century state spoils system, gave the governor—and other executive officials—significant power. This, however, can hardly be cited as a cause of the twentieth century increase in gubernatorial powers, for the recent trend has been away from patronage and toward the development of strict merit system procedures for hiring. While this has not gone very far in Florida, wherever it occurs it deprives the governor of one of the tools of leadership.

Possibly of fundamental importance have been the rapid growth of Florida's population and the nature of that growth. With unwieldy masses of people now concentrated in huge urban agglomerations and engaged in wage-earning occupations; with an ever-advancing technology transforming the face of the countryside and creating a complex and threatening economic giant; and with, as we have seen, a political condition tied to a creed that makes it difficult or impossible for the legislative body to adapt itself to drastically new needs and desires, the legislature has found itself bewildered by the onrush of events and the multiplicity of the demands on it. It is commonplace for critics of American government to remark that our antiquated legislatures seem unable to generate within themselves the leadership necessary to legislate effectively under modern conditions. Many commentators doubt that any possible reform in our legislative bodies would enable them to meet the need. These criticisms apply to Florida with, if anything, redoubled force.

Faced with such a situation, the public—and even the assembly—unwillingly have turned to an outside agency for the leadership they cannot find within the legislature. This leadership has largely sprung from the executive branch. It is not an usurpation of power, but an assumption of unused and necessary power.

As a part of this picture, these changing conditions have left Florida's state legislature unrepresentative in character. Earlier in this book we have enlarged on this fact. But at the same time the governorship has developed as the outstanding state-wide elective office, and with the growth of universal suffrage has taken on a representative quality which in one way rivals that of the legislature itself. For the governor, like the President, is elected by all the people (even many Negroes vote); he has become, in President Jackson's conception, the "tribune of the people." But perhaps of more direct significance, he is responsible to the urban majority—precisely the group which the unrepresentative legislature fails to represent quantitatively. It is natural, indeed inevitable, that groups denied proper representation in the legislature will seek it in the executive. In consequence, the governor is today invested with a representative quality for the entire state which can not be matched by the representative assembly. He is elected by, and speaks for, the entire state to a greater extent than the legislature itself. And by failing to provide for its own reapportionment, the legislature is gradually making its further decline even more certain.

Finally, the great changes in society have brought great changes in government. More than ever before, government today engages in vast services and regulatory functions embracing the entire economy and the living conditions of the people. In carrying out these programs, governmental administration has become the key factor. The governor and his executive associates are the men who run the administration of the state's regulatory and service activities. Being familiar with the actual conditions and the needs of these programs, these officials know much better than the legislature what is necessary to do a good job, where the loopholes are, and all the multifareous details which must be taken care of by legislation but which are known primarily to them rather than to the legislators.

When a governor, therefore, comes before the state legislature with proposals for legislation, he comes armed with a knowledge of the entire state and its needs, and of conditions and needs in the administrative arm of government, much greater than the legislature, for all its vaunted representativeness, can match. It may be said, therefore, that the great growth in executive influence in the Florida legislature is due fundamentally to the fact that *the executive occupies a more strategic position in society and government* than does the legislature, and thus it is in a better position to speak authoritatively of the needs and desires of the state. The legislature, knowing this (although not admitting it), can ignore him only at its peril.

The rather widespread popular disrepute of the state legislature has contributed to its relative decline, at the same time that it has been brought about by the circumstances outlined above. For while the popular executive has gained in public esteem the legislature, seemingly, has gone down. Public attitudes are doubtless the result of the ineptitude of the legislature; but such attitudes have a circular effect, for they are likely to be the cause of a further decline in the ability of the assembly to meet the demands upon it. The Florida state legislature seems to have been caught on a descending spiral from which only drastic action can rescue it.

The Executive Branch in Florida

As in most of the American states, the outstanding feature of the Florida executive is its plural nature, for there is no single person who can realistically be designated "the chief executive." Such reference is often made to the governor, but in reality he controls only part of the executive branch—possibly not even the major part. Each of the other cabinet officials, elected under constitutional mandate as they all are, is as much a chief executive in his own bailiwick as is the governor in his. And the institutionalized cabinet in Florida (a unique thing) has executive powers of its own which the governor must share with the rest of the cabinet's members.

In Florida there are six elected officials in addition to the governor: attorney general, secretary of state, treasurer, comptroller, commissioner of agriculture, and superintendent of public instruction. There is, in addition, a three man elected Railroad and Public Utilities Commission. The areas of control of these officials are indicated generally by their titles, although there are accrued functions of each which are not so indicated.

Such an arrangement, it has often been pointed out, may have the effect of reducing the degree to which officials can be held responsible for their conduct by the general public. This is due to the fact that the public gaze, rather than being concentrated on a single well-publicized individual, is split between seven officials most of whom are not subjected to a great deal of public attention (although particular interest groups may watch them closely).

Florida political custom further insulates these elected officials, except the governor, from the force of public opinion by providing for them almost certain life tenure. It is extremely rare for an incumbent to fail of re-election (with the possible exception of the utilities commissioners).

But the governor's position as chief executive is an anomalous one, for the public has a strong tendency to expect of him more than the powers of his office enable him to supply. The citizen looks to his governor not only for legislative leadership, but for active and effective control of the executive branch of the government. This the governor cannot provide, either constitutionally or in practice. Politically speaking, these public expectations tempt the gubernatorial candidate to run under false pretenses—he is likely to promise things in areas over which at best he has only partial control. In Florida politics the utter lack of any campaign slate or party platform compound the evil, for they prevent the candidate for governor from imposing even lip-service agreement with his views on the candidates for the other offices.

It can thus be seen that the Florida political system, while it provides the governor with most of the prestige of a chief executive, gives him comparatively little of the substance of that office. He thus can bring to the task of legislative leadership primarily his status as the principal state-wide elected official.

The Governor's Constitutional Role in Legislation

Even though the doctrine of separation of powers would seem to dictate an executive with no role to play in the process of lawmaking, American constitutions have seldom adhered to such a rigid separa-ion, nor does the Florida Constitution of 1885. Indeed, the entering wedge of legislative influence by the governor is a constitutional one. These constitutional powers are primarily the veto, the message to the legislature, the appointing power, and the power to call and adjourn special sessions.

The constitution provides that the governor may veto any legislation within five days of the time it reaches his desk during the session or twenty days from the session end if it comes before the five day period expires. Any bill which the governor neither signs nor vetoes becomes law without his signature at the expiration of this five or twenty day period.[2] He has, in addition, an item veto on appropriations bills.[3] Vetoes may be overriden by a vote of two-thirds of those present and voting in each house, and a bill vetoed after adjournment of one session must be laid before the legislature at the opening of the following session. These provisions vary only in details from those of most other states. A veto message ordinarily accompanies the notification of the veto.

The constitution also empowers—or perhaps better, requires—the governor to deliver messages to the legislature as he considers it desirable to do so.[4] The only regular message is the one always presented at the beginning of the session; it is unusual for messages to be delivered at any other time except perhaps when special sessions are convened.

The Florida governor has considerable appointing power, perhaps more than in the average state. Not only does he appoint the employees and officials who work under him and the members of a rather large number of boards and commissions, but he also has the constitutional duty of filling vacancies in all county offices—a task of some political importance.[5] The Florida governor has also a relatively large removal power, which may apply even to county and city officials;[6] but this has apparently little to do with his legislative position.

The power to call special sessions, discussed in Chapter 5, and to adjourn sessions is little different from that of any other governor.

In addition to the aforementioned disintegrated character of the executive branch, the governor of Florida suffers from at least one other constitutional disability which affects his role in lawmaking. This is his ineligibility for re-election,[7] the effects of which will be discussed later in connection with the significance of Florida's unique cabinet system. It is enough at this point to note that he loses the possible political influence to be had from the possibility of succeeding himself in office. He has no means of using his ideas as a standard by which individual legislators may be judged when they campaign for office.

Political Aspects of the Governor's Role

It has already been noted that the principal political asset brought to office by a Florida governor is the mere fact that he is the major state-wide elected official. The public support indicated by his election on such a basis is, on any reckoning, a formidable force in itself. His own personality may reinforce or detract from this original prestige, depending on whether it accords with legislative expectations as to the proper modes of gubernatorial activity in relation to lawmaking.

It must be repeated, however, even at the risk of boring the reader, that a governor has several political handicaps which seriously weaken his legislative position. He comes to office almost inevitably representing a radically different constituency than that to which the majority of the legislature is responsible. He consequently thinks in different terms and acts on different motives—a fertile source of misunderstanding and mistrust between executive and legislature. Further, he cannot use his popularity with the state's urban voters or his presumed knowledge of their needs with very great effect because of this difference in constituencies. Equally, however, he cannot merely give in and accept the views and actions of the rural-dominated legislature, for to do so would be to betray his platform and those who elected him.

Nor can the governor use the typical device of the American executive, the appeal to the people, with great effect. For obviously, the people to whom he may appeal are not the people who elect the legislative majority. The legislators can ignore such appeals with impunity and are likely (as with Governor Collins on the apportionment and constitutional revision questions) to react with hostility, so that the appeal has a negative effect; it makes even compromise difficult. Some legislators say, for instance, that Collins could have ob-

tained an "acceptable" reapportionment early in the extraordinary
session of 1955-56; but that his attempt to bypass the legislature by
going to the public had the effect of preventing any concessions at all
by the small-county people.

Allied with this is, of course, the almost total lack of that "tie that
binds" executive and legislature loosely in Washington and tightly
in London—the party organization with its campaign ticket and platform. Few legislators are beholden to the governor or the party for
election, for few citizens know or care about the lawmakers' attitudes
toward gubernatorial promises. The governor cannot be a party
leader under such circumstances: there is really no party to lead; he
cannot even be a real factional leader, for it seems impossible to
build up a faction in Florida. Since he cannot be re-elected, even
his personal charisma means little, for it cannot be transmuted—as
was that of Huey Long—into factional support.

It is also true, however, that the rather extreme tendency of legislators to concentrate on local issues and their subservience to local
interests leaves the field relatively open to the governor to formulate
the major state-wide issues and sponsor proposals for dealing with
them. The general conservatism of the legislature then may act as
a check to prevent change more fundamental than the lawmakers
desire.

The governor is thus reduced to the same sort of horse-trading
which must be practiced by any legislator sponsoring a bill. He must
scurry around the legislative hallways seeking what support he may
find, offering compromise here and pledging a return of favor there.
This is, of course, part of the stock in trade of all American executives, but the lack of organized, institutional ties between the governor and the legislature makes the process in Florida uniquely personal, and its success far from certain.

This personalized politics has made it difficult for governors even
to utilize legislative aides, for such intermediaries are looked on
with some distrust by the lawmakers, who in addition seem to feel
that they have a right to the governor's personal attentions, rather
than those of some subordinate.

Another major difficulty is the fact that the budget is controlled
by the entire cabinet, sitting as the State Budget Commission. This is,

to be sure, an executive budget, but it is not controllable by the governor, for he can be outvoted not only on budgetary items for cabinet departments but also on his own budget. So far, then, as budget-making affects policy-making, his position is relatively weak.

Not the least significant item in the political weakness of the governor is his "junior partner" status on the cabinet. Here he sits as chairman—but he is often the youngest man, either chronologically or in point of service, on the cabinet. He is accordingly inexperienced by comparison. He is not only a political tyro but an assuredly short-lived one at that. Secure in their life-tenure and in the absence of any legal subordination to the governor (except the requirements of reports and advice),[8] cabinet members may be forgiven if they show some condescension and pay relatively little attention to him. Because of the long tenure and the undifferentiated nature of his office, the cabinet member has effective access to the legislature in his own right; this will be emphasized later. The governor's legislative influence is correspondingly reduced if one or more cabinet members oppose his desires.

In discussing the political relations between governor and legislature, it would not do to ignore the race question as a factor. This *bête noir* of southern politics has had significant effects in recent years in tending to worsen executive-legislative relations. For one thing, it is at least partially responsible for the existence of the one-party system, which in Florida means a no-party system. If there is no party organization which can bridge the normal gap between legislature and governor, certainly the existence of race as a political issue is a major reason, as it has been since the 1890's. The issue, however, bulks greater today all over the South than it has for many decades, due to the school integration decision. In states of the "Deep South" and to an extent in Virginia and Arkansas, the looming crisis has brought governor and legislature closer together. But the nature of modern Florida has seemingly had the opposite effect (at least up to the time of the election of Farris Bryant in 1960). For if, as we have said, South Florida is northern and has the votes to elect governors, it seems to follow that governors will likely be moderates, for South Florida has too much invested in commerce and the tourist trade to want to make excessive sacrifices in the defense of segregation. At the same time the legislature is dominated by the North Florida Southerners, many of whom are as rabid on race questions as any Georgia Cracker. This leads to a cleavage of interest between the governor's mansion and the legislative chambers which tends to color all their relations with distrust. The experience of Governor Collins seemed to indicate this, and while Collins became well-known and rather popular in the North as a "moderate," in fact he had to make many concessions to the legislature on the race question—so many that by now Florida's laws on the subject are only slightly more moderate than those of Georgia, though there seems to be a certain degree of executive moderation in their enforcement.

Faced by such obstacles it seems a little surprising that the governor is able to get any of his legislative proposals adopted. That Florida governors are nevertheless fairly successful reflects, perhaps, their own willingness to compromise and to play the political game the legislature's way, but it also may merely indicate that most of the wise governor's proposals are so badly needed or so unexceptionable that their passage is not a matter of much doubt.

Techniques of Gubernatorial Leadership

What are the techniques and modes of operation open to the governor and how effectively may they be used? Confining the discussion to influences directly brought to bear on the legislature—we have already canvassed the appeal to the public as a technique—the following seem to be the more important available methods.

The techniques stemming from the governor's constitutional relationships with the legislature are the most obvious, and of these the veto power is the most notorious and—at least in a negative sense—effective. Not only can the governor by use of the veto prevent a bill's immediate passage, but by virtue of his position he makes it psychologically somewhat difficult for the legislature to override the veto. It is, perhaps, one measure of the weakness of Florida governors that Coleman Ransone's study of southern chief executives showed that in Florida from 1937 to 1947, the governor's vetoes were overridden 28.4 per cent of the time;[9] it appears that an abnormal situation in the 1939 session involving Governor Fred P. Cone and the legislature in a highway fight raised this figure, but our own study of the 1947 to 1953 sessions shows about 15 to 20 per cent of the vetoes overriden—which is still higher than in most southern states. The rate appears to be fairly constant; of the 1947 to 1953 sessions, only Governor Warren's first session in 1949 shows a significant drop. The figures cover four sessions and three governors (Caldwell, Warren, and McCarty), enough to give some assurance that the governor's personality is not a major factor.

Governors appear to use the veto rather freely; Ransone's figures show that the governors from 1937 to 1947 vetoed 2.8 per cent of the bills passed, a figure exceeded significantly among southern states only in Arkansas and Louisiana.[10] It is hard to say whether frequent vetoes are a mark of strength or weakness, although we are tempted to interpret it as a sign that the governor is too weak in the legislature to prevent it from passing bills he opposes so that he must call on the veto power fairly often. Certainly such an interpretation would accord with the large proportion of vetoes which are overriden.

The veto is of importance, of course, largely in a negative way; it does not constitute leadership but the failure thereof, for it indicates that the legislature has refused to follow the governor's advice. But the *threat* of the veto may at times have an affirmative effect, for it may be a significant influence in shaping the final form which a bill takes. Negatively, it may prevent a bill from being passed at all. Since there is no way of knowing how often either of these situations occur, the effectiveness of a threatened veto is largely a matter of conjecture. That it is not always effective was obvious in 1957 when the legislature passed the "last resort" bill despite Governor Collins' publicly expressed opposition.

The governor's message apparently has only a symbolic importance, for in itself it only states his aspirations; if it were not followed up by specific bills introduced by a friendly legislator, it is hardly likely that any credit would be due the governor even if legislation similar to his requests was passed. It does stand as a symbol of his right to suggest legislation, yet the suggestion is not meaningful if no influential action is taken to follow it up.

In the constitutional appointment power one finds a more significant weapon. Patronage is a time-honored (if not otherwise honored) American institution, and governors early discovered that a judicious use of it could open many doors and many otherwise closed minds. It may, of course, be used to cement political support; but more important in the present context, it may help to secure legislative support as well. The importance of patronage is great, but it has not been as effective in Florida as one might suppose, because there has grown up a sort of "courtesy" arrangement whereby many local appointments are actually left by custom to the senior member of the legislative delegation. In addition it is significant to note that Governor Collins—a firm believer in the merit system—foreclosed the future opportunity for the use of patronage as a weapon (at least by governors) by bringing the state employees under his control into the merit system as permitted by a 1955 statute.[11] Significantly, no other cabinet official took this step, which seems to prove how important patronage is thought to be as an item in political power.

A similar type of power is that heretofore exercised by the governor over the State Road Department in the location and maintenance of highways. The technique, of course, is to award or withhold new projects in the various counties in accordance with the attitudes of the legislative delegations concerned. Even Governor Collins with his deep belief in institutionalizing the operations of the executive branch, on at least one occasion—the turnpike bill in 1955—used highway location as a political lever to achieve the enactment of the bill. However, as in the case of patronage, Collins helped to weaken gubernatorial leadership by sponsoring in 1955 a bill by which highway allocation is decided under a formula, a device which takes the governor almost completely out of the picture.[12]

On the whole, the power to call special sessions seems of minor importance; it may in practice boomerang by creating an initial hostility in the legislature, and in any case the governor can wield no influence to force action during special session that is not also available during regular sessions. There is, perhaps, a greater psychological pressure on legislators during special sessions because of the public attention focused on them. Aside from this, there may be some significance in the fact that the governor defines the issues completely. He can thus dictate the questions, if not the answers thereto.

It seems that the constitution-based techniques so far surveyed do not add up to substantial leadership power. They are, however, reinforced by a fairly substantial set of extra-legal tactics which may, on occasion, be quite effective.

An extremely prominent device which seems to be expanding in its use is the study group. Sometimes the study committee will be legislatively authorized, with an accompanying appropriation to pay for it, as were the Citizens' Tax Council and the Fabisinski Committee on integration. But if he cannot get or does not wish to have legislative authorization, the governor may set up a governor's study commission, such as the Governor's Citizens Committees—twenty-nine of them—used in 1955 and 1956 by Governor Collins. The value of the study group is supposedly that its findings can be used in the preparation of legislative proposals which will then have the backing not only of the governor himself but of a substantial group of prominent citizens and even academic specialists which has seriously studied the question. It provides, also, a substitute for the inevitably inadequate committee hearings spawned by the short biennial session.

The effectiveness of this attempt to (in a sense) overwhelm the legislature with facts and statistics naturally varies with the issue. In a case like that of the integration question, in which legislators were desperately searching for something—anything—to do to forestall racial mixing in the schools, the study group's recommendations were followed with an alacrity which bordered on unseemly haste. On the other hand, the suggestions of the tax council were met with some frigidity. At times, indeed, it seems as though legislators are positively hostile to such influences: the fact that over forty states have central purchasing arrangements seemed to make no impression on Florida legislators considering the adoption of such a system.

Nevertheless on balance the use of study groups is a useful tool for the governor; the long-run hope for his proposals is, after all, considerably higher than his batting average in a single session might suggest. Conscientious legislators can never be completely impervious to the presentation of facts and figures when they issue from comparatively unbiased sources. Such studies, frequent as they already are, will doubtless become more common in the future.

The governor of Florida perhaps more than in any other state has to rely heavily on personal contacts with the legislators. He has no faction, party, or even personal-faction leaders to act as continuing floor leaders for his program. He is forced, consequently, to search until he finds a man—hopefully, a suitable one—who will sponsor each individual measure on the floor. The talents of such floor leaders, as one might expect, are not always of the best, and there is obviously no organization behind the effort. If he would be successful, a governor is wise to maximize his personal contacts not only with supporters but with his opponents as well. Governor Collins was often criticized by 1955 legislators for his aloofness and his tendencies to work through his legislative aides (he employed one for each house) rather than through direct contact. It was said—perhaps with some exaggeration—that some legislators became hostile to his program because of pique at his lack of attention to them. For the 1957 session he apparently tried to correct this fault by lining up his legislative floor leaders prior to the session through letters and personal conferences.

Legislative Expectations and the Governor's Role

It becomes clear, then, that the governor who attempts to lead the legislature openly and by institutionalized methods is courting trouble for his legislative program. To put it differently, a governor to be successful must act as little like a chief executive and as much like a legislator as possible. Members expect the governor to come to them personally to solicit support; they are piqued if he does not; they are openly angry if he goes over their heads to the public; they are suspicious if he tries to shower them with facts and figures. They want, and feel that they are entitled to, a man-to-man approach. While a governor fitting these specifications will "get along" with the legislature, it is probably only at the price of trading his program out of existence or accepting other laws against his better judgment. On the other hand, if he does not act in accordance with legislative expectations a definite coolness sets in and he becomes an outsider looking in. Any attempt to institutionalize his relations with the lawmaking body is resented, and his program, too, suffers. Damned whether he does or does not, it would not be surprising if—as some few have—the governor would sit on his hands and refuse to present a program, merely waiting for the legislature to act and using his veto power when necessary. That few governors do this is a measure of the necessity for political leadership in the modern legislature and their energy and devotion to duty.

The Status and Powers of the Cabinet

The institutional status of the cabinet comes initially from the constitutional provisions which constitute it (or parts of it) as an ex officio governing agency for four significant state functions. The entire cabinet sits as the Board of Commissioners of State Institutions,[13] which controls prisons and other such institutions, and various cabinet members make up the powerful State Board of Education,[14] the Pardon Board,[15] and the State Board of Administration.[16] Taking this constitutional hint, the legislature has by statute entrusted to some or all of the cabinet other administrative duties, of which the more important are its positions as State Budget Commission,[17] Board of Conservation,[18] Executive Board of the Department of Public Safety,[19] Trustees of the Internal Improvement Fund,[20] State Purchasing Commission,[21] and State Securities Commission.[22]

Setting up these functions in this manner means that the cabinet as a collective body holds a position of great importance, and in these functions the governor has only one vote as does any other member (although he has a veto power on the Pardon Board). This not only makes the institutional cabinet a power but also enhances the political positions of the other cabinet members at the same time that it tends to degrade that of the governor.

The cabinet has become an important factor in legislative leadership. In matters which come under its purview it can usually get what it wants from the legislature—providing it presents a united front. And correspondingly, it can often block actions which threaten to reduce its power. Because of these aspects of its position, there is a tendency in some cases for the governor to be opposed by the rest of the cabinet. As chief executive—particularly if he should be a believer in governmental efficiency and economy—a governor is likely to espouse the institutionalizing of administration. This is

204 The Politics of Mis-Representation

likely to involve such things as a state merit system, central purchasing, and central budgetary controls; but all of these would deprive the cabinet (and, more, its individual members) of highly prized prerogatives. These are apparently the reasons why the 1955 merit system act was made permissive so that no cabinet member would be forced to give up his patronage, and also why the 1957 central purchasing bill was so compromised as to become meaningless. In such battles the cabinet seems often to be the victor.

The Role of Cabinet Members as Individuals

It should not be forgotten, either, that each cabinet member is the executive head of a major state agency. As such, he occupies for that agency's functions a place vis-a-vis the legislature which is closely comparable to that of the governor. Within this relatively narrow area, in fact, the cabinet member seems to enjoy certain advantages in legislative contacts which are not available to the governor.

For one thing, since cabinet members are not in any sense responsible for a general program, as the governor is, they are not tempted to try to institutionalize their approaches to the legislature to the same extent. They are largely concerned not with programs but with individual and specific pieces of legislation, in support of which they will contact the key legislators personally, appear before committees, and in general act in ways which would be too time-consuming for a governor to use. They are thus able to use the very methods which accord most closely with the mode of operations in the legislature itself.

The indefinite re-eligibility for office of a cabinet official is a significant aid, for he gains the opportunity to build up his legislative support over long periods of time and with the older and more influential legislators. He also gains much experience and thus becomes adept in the use of the necessary persuasive techniques. The prestige and in some cases (of extreme longevity in office) even affection which come with the holding of important offices for long periods are certainly political assets. And such longevity, finally, provides the opportunity through patronage to build up a machine which helps to entrench the cabinet official still more firmly in the office and in the legislature.

Many of the cabinet members also gain strength from the fact that they have state-wide clienteles and thus state-wide support. They are very careful—as is noted in the chapter on lobbying—to represent these private or semiprivate groups so as to maintain this support, and often they will act as very effective lobbyists for their clientele groups. In return, they can count on support from these groups when they require it. The fact that the support will come from practically every county in the state, and always from county officials or leading citizens, makes this very effective with the legislature, as was indicated in Chapter 2. Consequently, these relations are assiduously cultivated. Seemingly only the governor and the secretary of state, then, are without highly-organized state-wide clientele groups.

Executive Leadership: A Summary

The problem of legislative leadership (at least in a programmatic sense) is a difficult one in Florida. Not only is the legislature itself unable to provide such leadership, but no party or other political organization is able to do so. The governor has, as in most states, assumed the responsibility for developing and sponsoring a program of legislation for "development of the state's human and natural resources."[23] He has done so because of the obvious need for such planning and the people's expectation that he will perform this role. "They have come to expect the governor to attempt to carry out his campaign promises, and there is considerable evidence to show that the governor in most cases actually makes such an attempt. . . ."[24] The advantages of such planning in the governor's hands are fairly obvious; they include, Ransone believes:

1. "More time and greater facilities to collect the data necessary for sound legislation";
2. "Access to the state's best advice in technical fields";
3. "A trained staff for the actual drafting";
4. "The best cooperative thinking" of the agencies concerned.[25]

Yet in Florida the governor is unable to make the most of these advantages, for the powers and perquisites of his offices are largely negated by its limitations. The result is that even a well-planned and (on the whole) desirable program presented by any governor will be looked at piecemeal as is the legislature's habit. The less contro-

versial proposals, it is likely, will pass; but those which are controversial or which trench on privileges of groups best represented
in the legislature—and these may often be the most significant proposals—are likely to run into heavy sailing.

No one in American politics would propose that the legislature
should be a rubber stamp for the executive, and there is, except in
crises, little danger of such an eventuality. But to be effective, leadership must be respected; it must have the necessary tools, and its
proposals must be given friendly rather than hostile or merely
"courtesy" consideration. It is not enough to say, as one legislative
leader did, that the legislature has a duty to "consider" the governor's
proposals; they must be considered seriously and with benefit of the
prestige that should be attached to pronouncements of the chief executive, backed as he is by the four advantages listed above. If after
such serious consideration the legislature—assuming now that it is a
truly representative body—comes to the conclusion that the proposal
is unworkable or undesirable, the governor and people have no cause
for complaint. But of course it should be remembered that one of the
major causes for the governor's asumption of leadership is the fact
that the legislature is *not* representative; thus the governor's legislative program perhaps has a greater presumptive validity as "the will
of the people" than whatever the legislature might do with it.

Legislative Control of Administration

Legislative-executive relations are, of course, a two-way proposition.
If the executive is expected in modern times to lead the legislature,
the law-making body is equally bound to try to see that the laws are
faithfully, effectively, and efficiently carried out by the executive.
Indeed, this is universally regarded as a most important legislative
duty.

At the same time, the American idea of separation of powers makes
the performance of this duty difficult. The difficulty is a constitutional
one to a large extent, for the executive not only is constitutionally
charged with the direct responsibility to "take care that the laws be
faithfully executed,"[26] wording which could be construed to deny
to the legislature any supervisory duty; but the executive's elective

and independent position also makes it hard for the legislature to exercise much beyond indirect controls.

Other difficulties are presented by the general failure of legislatures to organize themselves properly for supervision of administration. In part this failure is due to a misconstruction of their proper function; instead of organizing for effective oversight, "our legislative bodies show a strong tendency to attempt to exercise detailed supervision."[27]

The Zeller report on state legislatures lists three essentials for effective legislative oversight: it must provide itself with "the necessary organizational machinery; its supervisory techniques . . . [must be] geared to its role as a deliberate body that meets infrequently"; and finally, the executive branch itself must be organized in such a way as to permit effective administration.[28] Inasmuch as a great part of the administrative structure of a state is constitutionally mandatory, the last of these is at least partially outside the direct control of the legislature. But in Florida the legislature must approve all constitutional changes and it appears to be almost completely satisfied with the present disintegrated executive structure.

Perhaps the most effective tool for legislative supervision lies in its control of the purse strings of the state. The shaping of the budget is in the first instance, as we have seen, in the hands of the cabinet acting as the state budget commission. But the legislature remains as the agency which must finally approve the figures and pass the appropriations bills without which no governmental agency could operate. It is not consonant with the purpose of this book to deal in detail with the executive budget, but it may be important to note that Florida is one of those backward states which still clings to the use of the "item of expenditure" rather than the "program" budget. This has the effect of making it difficult, if not impossible, for the legislature to look at the budget in programmatic terms. Within this major qualification it appears that Florida compares rather favorably with the average state in effective legislative review of the budget, at least since the development of the presession activities of the appropriations committees outlined in Chapter 5. Even so the situation is far from ideal. Staff aid to the appropriations committees is rather slight, although more adequate than for most other committees. And in spite of the fact that the house rules require that appropriations for new activities must be referred to a subject matter committee as well as to the appropriations group,[29] the senate does not even require this much,[30] and in neither house do the rules require subject matter committees to approve the policy of the new program before the appropriations committee approves the money. It appears obvious that good practice would demand a prior approval of new policies so that real consideration could be given to the proposal before the appropriations committee needs to spend its time on the matter. In addition it appears unwise to approve an appropriation before the function it is to implement has been authorized.[31] Regardless of the rules, the Florida legislature appears to abide by this principle most of the time.

Perhaps the greatest defect in the legislature's treatment of the budget stems from lack of time to do more than cursorily review the proposals. The result is a tendency to use a meat ax approach when economy is desired—that is, to cut appropriations across the board rather than looking to see where reductions can best be justified. The 1959 legislature was a prominent case of the meat ax approach. In other cases the legislature may actually abdicate its responsibility; in 1957 when the claim was made that revenues would not meet the level of appropriations, the legislature decided to leave the cuts to the discretion of the budget commission rather than undertake them itself. In a number of cases members of the finance and taxation committees remarked that a deficiency in estimated income relative to appropriations might be just the thing for "keeping the agencies on their toes."

Another form of abdication of legislative responsibility in the fiscal field is the use of dedicated revenues, that is, of revenues which instead of going into the general revenue fund of the state are earmarked for only certain specific uses. Some dedication is included in the Florida constitution, such as the uses to which parts of the gasoline tax may be put,[32] but more commonly it is done by statute.[33] The Zeller report criticized the earmarking of specific revenues in severe terms:

It prevents any over-all planning of the fiscal program of the governmental unit as a whole; the money is there, but the hands

of management are tied. Moreover, the legislature whose responsibility it is not only to lay and collect taxes but to spend the receipts in the best interests of all the people, abdicates its authority
and responsibility every time it submits to the demands of a persistent pressure group. . . . [The] system makes needlessly difficult
the payment of the state's bills when due. . . . Finally, the system
may lead to . . . the expenditure of a major portion of the government's total receipts by an agency supported by earmarked
revenues.[34]

Legislative post audit of fiscal transactions is another essential if
the lawmakers wish to know whether the appropriations and laws
have been carried out. The best practice is considered to be the creation of an auditing agency under the aegis of the legislature itself;
but the usual procedure is to have a state auditor appointed by and
responsible to the governor, as in Florida, or elected by the people, as
in Illinois. The Florida practice does not leave the auditor independent
of the governor whose expenditures he is to audit.[35]

It appears, then, that the Florida legislature is not well equipped
to deal with budgetary control. Furthermore, there appears to be no
feeling among legislators that any change is needed: they do not
seem to realize that the legitimate power of the legislature in these
matters is not being effectively used.

Finally, in the matter of legislative supervision of administration,
care should be exercised to draft statutes in such a way that they
can be effectively administered. This involves to some extent a realization by the lawmakers that they cannot write all administrative details
into the law; that they should not prescribe the organizational structure of administrative agencies in detail; that administrative responsibility under any one statute should not be split among several
agencies; and that the purpose of the legislation should be clearly
stated in the law as a guide to its administration.[36] Legislative performance on these matters varies a great deal, but the Florida legislature, like that in most states, seems inclined to express a general
distrust of the administrative hierarchy by attempting much of the
time to tie administrators' hands so as to deprive them of desirable
flexibility.

On the whole it cannot be said that the Florida legislature exercises effectively its power and duty of overseeing the administration of legislative policies. It cannot even be said with any confidence that the legislature is aware of the need for such oversight. Paradoxically, the legislature distrusts the executive so much that executive leadership of the process of legislation is difficult; while at the same time it refuses to accept the burden of checking to see that its own policies are actually carried out by that executive.

Chapter 8

Lobbying and the Florida Legislature

T HE modern writer is in little danger of underestimating the importance of the "interests." Under the influence of Arthur F. Bentley, it is now agreed that "a discussion of the work and defects of a state legislature carries one nowhere, as long as the legislature is taken [only?] for what it purports to be—a body of men who deliberate upon and adopt laws."[1]

Lobbying is practiced primarily because American legislatures operate as the most significant political decision-makers in our governments and are thus the fundamental loci of power which must be influenced if interest groups are to be successful in promoting and protecting themselves.[2]

Granted that lobbying will persist, the nature of our party system seems to encourage its effectiveness. American parties are primarily loose affiliations concerned more with elections and organizing the government than with consensus on issues, and they can seldom bind legislators to any particular policies. We prize greatly the "independence" of our lawmakers, but we may pay the penalty of having the legislator become too dependent on private-spirited pressure groups, especially those which are strong in his constituency. This has the effect of allowing the pressure group to approach him in his most vulnerable spot, his chances for re-election, without needing to surmount any of the protection given by a strong party organization. And it allows the pressure group to do this with no risk to itself, for its operations are shielded from the public gaze and are never voted on; they are not subjected to the moderating force of public opinion.

Another factor bearing on the nature of pressure politics is the basis of our representative systems. American representation is usually based on the idea that population and area are the units to be represented. In state politics the unit used is almost always the county. This means, in practice, that economic and social interests are not directly represented in our legislatures. They may be represented indirectly if they are regionally differentiated, as farmers may be said to be represented by the legislator from Jackson County, Florida; but these regional variations, since they are informal and accidental, do not often become formalized organizationally in our legislatures. The result is that the innumerable legitimate interests of society—economic, social, and other—find the organization of special groups a necessity if they are to receive proper consideration in the process of political decision-making.

Our system of representation, then, *forces* the growth of lobbies. The major legitimate social and economic interests of a society must and will be heard, for they are too important to ignore. If they are given no formal representation they will construct their own channels of informal activity. It is necessary that they *be* represented if their interests are to receive attention, and democratic theory presupposes that all significant groups *should* be represented.

The Role of Lobbying in the Legislative Process

The foregoing paragraphs indicate briefly the *raison d'etre* of the pressure group; it remains to touch upon the actual effects that the existence of these groups has on legislative behavior. The lawmaker is likely to value and use pressure groups for two major purposes. One is that in a state like Florida the limited length of the session and the lack of adequate research staffs attached to the legislature leave the average legislator comparatively uninformed about the matters on which he must act. While a professional in politics, he is a mere amateur on most subjects which come before the assembly. He is forced to rely on whatever sources of information are available, and private groups are not backward in making their availability known. The information they supply naturally is often biased or partial. The system, in order to work for the benefit of the public, depends a great deal on the sophistication of the legislators and on the existence of other pressure groups which will correct the bias or fill in the void. Both of these are factors which, unfortunately, are more accidental than certain. Nevertheless, the supplying of necessary statistics and other data has long been considered a proper and desirable function of interest groups. Certainly few would question the legitimacy of allowing such groups to appear at legislative hearings and present such information as they see fit; this is part of the right of petition which is so basic to the Anglo-American tradition. The difficulty lies in the frequent inability of the legislature to separate the valuable from the merely selfish.

Then too, the pressure group may provide significant clues to attitudes of sections of the public. Groups thus play a role in the complex process by which public opinion represents itself to the representative assembly. Here too, however, there is danger, for the representative is often unable to distinguish between the voice of a minority group and that of the people. As a result the interests of the articulate sections of the public may be substituted for those of the generality. The presence or absence of opposing groups becomes crucial, for in their absence no legislator can be blamed if he sometimes mistakes the whisper of a lobbyist for the voice of the people.

In short, the pressure group plays a legitimate but at the same time dangerous part in our politics; the more dangerous since the checks presented by a strong party system or a strong popular executive are often missing.

The Lobby in Florida

Perhaps the major fact affecting pressure group activity in Florida is the lack of an effectively functioning party system. For such a system, complete with some element of discipline, a platform, and a set of principles, provides a legislator with something on which to rely for voting guidance.

Without such guidance and since "the legislator's tenure in office depends on no overarching party organization, he is accessible to whatever influences are outstanding in his local constituency almost regardless of more inclusive claims."[3] This produces local orientation with a vengeance, but it is as important to note that on many of the most important legislative issues there is little ascertainable local feeling, which leaves the legislator free, not only of party philosophy and discipline, but also of local mandate. In such a situation he may be (at least figuratively) for sale to the highest bidder, in the sense that the most persuasive, persistent, or in extreme cases, well-heeled, lobbyist may be able to secure his vote. So long as he violates no serious local desire he is in little danger of failure to be re-elected, and there are no forces aside from his conscience and intelligence leading him to consider the welfare of the state as a whole. Fortunately for Florida's well-being, conscience and intelligence often stand in good stead; but even so, the general interest is so vague in the specific instance that a legislator is hardly to be blamed if at times he tends to take a lobby's word for it.

Nor can a legislator in Florida ordinarily look to the executive for much policy guidance. True enough the governor is a representative of the entire voting population; he runs on something resembling a platform, and he is the "chief executive." But his representative capacity is vitiated by the rural domination of the legislature as contrasted to his own dependence on the cities for votes. Consequently his "platform" must be moderated to meet rural demands, and in any case, no legislator is ever forced to run on the governor's platform. There is no moral obligation to support the governor. And, as we have seen, the governor has few weapons with which to influence legislators.

This lack of both effective party and executive leadership leaves an "influence vacuum" into which pressure groups are happy to move. One may add to this the fact that in recent times in Florida, as elsewhere, the expanding functions and expenses—and thus taxes—of the state make the stakes of political pressure higher than ever before. There is more incentive than ever for groups to organize, since their welfare may be intimately affected by the actions taken in the lawmaking body.

The factors making for weakness in the structure of Florida's legislative system, combined with this enormous incentive for lobbying activity, produce a situation in which the various pressure groups have been able to gain an extensive control over the legislative process. Complex as the analysis already is, however, there are many other factors to be considered.

Florida is one of the states, as we have seen, which still retains a constitutionally-limited biennial legislative session. But as we have also seen, one of the springs of pressure group influence is the ability to provide the basic source data on which legislation must be based. In this connection Florida's sixty-day biennial session tends to aid the lobbyist, for the sessions are too short and too infrequent for the legislature to give each bill adequate study and consideration. An average session produces well in excess of three thousand bills; it is obviously impossible for even the most conscientious body of 133 people to consider this number of bills with proper care. Even major legislation is often hurried through because of time limitations, as were the tax bills in the extended session of 1957. In such circumstances lobbyists tend to exert a disproportionate influence; they are there, and the information they hold is readily accessible to all.

The almost complete lack of staff and research facilities compounds the defects of the short session, for as one observer remarked of the the New Jersey legislature, "the absence of a legislative reference library, the impossibility of retaining technical staff on a legislator's salary, and the failure of the State Government to provide such services as information on the progress of pending bills, [gives] privileged access to groups . . . prepared to perform such functions."[4] There is not only little time for study but also no one to conduct the study anyway, except the ubiquitous lobbyist.

The relative lack of legislative experience of Florida lawmakers is still another element which weakens resistance to lobbying. Ordinarily at least one-third of the membership consists of members serving their first terms—many of whom will be replaced in the next session by other freshmen. Such a member is likely to attach himself readily to the first friendly face, be it a legislative faction or a lobbyist.

If the attempted seduction is successful, it probably works best with the new legislator who is just taking up residence in a strange community. Having been a fairly large frog in a comparatively small pond, he suddenly finds the situation reversed. He may be disturbed by the abrupt interruption of his accustomed social relationship and feel the need for adequate substitutes. These may be supplied by the dinner and golf games of a "social set" or by the poker games and other diversions offered by an interest group representative. The implied penalty for sharp political disagreement is ostracism from the friendly group, and the legislator may quite unconsciously find himself avoiding this penalty by conforming.[5]

Older hands, on the other hand, through experience may have gained a certain degree of independence—though it is not unlikely that most legislators' first terms set the patterns for their future actions. As David B. Truman points out, the penalty for nonconformity may go beyond social ostracism: it may make it difficult to obtain support for one's own bills within the house.[6]

Some commentators believe that the bicameral legislature also encourages pressure group activity. Zeller, for instance, remarks that bicameralism "enhances the influence and enlarges the activity of pressure groups in enabling them to block legislation in one of the chambers and to play an important role in adjusting the inevitable differences between the two chambers."[7] For instance, the inability of the Florida legislature to pass a severance tax is apparently largely due to the strength of the phosphate and pulpwood lobbies in the senate; for while such taxes have several times (notably a minerals tax in 1957) been approved by the house, the senate has always killed them. Conversely, the house in 1957 killed a 3 per cent auto sales tax proposal which had passed the senate.

The very differences between the structure of leadership and power in the two chambers give advantages to some interest groups in the senate and to others in the house. The smaller and somewhat more rural-oriented senate tends to be rather tightly controlled by an oligarchical leadership. Pressure influence in the senate is therefore at last partially dependent on access to this ruling clique, which apparently always includes the president of the senate, who owes his power not only to his position as president but also to his place in the oligarchy. A pressure group—like the phosphate industry in recent sessions—which can reach the president and the oligarchy, is fairly certain of attaining its ends.

The structure of power is much looser in the house of representatives so that the problem of access by lobbyists is consequently more complicated, and successful action less certain than in the senate. But the situation in the house at times verges on the chaotic, which may allow clever lobbyists to use "sneak" tactics with some effect. At times lobbyists are even charged with being on the house floor master-minding operations or in the galleries signaling to representatives on the floor.[8]

Although the problem of malapportionment has been thoroughly discussed earlier, it should be noted that this basic problem also has repercussions on lobbying. It obviously gives some pressure groups privileged access to the legislature by providing them with a sure bloc of friendly legislators who hold a majority or close to it. This is clearly the case in Florida with those pressure groups which are strong in the rural areas: the farm bureau, the phosphate and wood-pulp industries, and others. In contrast, those groups which are primarily urban suffer an initial handicap which may be difficult to overcome. This has been particularly true in Florida of organized labor, which suffers the additional handicap of being unpopular with the general public.

A factor of great importance, especially in Florida, is the fact that the presiding officers of both houses hold the power of appointing all committees—a power which, combined with the power to refer bills, gives them great influence. This power is held in check neither by party nor factional ties; it is a purely personal attribute. But it results in the fact that whatever group interests the presiding officer favors will be able to get committees stacked and bills referred to the stacked committees. Although this is sufficiently obvious, it is not always as explicit as on the occasion in 1957 when the senate president used the reference power to kill three bills which would have imposed a severance tax on phosphate, citrus, and celery by referring the bills to five different committees.[9] Multiple reference is usually regarded as a death blow because the bill is then considered seriatim rather than simultaneously, and there is not time to get it through the com-mittee stage before the session ends. The fact that the president was a leading celery farmer and also has phosphate interests will indicate how great an advantage certain groups may gain from privileged access to the presiding officer.

As this incident suggests, the group affiliations of legislators are another element of great importance to the interest groups, for as George B. Galloway points out, legislators "retain after election the private interests, group affiliations, and social attitudes acquired from their previous experience and associations."[10] Some groups thus have considerable "built-in" strength in either or both chambers. The fact that 59 of the 133 legislators in 1957 were lawyers gave an obvious advantage to the Florida Bar Association and the University of Florida Law School. The fact that there were 32 farmers, 12 real estate dealers, 48 Baptists, and 67 alumni of the University of Florida is also revelatory of much in the way of access to the legislature.[11] Madison's statement is as true today as in 1789 that legislators are often "but advocates and parties to the causes which they determine."[12]

The relations of members with each other and their ideas of what conduct is to be expected of legislators are further important factors. These will be considered in greater detail a little farther on; only one instance will be given here. The house of representatives has a quaint custom that all ex-members are allowed on the floor during sessions. Since many ex-members become lobbyists, this has the effect of permitting lobbyists for some groups to carry out their tasks right in the legislative chamber. Former Representative "Bill" Lantaff, for instance, was lobbying for Hialeah race track in 1957, although it was reported that he scrupulously stayed off the floor.[13] Among other prominent former legislators active as lobbyists was Raeburn C. Horne, for the small-loans people, who was accused of giving hand signals from the gallery.[14]

The ethical standards of the legislature may also play a role. The senate, observers feel, is less careful to protect itself from unethical lobbying than the house—even to the extent, rumors say, of at times allowing lobbyists to cast the proxy votes of absent committee members. The house in 1955 adopted a rule prohibiting all proxy voting. It is worth noting, too, that pressure groups have various places in a "prestige hierarchy." That is, some groups have the advantage of representing interests that are in high favor in society or in the legislature (or both). In Florida such a group is the Florida Education Association, for public education is so firmly a part of the American dream that no legislator feels able openly to oppose it. On the other hand the race-track and small-loans lobbies enjoy no such unanimous public support. As Truman remarks, "the high-status group is aided by the large proportion of key officials . . . whose class backgrounds are such that they have similar values, manners, and preconceptions."[15]

Another point at which certain types of pressures may easily enter into legislation lies in the passage of local bills. This practice has the effect of removing political pressures from the city or county where interested citizens can watch and take an active part in developments and relocating them in Tallahassee, where organized groups can work relatively unseen by the people back home. It is no exaggeration to say that even the interested citizen has little chance to find out in detail what kind of local bills are passed for his own city or county. This absence of public knowledge is an open invitation to the more arrantly selfish local interests and gives even more than the usual advantage to those who are organized and know the political ropes.

Taking all of the foregoing considerations together, it becomes clear that pressure groups in Florida are aided by the existence of a wide variety of points of access to the legislature. The most powerful groups, it must be supposed, are those which can take effective advantage of the most possible access points, but almost any group can find access somewhere. This fact increases the effective representative qualities of the lobbying element in the legislative process, and it also provides some protection from extreme pressure demands by multiplying the number of competitors. At the same time, it may increase the already existing babel of dissonant voices to a point at which·no harmony can be discerned amid the cacophony.

> Besieged by all these competing pressures, a [legislator] is often faced with the choice of compromising between various pressures, of trading votes, of resisting special interests of one sort or another, of staying off the floor when a vote is taken on some measure he prefers not to take a stand on, of getting support here and at the same time running the risk of losing support there. Dealing with pressure blocs is a problem in political psychology that involves a careful calculation of the power of the blocs, the reaction of the voters on election day, and the long-haul interests of the district [and state]. . . .[16]

It is no surprise that some of the time—more often than one likes to think—"all these competing pressures" work out in ways that have little resemblance to the public interest. If organized private interests are close to taking over the Florida government, as some alarmists claim, the blame rests with a political and legislative structure which does little to impede their operations but much to aid them. Florida seems to have in relatively advanced degree a diversity of interests so great, and an integrating consensus so vague, that the entire political structure is in danger of ceasing to perform its representative functions satisfactorily.

Groups Represented in Florida

No one knows how many groups are represented at a legislative session; even the registration requirements of the lower house fail to give an accurate picture, for they are inadequately drafted and poorly enforced. A survey of the registrants may give a rough idea of the members involved and a fairly precise idea of the *private* groups represented; but it fails completely to make any distinction between the powerful and the inconsequential, nor does it adequately suggest the role of official groups except in a very general way. Within these limitations, the following data from the registration lists of the 1957 session may be instructive. There were—allowing for an undetermined number of multiple registrations—about 450 individuals officially engaged in lobbying. They represented roughly 32 local government units, 14 state-wide associations of county or municipal officials, 33 state government agencies, and 275 private groups. Among the private organizations, the most numerous were those representing the insurance business (28), labor (23), public utilities (including LP gas) (40), and medicine and health (18). But by broad divisions of interest, private business was by far the best represented, for at least 164 private business organizations had registered lobbyists.[17]

The scope of interests represented was extremely broad, from the picturesque Gainesville resident (locally known as "Bloomer Nell") who registered as a representative of "self and personal friends," to the Florida AFL-CIO, the Florida Manufacturers' Association, and the Florida Farm Bureau. Government groups were as broadly represented, from the governor's office through the Game and Fresh

Water Fish Commission on down to the Stephen Foster Memorial
Commission.

Such statistics, while interesting, are necessarily misleading. Many
persons engage in lobbying without registering because they do not
intend to appear before a committee hearing; for instance, there
was a lawyer lobbying for the reincorporation of the town of LaCrosse
(Alachua County) who buttonholed the Alachua delegation to support the bill, but he was not registered.

The only substantial minority interest that remains unrepresented
amid this welter of lobbyists is the Negro; at least in the 1957 session,
neither the NAACP nor the Urban League was registered, nor were
any other Negro groups. Considering the seriousness of the race question, the fact that legislative action is a major determinant of solu-
tions, and the lack of efficacy of the Negro vote—all factors which
would ordinarily lead a group to adopt lobbying tactics—this may
seem a peculiar omission, as it obviously is a serious one. Negro
leaders undoubtedly feel that for many reasons they lack effective
access to the seats of legislative power, and they have therefore felt it
wiser to concentrate on the courts.[18] The legislature has responded
to this neglect by attempting to cut off the access of these groups to
the courts as well.

The Private Lobby

Pressure groups are often divided into classifications, but in order
to cover all groups these soon become extremely complex, and it
seems adequate here to confine our classification to the rather common distinction between public and private groups.

The private lobby in Florida, as indicated above, is very broad in
scope. It varies somewhat from session to session depending on what
issues come up. But it can be assumed that any legislature will consider some legislation affecting the interests of all major economic
groups; consequently these groups will always send lobbyists to
Tallahassee. It is rather surprising to note the rather large number
of national businesses which lobby in the state. One news report
listed the following: Sperry and Hutchinson (a national trading
stamp outfit), Armour and Company, International Minerals and

Chemical Company, Prudential and several other national insurance companies, St. Regis and International Paper companies. These are, of course, all concerns which have large and legitimate business dealings in Florida so that their interest in legislative action is the same as that of a local company.

Some more unselfish pressure groups exist side-by-side with the economic interest groups. Possibly the finest example of such a group in Florida is the League of Women Voters, which has no group "self-interest" ax to grind, but nevertheless conscientiously (not to say enthusiastically) covers every session of the legislature, testifying for governmental reform more than on any other type of issue.

Since there are no easy ways of measuring it, the relative strength of the various pressure groups can only be guessed. The determinants of strength are many and varied. They include such obvious considerations as the group's size or wealth; its access to the press; public attitudes toward it; its relationships with other groups; the ability of its leaders; the degree to which it represents a primary interest of its members; how well organized it is; the degree of internal cohesion it maintains; where, geographically, its strength lies; and many others. Using these criteria, observers can arrive at rough estimates of the strength of various groups. It should be added that these strengths may not always lead to success, for in specific matters the lineup of the opposition may be strong enough to defeat even a powerful group. With no pretense of completeness and in no particular rank order, the following may be listed as among the more powerful private lobbies in Tallahassee as of the 1957 session:

1. Florida Milk Producers Association. This group is a combination of dairy farmers and milk producers; the 1957 speaker (now commissioner of agriculture) and the chairman of the rules committee (who became the 1959 speaker and has been a power in the house for years) were both men with dairy interests.

2. Agriculture. The agriculture lobby encompasses both the general Florida Farm Bureau Federation and various powerful commodity groups such as the Florida Citrus Mutual, the Cattlemen's Association, etc.

3. Truckers and other transportation interests. These interests are said to have one of Tallahassee's favorite lobbyists, Major A. D.

Tomasello, who is famous for merely sitting around hotel lobbies, etc., talking to legislators casually as they come in and
out and for buying the breakfasts of rural legislators who arise
before 6:00 A.M.!

4. The Rose Printing Company. This company, a Tallahassee firm
   which does at least half of the state's official printing, is one of
   the leading "social lobbies" and powerful enough to prevent
   the inclusion of printing in the central purchasing bill in 1957
   —though not in 1959.

5. Liquor interests. This group successfully lobbied through a
   liquor "price-fixing" bill in 1957 which Senator Charley Johns
   called the "most-lobbied bill" of the session.

6. Race tracks. Although often in conflict, they are very powerful
   when Hialeah, Tropical Park, and Gulfstream get together
   and especially when they combine with the dog track people.

7. Trading stamp companies. This lobby is possibly a temporary
   phenomenon. The 1957 legislature heatedly debated trading
   stamps, but the companies issuing them managed to put together enough strength to stave off damaging legislation.

8. Small-loan companies. These companies have fought off attacks for several successive sessions and even succeeded in 1957
   in obtaining a law doubling the legal loan limit—to $600—
   in return for a minor scaling down of interest charges.

9. The Florida Education Association. With a highly organized
   bureaucracy, a cabinet post, a united membership of over thirty
   thousand, the FEA is aided by some former teachers in the
   legislature and some members whose wives are teachers.

10. The insurance business. Florida has made a special effort to
    attract national insurance companies' regional offices and as
    a result has shown a tender regard for their interests. Quite a
    few county seat legislators, including the 1957 house speaker
    and former Senate President Charley Johns, operate insurance
    businesses.

11. The Associated Industries of Florida. Although Florida is not
    a leading industrial state, the state unit of the National Asso-
    ciation of Manufacturers is powerful. The state wants to attract
    industry; several districts have important industrial establish-
    ments, and the AIF has maintained close working relationships

with many other state business organizations such as the Florida Hotel Association through a trade organization known as The Trade and Industrial Council of Florida.

12. The woodpulp industry. This industry keeps quite a few North Florida counties afloat economically and is important in many other counties as well. St. Joe Paper is a subsidiary of the Florida branch of the DuPont family, and its head, Ed Ball, has long been one of the most active and powerful behind-the-scenes figures in Florida politics.

13. Automobile dealers. It is difficult to figure out just why the automobile people should be powerful, but it is nevertheless commonly agreed that they are. Those "in the know" were distinctly surprised when the legislature in 1957 imposed a one per cent tax on automobile sales, although this was a reduction from the original 3 per cent proposed.

14. Southern Bell Telephone. The telephone company is extremely powerful in Florida, as it is in most states.

15. Phosphate mining and processing. Since Florida's only important mineral product is phosphate, the operators have been careful to keep their legislative fences mended. Their success in avoiding a severance tax has been notable. One legislator, when asked, said the legislature *could not* pass a severance tax because "the phosphate boys wouldn't stand for it."

16. The power companies. The power companies, principally Florida Power and Light Company and the Florida Power Corporation, are very powerful, as they are in most states.

17. The bankers. Any group with as strategic a position in the economy as the bankers is certain to be powerful. Several legislators are in the banking business, including the chairman of the 1957 House Banking Committee. Only four legislators call themselves "bankers," but an unascertainable number of others undoubtedly own stock in local banks. The bankers are so powerful that they have been able (notably in 1959) to keep the legislature from forcing them to give up moneys which have, under the law, escheated to the state. Nor do they pay interest on state deposits.

The great predominance of business and commercial groups is a noticeable feature of this listing. While this is true in all states to some degree, the weakness of labor and of racial or nationality groups eliminates to some extent one of the major safeguards against the dangers of pressure groups—the opposition of group to group. If it be true that power checks power, it might be better for Florida if there were one or more really strong countervailing powers to that of business (which for many purposes nowadays is in league with agriculture, especially in the South Florida corporation farming area).

Some of the groups mentioned above are particularly liable to a limitation which applies in some degree to all: that their power is confined largely to particular subjects, and if and when they try to exert influence beyond those matters, their influence dwindles rapidly. This would obviously be true of the Florida Education Association, but it is more or less true of many groups.

Pressure Groups and the Rural-Urban Cleavage

Although it may already be obvious, one feature of the activities of pressure groups which calls for comment is the fact that the strong pressure groups are usually those which have (or can gain) "privileged access" to the majority or to the leaders in the legislature. Since these power centers are largely rural, it would seem to follow that those interests which are strong in rural areas would be the strongest influences on legislation. A glance back at the preceding list of powerful groups will illustrate this point. Except for the race-tracks, every single one of the listed groups is either peculiarly agricultural or else is broadly spread over the whole state so that it has access to rural legislators. No one familiar with rural life in America doubts the power of the local banker, the telephone company, or the power and light company, although none of them is peculiarly rural in its nature. This accounts perhaps for the rather special constellation of interests held by the courthouse leader of the county seats referred to in Chapter 2, for while such groups are interested (among other things) in low taxes, *as groups* they are not often interested in the things which tax money supplies, such as social services and education.

Thus, while there may be nothing particularly "rural" about the interests of these groups, the fact that they are powerful in rural areas puts them in position to influence legislators from those areas.

Conversely, groups which are powerful only in urban zones have little influence in Florida state politics. Organizations such as the AFL-CIO and even (surprisingly) the tourist industries are not very successful; the race-track and tourist lobbies are mostly engaged in a battle against the rural legislators' tendencies to use them as sources of new revenue—a tendency which is reinforced by the fact that the average rural lawmaker is not very sure he even wants them in Florida: taxation expresses to some extent a moral judgment against them.

The Official Lobby

The public (or "official") lobby is less well known to the general public. In Florida, it consists of four more-or-less well-identified types of groups. Most obviously, there is the high state official himself— the governor, budget director, attorney general, etc. This category will be ignored here; it is not usually considered a lobby, for its work with the legislature is a normal part of the interplay between the legislative branch of the government and the executive-administrative branch. Nevertheless, when Governor Collins testified before the senate committee considering constitutional revision, giving his views on the executive article, he was, in effect, lobbying, as was Attorney General Richard Ervin when he spoke to a senate committee urging the passage of the interposition resolution.

Secondly, there are the representatives of the various state governmental bureaus and agencies. Every major agency in Florida assigns someone to the legislature while it is in session, despite frequent protests from legislators concerned about the "misuse" of tax money to pay such lobbyists. The house registration lists in 1957 showed that thirty-three separate state agencies were represented, from the governor's office on down to the State Fire Marshal and the State Board of Beauty Culture. The state universities are an important subgroup within this category. These agencies, of course, vary widely in importance and in legislative influence. Their job is to protect their agency and promote its interests (by expanding its power or functions and increasing its budget)—a task which includes the perfectly proper aim of securing legislation to enable them to serve the public well—and to promote the interests of their private clienteles if they have them. The Florida Livestock Board and the department of agriculture are two agencies with rather obvious clientele interests.

Another type of official lobby is that of the local governmental units within the state: the cities, counties, and other local areas. Since much of their lobbying is unregistered it is difficult to gauge how active these governments are, but while only thirty-two were registered in 1957, a glance at the number of local bills (in hundreds) affecting these units directly indicates a tremendous amount of effort. The job of such lobbyists is made easy by the fact that most bills they want are of interest only to themselves and are noncontroversial. They need not, in most cases, even go to Tallahassee, since they only have to contact their own legislative delegation, which is easy to do at home. Rarely, a controversial issue arises in which there will be a floor fight even on a local bill, such as the Orlando Utilities Commission's fight over its plant in nearby Brevard County.

A fourth, and vastly important, public lobby is that composed of the various state-wide organizations of local officials, such as the Florida League of Municipalities and the Association of County Commissioners. Many of these organizations (there were fourteen registered in 1957) are very powerful within their own spheres of interest: it was the opposition of the county assessors which prevented the adoption of the Citizen's Tax Council—itself a pressure group—recommendation of a state agency to oversee assessment practices, and the sheriff's association has succeeded in blocking the development of the State Highway Patrol into a police force by setting up—with *state* funds—a state sheriff's bureau which co-ordinates activities and maintains a crime laboratory with detection facilities.

Two other public groups had registered lobbyists in Tallahassee in 1957. One illustrates the potentialities of lobbying—for it was a federal agency, the Social Security Board. The other was a peculiar phenomenon brought on by the no-party nature of the legislature: the State Democratic Executive Committee found it necessary to lobby for party loyalty bills, although the legislature was almost entirely Democratic.

The Role of the Press

The role of the press as an influence on the Florida legislature is at present largely a matter of guesswork. No thorough study has been made of the subject; only scattered and unauthenticated comments by observers and participants are available. But since the general public—at the state level particularly—is almost completely dependent for information on the larger city daily newspapers (there is no magazine press for state politics), the part played by these papers is a crucial one.

The daily newspaper in Florida is largely a metropolitan phenomenon. It is true that quite a few smaller cities have dailies, but they tend to supplement rather than compete with the metropolitan papers. The papers in the large cities circulate widely over the state; there is probably no town of any size where a metropolitan paper is not available on the day of publication. The *Florida Times-Union* of Jacksonville, for instance, sells the same day all over North Florida at least as far west as Tallahassee. The other more important papers (state-wide) are the Miami *Herald*, Orlando *Sentinel*, Tampa *Tribune*, and St. Petersburg *Times*; there are several others of lesser but still considerable significance.

Two points may be emphasized about these papers. Most obviously, as papers in metropolitan areas, they express the attitudes and desires of urban residents. This means that the major sources of information and opinion, even in rural areas, are urban-oriented. How much influence this has or may have in the future on legislative action is problematical. It does, however, seem to inspire a certain amount of fear and hostility in the small-county legislators, who often refer to the big city press as one of their chief antagonists. The small-county people are likely to seize whatever occasion offers to try to trim the papers down to size. Such an occasion, it was rumored, arose in 1957. The legislature had authorized the creation of a new state university at Temple Terrace, in the Tampa suburbs, and was considering an appropriation for the establishment of the institution. The Tampa *Tribune* has for some years been one of the most vocal critics of the small-county people, but it was one of the loudest backers of the new university. The small-county legislators, the story goes, threatened to slice the university's appropriation unless the *Tribune* soft-pedalled its attacks on them. A substantial appropriation went through, but it is impossible to say whether this reported deal had anything to do with it.

The second factor of interest is that all the papers mentioned above except one—and almost all other Florida papers—are conservative, many of them verging on a right-wing Republicanism even though (being southern) they call themselves Democratic. The St. Petersburg *Times* is the only metropolitan paper which could be called liberal by any stretch of imagination. In state affairs the others all adopt the standard Chamber of Commerce attitude, which is "that government is best which spends least" except when the money is to be spent locally and obtained elsewhere. This fits in well with the dominant ideas of the urban Florida legislators and makes successful liberalism in the halls of the legislature even more difficult. One principal effect, then, is that the Florida press to a large extent reinforces the commercial lobby in Tallahassee.

Nevertheless, the newspapers through publicity sometimes can exercise a more positive role. It is quite probable that the decline of the more obviously unethical lobbying practices, such as bribery, is due at least partly to the watchfulness of the able press correspondents stationed in Tallahassee during legislative sessions. Some of these— Allen Morris, Jim Hardee, and Martin Waldron are examples—have been in Tallahassee long enough so that they have built up excellent contacts, and thus can spot what is happening even behind many closed doors. There is no doubt that in many cases they know better what is going on in the legislature than do many of the lawmakers themselves.

The High Cost of Lobbying

Lobbying is not always cheap. There are no official sources on lobbying expenses in Florida, however, so that estimates are largely guesswork. The small or occasional lobbyist will spend little beyond transportation. But the lobbyist working for a powerful group may spend thousands of dollars, and his employer may spend even more.

A good lobbyist may be paid $100 a day or more; some large groups employ two or more of these "influence specialists." The *Wall*

Street Journal has estimated that some large pressure interests may spend as much as $20,000 during the session.[19] Whether this includes the cost of bringing large numbers of officials to Tallahassee to put on a show of force at strategic times, as the Milk Producers' Association does, is not known. Payments for legal counsel and research add to the bill. Entertaining is another item. Some powerful groups, especially in the official lobby, do not spend much. They can send a regular employee to the capitol on his regular salary.

No one is in a position even to estimate the total amount spent for lobbying at an average session. It quite obviously runs into the hundreds of thousands of dollars, perhaps higher—a fact which underscores the importance to the "interests" of what the legislature does, for even a large company does not spend over $20,000 without the solid hope that such bread, cast upon the legislative waters, will return a hundredfold.

The Techniques of Lobbying

The techniques of the lobbyist are many and varied. None of them, it should be emphasized, provide any guarantee of success. In fact, some observers profess to believe that *lobbying as a technique* seldom influences the course of legislation, because, they say, it is the strength of the pressure group in a particular subject-matter area that counts, not its lobbying techniques. This is probably extreme, however, for as Truman points out, "an important determinant of the interest group's success" seems to be "the skill with which it and its 'members' in the legislature are able to exploit their position."[20]

"Because the position of no two groups is precisely identical," Truman continues, "and because the resources of any single group are in part altered by the presence of other groups operating in the same area, techniques appropriate at one time may be inappropriate or unavailable at another."[21] Consequently, no complete list of techniques can be drawn up nor can the frequency of their use be judged. What will be done here is merely to suggest the range and types of techniques which appear to be most typical in the Florida situation. Most are familiar elsewhere; therefore little need be said of them.

It should be noted at the outset that, while pressure groups operate both offensively (to get what they want) and defensively (to prevent action they judge harmful), the defense gains a certain advantage. This seems to be based, Truman believes, on two factors: social inertia and the obstructive opportunities present in the legislative process.[22]

Any change "involves an alteration of existing relationships within the society."[23] It is the uncertainty as to just what kind and degree of change—the fear of loss of present benefits in exchange for an uncertain future—which makes changes difficult.

The nature of the Florida legislature provides a further defensive advantage. Its bicameral organization and the operation of the separation of powers were deliberately intended to obstruct action, and they do. The absence of strict limits on the length of debate gives the opponent of legislation many chances to obstruct, and, as has already been amply illustrated, the lack of leadership furnishes "abundant opportunities for obstruction and delay."

Those with the advantage do not always win, and there are often other advantages in the hands of the proponents of legislation; otherwise few laws would be passed. Nevertheless the determined obstructionist is in a fair way to defeat or emasculate even the best bill, as the watering down of the bills to create a central purchasing system and abolish the practice of naturopathy indicates.[24]

Every day during the session a legislator finds his desk piled with letters and telegrams. While a certain number of these represent merely individual constituents, most of them are connected with pressure groups directly or indirectly; telephone calls fall in the same category. The effectiveness of this technique depends on several factors, of which the most obvious but perhaps the least significant is the volume of such communications concerning a particular bill. Volume is so imprecise as an indicator of public opinion that many lawmakers pay little attention to it unless it is unusually high or unusually unanimous. It is quite probable that the large mail received in the 1957 session of the legislature on the teacher pay issue had something to do with the rather surprising willingness of the assembly to vote the new taxes required to pay part of the increase. When mail is heavy and apparently genuine, legislators will respond although the communications represent the views of a single interest, and if there is any indication of mass support in the local district, some response is always forthcoming.

The practices of forming alliances and logrolling are invariably useful to the lobbyist, for the greater the battalions on his side the more likely he is to win. In this the various business groups have a distinct advantage, for on many issues their alliance is natural and automatic. Perhaps of particular significance are the more or less permanent alliances between a private and an official lobby, like that between the attorney general's office and the state association of prosecuting attorneys, for such alliances are based on an almost perpetual identity of interest. Logrolling is, of course, basic to the maintenance of any alliance, be it international or pressure group; for unless mutual aims exist, support *for* a group's bills must be purchased at the price of its support for those of some other group. In effect, the University of Florida's appropriations are the result of logrolling, for the Alachua County delegation always finds it easier to get the university budget through if it is reasonable about some of the things other delegations want. There are indications, for instance, that approval for the unusually large appropriation for 1957-59 was at least partly the result of an agreement by the Alachua delegation to support the Hillsborough delegation's hopes for the new school at Tampa. Such instances are part of the everyday stuff of the legislative process; to multiply examples is needless. Sometimes such success boomerangs at the next session: in 1959 the university got almost nothing from the legislature.

It is ordinarily stated that in the national Congress the primary effort of a lobby is concentrated on the testimony at committee hearings. This seems not to be so true of the Florida legislature, for with the short session and crowded calendar, committee sessions tend to be more perfunctory. It seems more likely that personal contacts by the lobbyist with individual committee members *before* committee meetings to some extent replace or at least supplement formal appearances. A factor in this is that at times open lobbying does more harm than good: the representatives of the NAACP, for example, were probably well advised not to testify before the legislature's interim committee on race relations in 1956. Many times a spokesman *in* the legislature can do more good than one *before* the legislature.

The senate president was once reported to have told the board chairman of the Florida Power and Light Company (of which he was himself a director) to leave Tallahassee because he was "such a colorful and well-known figure that he was attracting much attention to the power company's bills" and thus harming the cause.[25] It probably should be added that the practice of committee stacking makes the deliberations of many committees upon many subjects mere formalities; it was, as noted earlier, ridiculous to expect the senate's forestry committee to give serious attention to a proposal to tax the pulpwood industry!

The use of parliamentary procedure by a lobby obviously depends on having a legislator tied to the lobby and occupying a legislative position through which he can use the desired techniques. This puts speaker, president, rules committee chairmen and other chairmen in particularly strategic positions for reasons that do not need repeating. But any legislator can use some parliamentary tactics, such as the motion for reconsideration, filibustering by offering many amendments, or the motion to amend by striking the enactment clause or all but the enactment clause. These are merely illustrative of the numerous opportunities to delay or obfuscate. A life insurance official once described one of his organization's parliamentary techniques in this manner: "If we do not succeed in getting a bill adversed [in committee], we try to introduce another bill, hoping that the whole thing will wind up in a row, to be plain about it. . . . If a bill passes either house and goes to the other house, we try to repeat the above tactics."[26]

Since the use of these techniques for the benefit of a lobbyist is dependent upon the existence of compliant legislators, one is reminded of the verse regarding the incorruptible British press:

> You cannot hope to bribe or twist,
> Thank God, the British journalist;
> But seeing what the man will do
> Unbribed, there's no occasion to.

When persuasion is necessary, it is best accomplished through someone or some group in the lawmaker's home district. When the comptroller wants to stop a bill in the legislature, many members receive telephone calls from local bankers on the subject; when the farm bureau puts on the pressure, it uses three or four key farm leaders in each county who can approach that county's delegation; when the Veterans of Foreign Wars scented trouble in an appropriations committee, they secured men from each district which had a man on the committee to contact the panel members. Such pressure is of course most effective when the local citizens serving as "contact men" are prominent and influential in the community. Sometimes persuasion is largely a matter of merely providing a legislator with relevant information—opposition to an appropriation for a VFW encampment evaporated when it was pointed out to legislators that other veterans' groups had secured such favors in the past.

Some methods of lobby influence are more devious and less legitimate than those so far noted. No one knows exactly how common the following practices are, but the talk about them is sufficiently specific that there seems to be some solid substance to it.

It has apparently not been unknown, particularly in the senate, for lobbyists to gain and cast proxy votes in committee hearings, but this does not seem to have happened in at least the last few sessions. It is probably so rare that it demands little attention. More significant is the fairly common practice of paying a legislator "expense money" while he is attending the session in Tallahassee; some local Chambers of Commerce are known to do this. It is not considered bribery, nor apparently even frowned upon, although there is no attempt to publicize the practice.

Some organizations will pay campaign expenses—a practice not, presumably, as widespread as it used to be, since Florida has now enacted a campaign expense report and regulation statute. According to reports, not too long ago a DuPont representative paid such expenses for quite a few legislators; then he went to Tallahassee and held "DuPont caucuses" to advise them how to vote. More recently it was reported in the press that a Dade County representative owed support to the small-loans lobby in return for its electoral help. The threat to withhold future campaign support is sometimes known as "turning a blow-torch on the navel of the blue hens."[27]

Approaching bribery—except that it is attached to no specific legislation—is the rather common practice of paying legal retainer fees, insurance brokerage fees, and similar emoluments to legislators regardless of business services rendered but doubtless in expectation of political services. Particularly involved in this practice, reputedly, are the power companies, which (since they do business in many counties) have need for widespread legal services! Legislators who are not lawyers believe that such retainers are paid to a very substantial bloc of legislators, but there appears to be no way of verifying the accuracy of such observations.

Finally, there is the possibility of bribery. While no one will admit that this is still practiced, even very respectable legislators known for their integrity can cite instances of its use in the past. The "going price" for a race-track bill in 1953 is said to have been $3,000; the story goes that one rather unprincipled lawmaker after having pledged his vote for that fee, came back to the lobbyist saying he knew someone else whom he could persuade to do likewise. He secured the extra vote but kept the extra $3,000! Farther back is the case mentioned publicly by old-time legislator and lobbyist McQueen Chaires. According to him, he collected $500 (a good many years ago) to secure votes for a capitol expansion appropriation.[28] Even at worst, however, bribery is a limited method; it is risky; it may cost too much; it may boomerang. It will be used, if at all, only in exceptional cases.

No discussion of lobbying techniques would be complete without mention of the "social lobby." There has been a pronounced tendency of writers on pressure groups to play down its importance, but our own observations tend to indicate that the operations of the social lobby in Florida are considerably more significant than Truman's offhand remarks about the situation in Washington, D.C. might indicate.[29] The very volume and intensity of social activity in Tallahassee during legislative sessions would lead one to conclude it has some importance, for these activities are expensive and would hardly be undertaken without some hope of gain thereby. Nevertheless it is true that little or no direct lobbying is performed at these social functions; the idea seems to be that of making friends and cementing relationships. As one Florida lobbyist put it,

Why do lobbyists spend so much time taking people out to dinner and having them to cocktail parties? Well, the answer to that is simple; if I want to talk to a Senator or Representative, it's certainly a lot better for me to be on a "Bill"-"Jack" basis than to meet him as a total stranger.—[It] does give you an opportunity to know the man and for him to know you. As a result when you come to see him on business the next week or so he's already had a social evening with you and he knows you and your family and you know his likes and dislikes and you get along better.[30]

The activities of the Tallahassee social lobby range from the intimate to the grandiose and from the "high society" type to the barbecue. Not all lobbyists use the more formal types, but almost all will on occasion buy meals or drinks. One legislator says he never worries about meal expenses during sessions because try as he will he can never spend over a dollar a day on them—"somebody always picks up the check." Other lobbies run formal permanent establishments; one alliance of them rents a whole hotel floor and has set up a self-service bar and restaurant which is open at all hours. In 1957, the milk producers rented a house on the outskirts of town and set up a bar there—with signs on the highway pointing "this way to E. T. Lay" (the name of the lobbyist). The house was very crowded when the bill to abolish the price-fixing powers of the milk commission was being discussed.[31]

Perhaps the most dramatic events of the session's social lobby are the series of parties given at each session by the Rosenbergs, who own the Rose Printing Company. These parties are often costume balls—in 1953 one was a Roman party at which the legislators came appropriately dressed in togas; in 1955 one was a Li'l Abner costume party, and a caterer was flown in from New York for the occasion. On another occasion the Tallahassee Chamber of Commerce served dinner to 750 guests at the state-owned Killearn Gardens.[32]

Other activities of the social lobby vary greatly. Dixie Lily Company has put packages of its products on legislative desks. The small-loan lobbyist, Raeburn Horne, opens his fishing camp near Tallahassee for free use by legislators. Trips to the Kentucky Derby were paid for in one recent session. A power company finances a weekend in Gainesville for legislators desiring to attend homecoming festivities at the University of Florida. And—inevitably—the story is heard that one lobby in 1953 operated a call-girl set-up with imported (that is, not local) prostitutes.

While resourceful use of these techniques aids the skillful lobbyist, it probably remains true that the inherent strength of his group—providing it is properly marshalled—counts far more than does the skill of the lobbyist. For this reason only brief mention will be given to the man who plays this role.

The lobbyist—they sometimes prefer to be called "legislative representatives"—is typically a smiling and affable man. He may be a "free-lance" who picks up clients as he can; he may be hired for each session by the same group (or groups, for many lobbyists serve more than one); alternatively, he may be a permanent employee or official of a business organization or government agency, part of whose job entails lobbying during sessions.

Although it is by no means a requirement, a certain advantage accrues from the use of ex-legislators. In addition to Lantaff and Horne, who have been mentioned previously, other prominent ex-legislators who served as lobbyists in 1957 were former Senators "Bun" Gautier, G. W. Sanchez, and Pat Whitaker; and ex-Representatives H. T. Cook, Charles Andrews, and Wallace Sturgis. Others have formerly served the state in executive capacities—former Governor Fuller Warren was a lobbyist for labor in the 1953 session, and Everett McKinney, former state beverage director, was a principal lobbyist for the retail liquor dealers in 1957. The advantages of such connections are obvious: ex-legislators have the privilege of the floor, and all those mentioned have many acquaintances in the legislature, particularly in the senate. Whatever handicaps other lobbyists have in lack of acquaintance can be made up by long service as a lobbyist. Allen Morris reports that at least four 1957 lobbyists had been in "continuous service since the 1929 session—one of them since 1921."[33]

Regulation of Lobbying Activities

Like most states, as well as the federal government, Florida has made a few half-hearted efforts to regulate certain aspects of lobbying. These are neither very comprehensive, very effective, nor very strictly enforced. The only law on the subject provides merely that any lobbyist testifying before a committee *may be* required by the committee to state upon oath whether he represents anyone besides himself, if so whom, and whether he is receiving any compensation

for his services. This information is to be printed in the journals of
both houses. Misstatement of fact is punishable by a prison sentence
of up to twenty-five years.[34] It will be noted that the oath is permissive,
not mandatory; and legislative practice in Florida seldom requires a
lobbyist to take the oath. It is, however, customary for lobbyists to
divulge orally and informally to the committee the groups they represent.

Senate rules do not go beyond this statute; but the house requires
written registration of all lobbyists, in which they tell (under oath)
the groups they represent and the legislation in which they are interested.[35] This information is tabulated in the *Journal* every Monday
during sessions. Individuals representing only themselves are not required to register, and the only penalty for failure to register is loss
of the lobbying privilege for the duration of the session. So far as we
are aware even this penalty has never been imposed, and there seems
to be little or no real attempt to enforce the rule, although apparently
all the "regular" lobbyists observe it.

These are merely "disclosure" laws, which in reality do not in any
way affect lobbying activities. There is nothing a lobbyist could do
before their adoption which he cannot do now. Aside from the possibility that scholars may glean from the tabulations some valuable
information as to extent of lobbying, there seems to be little or no
practical effect of such provisions. Whether more drastic regulation
is either desirable, necessary, or possible is a moot question.

Legislative Defenses Against Lobbying

It remains to consider briefly the extent to which the legislature
is in a position to defend itself against at least the more extreme or
illegitimate lobbying tactics. There are some such defenses; how effective they are seems to vary with the individual case. Perhaps the
chief defense is the existence of opposing pressure groups, which
permits the legislature to play one off against another. But as E. P.
Herring points out, "in questions that seem to affect the groups requesting governmental action and no other interests, the legislative
agents are usually successful. . . . In such a case the chief virtue is
persistence."[36]

Other defense mechanisms are listed by George Galloway—and

though he is speaking of Congress what he says is applicable also to the legislature of Florida. "One house," he says, "may pass the lobbyists' bill and rely on the other house or the conferees to amend it so as to nullify its effects"[37]—or, it might be added, to knock it out completely. This is a technique frequently used, several examples of which were cited earlier in this chapter. The fact that their differing apportionments make the two houses responsive to slightly different pressures aids in the use of this device, but the lack of substantial party or factional discipline makes it somewhat hazardous, for one can seldom be quite sure what the other house will do.

Galloway continues to point out that some bills may be passed to satisfy pressures, relying on the governor to veto the measure.[38] This is an effective political tactic, for it defeats the bill but enables the lawmakers to go back to the pressure group or home constituency and say they supported it. There is little doubt that some representatives in 1957 voted for the "last-resort" school bill secure in the conviction that the governor would not allow it to become law. How many measures receive such treatment is impossible to judge.

Again, a bill may be "lost" in multiple committees and never found again, so that actually no one has to take any stand on it. Committee hearings may be used as safety valves to satisfy groups that their wishes received due consideration although no action results.

"Judicious amendments of bills may be adopted in . . . conferences held behind doors closed to press and public alike."[39] Such informal conferences are a regular—and necessary—part of the deliberations of any legislative body; they make it possible for a committee to present a united front as a collective body so that pressures cannot mount too strongly against individual members.

"Bills to which there is strong opposition may be recommitted, relying on the tactics of delay to postpone difficult decisions."[40] This device is especially effective in a short session, and such tactics seem to have been largely responsible for the failure of the 1957 legislature to adopt any measure regulating the issuance of trading stamps, although strong pressure was applied to do so.

Lobbying and Legislative Ethics

Leaving aside any question of the general legitimacy of pressure group tactics, or of their effectiveness, it still seems to be true that some lobbying tactics are unethical without being illegal and that they are likely to taint legislative action with the brush of corruption even though few of those involved fully realize it. This is most clearly true of the givers and receivers of contributions, retainer fees, and similar emoluments which, without being bribes, are likely to produce a feeling of obligation on the part of the beneficiary. It was with this thought in mind that United States Senator Paul Douglas cautioned his fellow lawmakers:

> [Legislators] certainly should not accept costly gifts and entertainment from private parties and should avoid being put under obligation to those who have an open or secret axe to grind. They should not vote for measures in which they have an appreciable and direct private interest but should rather disqualify themselves, if they find their public judgment being seriously influenced by considerations of private benefit. Upon retiring from office they should be very chary about using their experience or friendships as paid lobbyists for legislation and if they do take such work, they should confine themselves, as would lawyers before a court, to appearances before committees and should refrain from attempting to sway individuals. In no circumstances should they use their rights to the floor of [the legislature] for a specific measure in which they are interested.[41]

This is a hard discipline; not many will fully attain it under the best circumstances. But Florida does not appear to provide the best circumstances, for the effects of the political system and practices of lobbying as we have seen them do little or nothing to institutionalize power or to institutionalize this high ideal of legislative conduct. Instead, the Florida ideal seems to be one of personalized and irresponsible power, and such a system puts an intolerable moral burden on the legislator.

It becomes easier and easier to identify the public interest with special interest, and more and more difficult to keep his broad public perspective. As his position strengthens, continued exercise of personal power tends to make even the most conscientious legislator less careful in exercising his power only for public ends. Irresponsible personal power is inevitably corrupting in its influence, and a system of personal power is essentially immoral.[42]

It is not the existence of pressure groups which poses this problem: it is the tolerance and acceptance of their more unethical tactics by the legislator and more broadly by the public. A legislature will not rise very far above the moral level of the community it represents: "The faults we see in government are all too often the reflection of our own moral failures."[43] There is nothing dangerous about pressure groups which could not be rendered largely innocuous if the code of public and private morality refused to permit the existence of such personalized power.

Chapter 9

The Problems and Prospects in Summary

I N the foregoing chapters we have subjected the Florida legislature to a fairly stringent examination. If we have appeared hypercritical at times, we can only plead our calling: when the academician ceases to be a gadfly in a one-party (or "no"-party) state, who is left to perform the vital function of criticism? At the same time we have made every effort to avoid two snares that occasionally trap those who try to analyze institutions—the use of manufactured criticism and the failure either to develop or to reveal the standards of critical evaluation applied. The standards used to measure the Florida legislature were those which have been developed in American political theory, either through formal writings or in the historical accretions by which the lacunae in our conception of institutions have been filled. Above all, we have tried to apply to a single representative institution the standards which appear to derive from the American legislative assembly in the generic sense. To a great extent, therefore, the criticisms offered here have grown out of the contrast between theory and practice, a contrast which, although common to all human activity, gives no cause in itself for repudiating the theory.

Professor George Graham has argued persuasively that "representativeness, responsibility, and rationality are the bases for the moral authority of legislative bodies."[1] In terms of these criteria the moral authority of the Florida legislature compares very unfavorably with the authority legally vested in it.

The legislature is not representative according to the standard most common to democratic societies—proportionality of population. If this formal standard alone had been violated and the legislature, despite the disproportionate allocation of its members, still assumed responsibility for public policy within a conceptual framework which embraced the state as a whole, the violation of the representative ideal would be less complete. Unfortunately this is not the case, for the system of malapportionment is not a mere distortion of numbers; it goes to the very heart of the governmental process in Florida. The current political style of the state depends to a great extent upon a legislature which settles general issues by trading votes for local concessions, on legislators whose main service is as political brokers for their constituencies and for selected economic interests, and on a dispersal of both executive and legislative authority so that effective patterns of institutional leadership and a majority consensus are precluded from politics. While malapportionment in its simplest form may not be said to be the cause of these things, it has certainly contributed to them, and perhaps its greatest contribution has been toward the preservation of this type of politics in the face of vast changes in the society and long after personalism has ceased to serve the needs of the state adequately.

We are assuming, of course, that the main advantage of a properly working representative system is that it translates democratic ideals into workability by making possible a high degree of congruity between the requirements and aspirations of the public and the policy of the government. Such a correspondence between public opinion and governmental action can be produced only if the institutional arrangement is designed so that the public is offered an opportunity to make its desires intelligible and the representative assembly is able to translate these public expressions into law. A responsible and rational system of representative government is not achieved by adherence to certain external forms and the espousal of a series of ideals which are explicitly denied in practice.

It is difficult to see how a high positive correlation can exist between public opinion and public policy when a majority of the legislature not only is elected by a small percentage of the population, but also openly defies the demand for adjustment of the state of malapportionment and frames policy which is admittedly grounded in distrust of the cultural traits of the populous areas.

Much of the organization and procedure of the Florida legislature has been pressed into the service of the political groups which have become dominant through the geographical system of apportionment. Legislative elections, for example, should afford the voters an opportunity for rational selection of individual legislators who will then be in a position to exercise collective responsibility. But the practice in Florida is quite different: the alleged independence of candidates, the emphasis in the campaign on personal characteristics which may have little relation to fitness for legislative service, the complete subordination of state-wide issues to local issues in the election literature and speeches, and the absence of acknowledged party or factional stands on issues are barriers against the possibility of responsibility to the electorate. The electoral process in this state is not a contest in which the strengths and weaknesses of the candidates and their parties are revealed to the public as the contestants sharpen their conceptions of policy through abrasive competition. In an ideal representative system the election process and service in the legislature should merge into a political continuum. In Florida the election is a more or less disagreeable means of entry into the real world of politics, which consists almost exclusively of the personal relations among those who have been admitted to the inner circle.

In a democracy every election should be a stage in the political education of the voting public; the method is presumed to be dialectic and the result is a clarification of the effects of the policy of the recent past and the projection of suggested policy into the future. Elections which are won on other terms—and especially through deliberate obscuration—are lessons in irresponsibility, since such activities deny the voter the basis for rational choice of governmental officials, relieve him of the possibility of effective control, and gradually deaden his sensitivity to the full implications of popular government.

The orientation of the legislator to his duties also serves to stabilize the mode of politics prevailing in the state. Without a party or factional organization which he can look to for support and guidance (and can influence reciprocally), the slender new legislative reed can soon be bent in the direction in which the legislative leaders wish it to grow. It is easier to adapt and conform than to rebel and assert independence because conformity affords protection against all sorts

of political pitfalls and, in time, may even procure a certain measure
of influence, whereas independence may result in loss of status and
in some cases of the legislative seat itself. Being almost infinitely
adaptable, the human species can soon learn to justify the new attitudes it has been constrained to adopt.

The organization of the legislature is also malleable and has been
shaped to the demands of the system. The influence of the leadership
and the conditions for achieving influential positions help to preserve
the system of interpersonal control, a type of control which can nearly
always be made to assume the form of absence of control. The appearance of near anarchy has great appeal to the antigovernmental
sentiments of Americans; as a result governmental negativism is a
very useful cloak behind which the effective use of political power
may be carried on anonymously. The wide dispersal of committees
and committee assignments, for example, makes it very difficult to
detect such activities as committee stacking and concentration of legislative control through interlocking directorates on the more important
committees. The plethoric nature of committee responsibilities, the
adroit use of the power of committee reference (especially in the
senate), and the skillful appointment of the membership of conference and certain types of interim committees are other means of
consolidating the legislative position. In the absence of clearly recognized institutionalized leadership and in the face of shifting alignments based on interpersonal agreements, it is very difficult to fix
responsibility for the failure of a good piece of legislation or the
passage of a bad one. It is even more difficult to secure accountability
even if responsibility can be determined. A sort of Erewhon reversal
of justice may be forthcoming when knowledge of the full meaning
of legislative activity is so difficult to come by: a courageous and
independent action may cost a member his seat, whereas a consistently bad voting record may be very difficult to use with effect
against a man.

If the system of apportionment and the overtly vague, but quietly
efficient, power structure of the Florida legislature raise questions
about that organization's representativeness and responsibility, neither
do its processes permit much confidence in its rationality. The pace
at which the legislature moves does not allow for the kind of de-

liberation that not only probes into every aspect of each major piece of legislation, but also attempts to consider an individual measure in relation to the larger legislative program of which it is a part. To the handicap of a very short legislative session is added the inconvenience of trying to secure some degree of majoritarian agreement *after* the legislature has actually convened. If a two-party system were in operation or if the leadership that could be furnished by the governor were not vitiated by the strained relations between the legislative and executive branches in Florida, it is possible that some consensus could be worked out in the interim between sessions, tested and approved at the elections, and considered in detail and enacted during the session. Such is not the case, however; consequently the legislature must begin without much guidance and continue in ill-informed haste. It does not even use the program-planning possibilities of its legislative council. The more noticeable errors committed under such circumstances, such as the passage of both (rather than only one) companion bills or the approval of a new program while failing to make an appropriation for it, are relatively minor when compared with other considerations. In some respects, the conduct of the legislative function under the circumstances just described resembles the negativism characteristic of a multiparty parliamentary system: it is easy to secure a majority coalition against almost any program that is proposed but virtually impossible to secure positive action on anything but the minimum policies needed to carry on the government at all. Lacking even the permanent clarity of line of the ideological parties in a multiparty system, the Florida legislature must rely on personal leadership exercised in the manner described earlier, and this leadership is for the most part content with something short of positive government. Needless to say, the pressure groups are equally willing to operate in a situation in which programs and their interrelations are handled so casually and leadership is apparently so self-effacing.

The failure of the political institutions in Florida to come to grips with crucial problems is naturally most noticeable in those areas of governmental action for which the prevailing style of politics offers little outlet, particularly for the problems of urbanism. This state is already well on the way to developing two and possibly three of the nation's multicity agglomerations which are sometimes referred to as metropolitan regions. Much of the opportunity to prepare in advance for the coming of these new patterns of living has been lost, and the price of lack of foresight probably will continue to mount. The need for extensive planning legislation to enable the cities (in some cases in co-operation with the counties) to cope with their growth problems is manifest, and a greater measure of attention to the state's role in the planning field in areas where effective control is beyond the capacity of traditional local units is vitally important. These problems naturally spill over into practically all aspects of the state's activity— schools, highways, public health, conservation, state parks and recreation areas, and revenue and taxation are closely related to the process of planning for the future of urbanism.

An ancillary development resulting in part from the lack of correspondence between the state's needs and the area of responsibility that the legislature may be expected to cover under its present conditions is the march of power to Washington. A considerable upward movement of political power is inevitable in the face of the tremendous growth of private economic organizations and the resultant areal interdependence; this social phenomenon is the factor that has incapacitated the local units for effective performance of certain functions. But centralization is also due partly to the failure of the state and local units to cope with problems that are within the scope of their powers.[2] Anyone who has attended meetings of local officials and private organizations concerned with governmental action can attest to the naturalness of the tendency to look toward the federal government when no response is heard from appeals to the state. There is no "conspiracy" among federal officials to take over all the functions of government, but if one level of government fails to develop the conditions which make it sensitive and responsive to the issues that are overtly or implicitly dominant in the society, an outlet will be sought through other instrumentalities open to democratic processes. There is irony in the fact that many of those who most deplore the expansion of federal power also are assiduous in fostering the circumstances which make that expansion necessary.

If the institutional structure of representative government in Florida exhibits all these faults, it may very well be asked, "How does the legislature continue to function to the apparent satisfaction of the people of this state and without a serious crisis?" The answer to the question is remarkably simple: the legislature actually accomplishes a great deal in spite of the difficulties under which it functions. For instance, it passes the legislation and appropriations necessary to support the main functions of state government, although at times both the legal and financial support are minimal and new services which are badly needed may be very slow in coming. The representative assembly also raises the tax revenues necessary to maintain these services, although it may not always give sufficient consideration to the collateral effects of the type of taxes imposed. In quite a few instances, especially in cases in which the program has overwhelming public support and is long-standing, the legislature goes far beyond the limits of minimum support and creates the conditions for a very sound and efficient program.

It should also be noted that the members of the legislature are aware that the American legislative tradition makes certain demands on them, and even the members who are completely habituated to the more undesirable practices take great pains to make public obeisance to these demands. Even if the adherence to the traditional ideal is more talked about than practiced, the fact of its omnipresence gives continuing hope of more complete application.

The continuing urbanization (or suburbanization) of Florida's population will certainly make the reconciliation of the representative ideal with the unrepresentative reality more and more difficult. A point will be reached—perhaps it has already been reached—at which rural legislators must either give up the ideal, standing boldly on the platform of naked power, or make some concessions. Such concessions, when made, will almost certainly ramify into the whole political structure of the state. For as we have seen, there are three basic malfunctions responsible for the present quality of Florida politics: the rural-urban conflict, the lack of a party system, and the race question; of the three we regard the first as the most important—indeed, in some respects it is the cause of the others and the key to their improvement.

This is particularly obvious in the case of the racial conflict. We have seen that the urban areas have no special stake in the perpetuation of racial discrimination; indeed, the tensions and conflicts it produces can only harm them. Thus, while the urban counties particularly in South Florida do not actively *want* integration (many individuals certainly oppose it), neither will they act affirmatively to prevent it. It is quite likely that if they were properly represented in the legislature the problem of integration would by now be more nearly solved than in fact it is.

Similarly, as the preceding chapters have amply illustrated, nopartyism is, in Florida, a function of the type of rural interpersonal politics which the legislature exemplifies. Representatives of large heterogeneous populations are not likely to wish to (even if they could) maintain such a system. It seems inevitable to us that urban control of the legislature would gradually lead to the rise of a party system, and it is at least probable that such a party system would eventually be a two-party system, especially if (as we assume) race could no longer be used as a means of preventing the growth of a rival to the Democratic party.

It can be seen, then, that Florida's basic political dilemma is that of apportionment. As long as the rural legislative majority (which controls both the process of reapportionment and that of constitutional revision) is determined to remain in power it can do so. Will a social group, in power, be willing voluntarily to give up that power? Perhaps the great example of such a transfer of political power was the democratization which took place in England beginning with the Reform Act of 1832. The landed gentry in England, it is true, had a sort of public spirit which does not seem to be present among the rural legislators in Florida: in many ways, although "landed," it was not rural. It is, therefore, doubtful that the rural leaders in Florida, backed as they are by the powerful rural-based interest groups, are likely to reach such heights of self-immolation.

In this respect we can agree to some extent with Professor Michael Oakeshott in his view that politics is the "activity of attending to the general arrangements of a set of people," that it is a self-moved manner of activity, that in hereditary co-operative groups the activity is never open to infinite possibility, and that a "certain degree of shabbiness is joined with every real convenience."[3] Despite aberrations, the legislative processes in the United States are based on a workable tradition, and we are not faced with the task of creating a set of political institutions based on some extraneous model, an activity which probably would be futile anyway. Instead, it is necessary to explore the full implications of the tradition in order to make use of its very potentiality for attending *properly* to the arrangements of the society, while avoiding as much of the attendant shabbiness as possible. Regardless of the rigidities implicit in such doctrines as the separation of powers, American legislative practice can be quite adaptable and, under the proper impetus, can make good use of the country's experimental propensity.

Since all human accomplishment takes place to the accompaniment of error (or with a certain degree of shabbiness), the question seems to be, how defective can a political institution become and still survive and accomplish its purposes well enough to deserve survival? It is our feeling that the Florida legislative system is approaching the point at which a considerable measure of reform is needed if it is to continue to serve the people of Florida to their reasonable satisfaction. A rural legislature cannot forever fill the needs of an urban society, nor can methods and procedures developed under the social conditions and out of the social tensions of the nineteenth century always work well in the twentieth.

Although institutional reform is not the complete solution to the problems of the Florida legislature, we feel justified in setting out briefly some of the changes that need to take place if the legislature is to be fitted for its proper role as an instrument through which we attend to our general arrangements. Few, if any, of these suggestions are new; they are neither radical' nor untried. Some of them would require constitutional amendment to effect; others could be achieved through legislative initiative. Most of them would require strong public backing and a considerable shift in legislative attitudes before they could be adopted.

1. The first and most obvious need is for a more adequate system of reapportionment; a possible system is outlined in Appendix A to this volume.

2. The situation in Florida probably justifies a shift of state elections to odd-numbered years. This might have the salutary effect of broadening the discussion of issues.

3. The frequency and length of sessions should be left more open to the needs and discretion of the legislature.

4. Salaries of members of the legislature should be substantially increased, at least to the amount necessary to allow for service without financial loss.[4]

5. The committee system of the Florida legislature should be extensively overhauled: (a) a great reduction in number is called for; (b) an adequate description of the nature of the legislation that each committee shall handle should be included in the rules; (c) one method of reducing the amount of interpersonal control slightly might be to establish rotating chairmanships, coupled with some form of committee tenure. The system might call for the chairmanship of each committee to go to the senior member of the committee who has not previously served as chairman, except that in the case of freshmen the post could go to the former chairman who had served the longest since his chairmanship; (d) a rule should be developed which would seek to prevent the kind of stacking of committees by interest groups discussed in Chapter 5. There seems to be no adequate reason to fill practically every committee post with a man directly involved in the interests affected; perhaps such a rule could limit the proportions in which interested members (or members from areas where the relevant interest predominates) could serve. A further means of separating the interested from the expert would be to staff the committee (either permanently or temporarily) with individuals qualified to give relatively unbiased, expert advice; (e) more money should be made available, especially in the house of representatives, for adequate personal and committee staffs.

6. The Florida legislature needs to undertake a comprehensive study of its procedures, possibly through the legislative council. Particular attention should be given to the rules. Where possible the rules should be simplified, and in a number of cases clarification is needed.

7. Bills other than general bills should either be precluded from consideration or, where they are deemed absolutely necessary, handled by more generally responsible means.

8. More attention needs to be given to the ethical standards of the legislative assembly. For example, an act probably should be passed

making it a criminal offense for a legislator to receive fees and emoluments from private sources, except in cases in which he makes his living through such fees. Proxy voting in committees should be abolished in the senate and the rules on lobbying should be tightened and made uniform in both houses.

9. Steps are needed to improve the relations between the executive and legislative branches. Better overall co-ordination could be achieved and a more effective consolidation of authority and responsibility developed if all administrative proposals were to pass through the governor's office.[5]

10. The Legislative Council and Reference Bureau should be improved, so that they can function more adequately both in research and in the preparation of a policy program.

In presenting these generalized recommendations we must appear to be somewhat like Alice in Wonderland—the things that have been suggested sound an excellent plan, the only difficulty is in not having the smallest idea how to set about it. At first glance, change may appear not only difficult but virtually impossible to achieve, but there are clouds (perhaps even smaller than a man's hand) which may eventually gather sufficiently to wash out some aspects of the prevailing system.

There are, of course, serious legal obstacles to the alteration of legislative politics in Florida. The constitution, like many of the other state constitutions, does not permit the legislature much flexibility either in the organizational or policy sense, and any attempt to change it is at the mercy of those most satisfied with the status quo. Unfortunately, the practice of tying the legislature's hands through detailed constitutional provisions has such a long history that even proponents of change are timid in the face of proposals to deviate very far from the outlines of the basic law, however rigid it may be. Professor E. E. Schattschneider has pointed out that the United States is the "world's foremost example of government by lawyers";[6] therefore the native American propensity toward legitimation of almost every governmental device by elaborate legalistic pronouncements finds strong support in the practice of having a high proportion of lawyers among governmental personnel. In establishing and maintaining our state political institutions we have paid insufficient attention to Disraeli's aphoristic quip to the effect that "a precedent embalms a principle."

Among other factors, an excess of legalism has made us unaware of the value of extraconstitutional institutions such as the party system, and the absence of party government in Florida is, as we have seen, one of the most important barriers to legislative reform. The inability (and in many cases lack of desire) on the part of the legislature to break the pattern of localism and to perform the task of explaining state-wide issues to the public has worked indirectly to lower the prestige of the legislature, and the loss of prestige has in turn caused a large share of the public to lose interest in the state legislature and to turn elsewhere for a solution to public problems. In the absence of any sort of concept of the general interest such as a party develops, the individual legislator has no incentive to put over the hard facts of political life to the voting public. As candidates the legislators often find it advantageous to play up their opposition to taxes, extol the virtues of the state, and avoid the discussion of the more general problems; so when necessity forces additional taxes and services on the state, the public, not having been adequately prepared for them, tends to castigate the legislature. The consequences of leaving the public out of the decisions on broader aspects of policy in a democracy may be very severe, and not the least of its bad effects is public apathy in the face of the decline of legislative responsibility. We concur with Professor Herman Finer's judgment that responsible government is party government and can add from the Florida experience that deliberate effort to avoid the party struggle is both a symptom and a cause of extensive legislative shortcomings.

If legalism and the lack of a party system are serious drawbacks to changes which might bring the Florida legislature closer to the ideal, there are some offsetting factors. Many of these, such as creeping urbanization, the increasing openness of the fight over apportionment, and the omnipresence of the American representative ideal, have been referred to extensively. To the man of little patience, real political change in a working system may be so gradual as to appear to have no meaning, because it involves a readjustment of institutions and societal attitudes within the framework of a tradition which is both more and less than a rationally understood and operated process.

Nevertheless, very minor surface stirrings may augur disturbances that go very deeply into the system. Within the past five years, for example, the legislature (with popular approval) has made considerable concession to the need for more time, for greater compensation, and for more assistance in carrying out its tasks. In other directions, too, rifts are beginning to appear, although as yet they are very small and may even appear to be covered almost before they show. Thus, although the concern of the Democrats about the growth of Republicanism has thus far resulted only in an attempt to protect the old style of Florida politics, even the awareness of the necessity to do *something* as a unified party could be fraught with meaning for the future. Again, it is true that the legislature has offered more form than substance in its concessions to constitutional revision, and to some this may appear to be a minor tragedy, but the very fact that any action at all was taken is a tribute to the public pressures behind the movement. And there is much evidence to show that the popular forces supporting revision have not been taken in by the substitution of form for substance to the extent that some legislators had thought.

In holding out some hope for an adjustment of the Florida legislative assembly to the politics of the mid-twentieth century, we are neither whistling past the graveyard nor attempting to close on a sweeter note than is recorded on the score. But if democracy is self-corrective, if the states are still viable units, and if our representative tradition is as deep-rooted as we like to think it is, it is high time that the legislature be given an opportunity to resume its full role as the basic representative institution of state government and that its session no longer be looked upon as "a recurrent, unavoidable public calamity."[7]

Appendix A

A Proposed Reapportionment System

THE idea of popular sovereignty is the dominant feature of the American conception of government, and the notion is widely held that the representative assembly, because of its particular organization and functions, is the institution that most appropriately exemplifies this principle. Basic to the latter point of view, however, is the assumption that each individual should participate equally in the selection of representatives unless there are valid reasons for disqualification. Judged by any standard of equality of representation both houses of the Florida legislature are so seriously malapportioned that they seem to constitute an implicit denial of the ideal of popular sovereignty.

Although Florida has never had an apportionment based on the principle of equality, this situation probably worked no great hardship until the recent changes in the ecology of the state began to manifest themselves clearly. In the late nineteenth and early twentieth centuries neither the extreme degree of the disproportions in representation nor the north-south, rural-urban cleavages that exist today were in evidence. It is also unlikely that any substantial change in governmental organization, style of politics, or basic areas of public policy would have resulted from a more equitable reapportionment during that period. If the constitutional promise of popular sovereignty was not completely fulfilled, other factors such as inadequate education, lack of communication media, and racial discrimination were probably more influential in its restraint than the variations in the number of people represented by each senator and representative. Today that position is reversed; it is difficult to think of a single aspect of governmental organization, operation, or policy which is not directly or indirectly influenced by the system of legislative apportionment.

The very fact, however, that the question was not a central problem of Florida government in the earlier period increases its current aggravation. For the obstructive features of the present system and the style of politics that sustains it are products of a lengthy historical experience. Extreme decentralization and local identification of representatives, personalism, suspicion of institutionalization, and antipathy to party organization developed concurrently with and reciprocally influenced the growth of the ideas that county boundaries are sacrosanct in allocating legislative seats, that representation of any county regardless of other factors should not greatly exceed the representation of any other county, and that no county or for that matter no sitting member, should be deprived of a seat as a result of reapportionment. It was out of this experience, in other words, that the restrictions on the possibility of equitable apportionment developed.

Nor do the prospects for change appear too hopeful, except for the recently developed possibility that the case of *Baker* v. *Carr* holds out for judicial correction. Every proposal for reapportionment that has been seriously considered in recent years has been minimal in its anticipated effect on the existing apportionment and has carried over the restrictive constitutional arrangements that make an equitable apportionment impossible. The proponents of change have not taken the initiative in proposing measures based solely on equality of representation; they have usually had to start their bargaining from the narrow concessions offered by their opponents. The resulting legislative settlements inevitably have to be regarded as less than compromise; they are more accurately characterized as capitulation.

It may be argued, of course, that the sociological change that Florida is undergoing will soon overcome the lag in the distribution of political power. It is true that South Florida is gradually moving north and that urbanization is making inroads in many sectors of the state. It is, therefore, possible to envisage a time when these developments may affect the political habits of enough counties to cause a shift away from the present preponderance of rural or small county control. When and if such a change in equilibrium occurs, it may be possible to enact an apportionment plan that will ensure representation on the basis of population.

However, it is well not to be overly optimistic about such eventualities. The present imbalance is so great and the constitutional rigidity so pronounced that even a projection of the current rate of change would be slow to manifest its effects so broadly. In addition, ecological changes will not make their impact felt immediately and directly in areas with long-standing political traditions. As was noted earlier, the present urban areas of North Florida frequently return representatives whose outlook conforms more to the small rural-county type than to the larger county pattern. There are also several institutional factors which help to sustain the identification of the urban representative from these older areas with a rural type of politics. Included among them are the method of selecting legislative leaders, committee organization and membership, the one-party system, and general legislative mores.

Regardless of the pessimism engendered by the present allocation of political power in the Florida legislature, it is still possible to assume that democratic self-correction will take place before conditions become intolerable. One of the few hopeful signs of recent years has been the increasing difficulty of avoiding the eruption of controversy over reapportionment. The fight has been brought entirely into the open. Urban voters are less prone than any underrepresented group of an earlier period to accept under the label of "compromise" formal concessions that have little immediate, and no long-run, effect on the imbalance. Some of the small-county senators and representatives are discovering, too, that their sense of duty will not countenance the obvious tensions between the theory and practice of representative government in contemporary Florida.

It would be impossible, of course, to achieve an equal system of apportionment under the present constitutional formulae even if the movement of population or a break in the opposition to reapportionment would permit the maximum adjustment that the constitution allows. Any legislature of the future that is willing to provide for equal representation will, therefore, be faced with the twofold problem of securing a fair apportionment under prevailing conditions and preventing a natural recurrence of malapportionment at a later period. This apparently can be accomplished only by a constitutional amendment which completely changes the present system. Decennial reapportionment following each federal census and based on its findings would continue to be carried out, but both the basis and method need to be overhauled. The present limits on the number of house seats that may be allocated to a single county could not be retained. In view of the disproportion between the largest (935,047) and the smallest (2,800) county, it is impossible to see how the present guarantee of a member of the house to each county could be continued and an equitable apportionment established without increasing the house of representatives to an unwarrantable size. Similarly, the prohibition against dividing a county in the creation of single-member senatorial districts precludes equal representation in that body and would have to be abolished.

Furthermore, it would be desirable to place the system of apportionment on an automatic basis so that the actual determination of the distribution of representatives and senators would be removed from the discretion of the legislature. The criteria for distributing seats should also be drawn so clearly that any reapportionment act could be tested for validity by simple mathematical computation, thereby facilitating judicial review should. the question of noncompliance with the constitution be raised.

If all or most of these propositions could be agreed to, it would be possible to utilize the mathematical techniques that have been developed in connection with reapportioning seats in the United States House of Representatives. These methods are based on the establishment of priorities for additional seats after the allocation of one seat to each geographical unit which is entitled to representation.[1] Five formulae have been produced which are mathematically correct (i.e., they do not admit of internal contradiction in terms of the proportions they claim to maintain) and one of these—equal proportions—is now required by Congress for use in congressional apportionment. Although each of these formulae is designed to minimize the differences in representation from one area to another, they differ in terms of the standard that each takes as the criterion of equality. However, most competent students of legislation, and indeed, members of Congress, prefer the method of equal proportions because it provides for the smallest possible difference in representation of any two states when measured by both the relative difference in the average population per district and by the relative difference in the individual share in a representative. This preference appears to be based on two factors: the method of equal proportions provides for a minimum inequality of representation in terms of *two* criteria (each of the other methods affords a single criterion), and in most instances mathematical relationships seem to be more accurately expressed in relative rather than in gross or absolute terms. All of the methods can be utilized simply by applying a set series of multipliers to the population of each representative area and establishing a priority table on the basis of the results.

In order to illustrate what might be done in Florida through the use of the equal proportions methods we have appended to this study two tables showing the distribution of seats in the house of representatives under differing circumstances. Table 14 indicates the number of representatives that would be assigned to the counties in houses of various fixed sizes if the present guarantee of one representative to each county is continued. Table 15 lessens the differentiation still further by grouping the counties into multicounty districts prior to the application of the equal proportions formula. Counties are grouped so that no district contains a population (1958 estimates) more than 20 per cent below the natural ratio (43,100) for a representative in a 103 member house. The significant result shown in Table 15 is that 50.5 per cent of the population would elect 52, that is 51 per cent, of the representatives.

It would be feasible to provide a constitutional amendment which would embody the premises on which the apportionment in Table 15 is based and make its effectuation automatic. The amendment could provide, for instance, for the county groupings to be made (with the relative permissible deviation from the natural ratio stipulated) and the equal proportions formula to be applied by an agency other than the legislature. Either an officer of the executive branch—for example, the secretary of state—or a reapportionment commission of some type could be required to make these computations on the basis of each new federal census and to submit the results to the following legislative session. If the legislature should then fail to enact this proposed reapportionment, the latter would go into effect for the next election upon certification by the secretary of state. Since the duties of an executive agency may be compelled by a writ of mandamus and since both legislative enactments and executive actions are reviewable in the courts, the performance of the constitutional mandate on reapportionment could not be avoided with immunity from judicial remedy.

The establishment of an equitable, automatic apportionment plan for the Florida senate could also be achieved without foregoing the single-member district or greatly increasing the size of that body. Perhaps the simplest solution would be to remove the prohibition against dividing a county and add the requirement that the population of any district may not vary from the natural ratio by more than a stipulated percentage.[2] A reapportionment commission could then carry out the actual districting and submit its plan to the legislature under conditions similar to those outlined above for the house.

These suggestions illustrate the fact that, with a little ingenuity, a number of plans can be devised which would automatically provide for decennial reapportionment on an equitable basis and utilize the checks against abuse which are built into the constitutional machinery of American government. The acceptance of such a system would resolve many of the problems that grow out of the plethora of partisan involvements that beset a legislature in allocating its own seats. More than this, the adoption of a plan of the type offered here would help to fulfill a fundamental condition of democracy—the opportunity for the various components of the popular will to secure proportionate expression in the representative assembly. However difficult its achievement may be, this ideal is an abiding standard of the American constitutional tradition.

Table 14
Apportionment of the House of Representatives
By the Method of Equal Proportions
With One Member to Each County (1958 Population Estimates)

County	Population	No. of Seats		
		103 members*	115 members†	125 members‡
1. Dade	846,000	12	15	18
2. Duval	427,200	6	8	9
3. Hillsborough	359,300	5	7	7
4. Pinellas	296,100	4	5	6
5. Broward	265,900	4	5	6
6. Orange	237,600	4	4	5
7. Palm Beach	214,300	3	4	4
8. Polk	176,000	3	3	4
9. Escambia	166,400	3	3	4
10. Volusia	102,100	2	2	2
11. Brevard	86,200	1	2	2
12. Alachua	80,500	1	2	2
13. Leon	78,000	1	1	2
14. Bay	63,600	1	1	1
15. Okaloosa	59,500	1	1	1
16. Sarasota	59,000	1	1	1
17. Manatee	56,300	1	1	1
18. Lake	52,200	1	1	1
19. Marion	47,500	1	1	1
20. Gadsden	46,700	1	1	1
21. Monroe	46,300	1	1	1
22. Seminole	46,200	1	1	1
23. Lee	40,800	1	1	1
24. Jackson	34,100	1	1	1
25. St. Lucie	33,600	1	1	1
26. Putnam	33,500	1	1	1
27. St. Johns	31,300	1	1	1
28. Pasco	30,800	1	1	1
29. Santa Rosa	25,200	1	1	1
30. Indian River	23,100	1	1	1
31. Clay	19,700	1	1	1
32. Columbia	18,600	1	1	1
33. Highlands	17,400	1	1	1
34. Osceola	16,300	1	1	1
35. Nassau	14,900	1	1	1

Table 14—(Continued)

County	Population	No. of Seats		
		103 members*	115 members†	125 members‡
36. Madison	14,200	1	1	1
37. Walton	14,200	1	1	1
38. Suwanee	14,100	1	1	1
39. Taylor	14,000	1	1	1
40. Collier	13,900	1	1	1
41. Hardee	13,600	1	1	1
42. Martin	13,100	1	1	1
43. Bradford	12,200	1	1	1
44. Holmes	11,600	1	1	1
45. Sumter	11,500	1	1	1
46. De Soto	11,000	1	1	1
47. Washington	10,900	1	1	1
48. Levy	9,900	1	1	1
49. Hernando	9,800	1	1	1
50. Jefferson	9,500	1	1	1
51. Union	9,100	1	1	1
52. Gulf	8,900	1	1	1
53. Citrus	8,400	1	1	1
54. Hamilton	8,300	1	1	1
55. Calhoun	7,800	1	1	1
56. Charlotte	7,200	1	1	1
57. Hendry	7,200	1	1	1
58. Baker	6,800	1	1	1
59. Franklin	5,700	1	1	1
60. Flagler	5,300	1	1	1
61. Okeechobee	5,100	1	1	1
62. Wakulla	5,100	1	1	1
63. Dixie	4,400	1	1	1
64. Gilchrist	3,300	1	1	1
65. Glades	3,100	1	1	1
66. Lafayette	2,800	1	1	1
67. Liberty	2,800	1	1	1

*With a 103 member house 22 per cent of the population could elect a majority under the equal proportions formula.
†With a 115 member house 29.4 per cent of the population could elect a majority under the equal proportions formula.
‡With a 125 member house 33.5 per cent of the population could elect a majority under the equal proportions formula.

Table 15

Apportionment of the House of Representatives by the Method of Equal Proportions, Counties Grouped in Districts (No District Below 20 Per Cent of Representative Ratio for 103 Members) 103 Seats*

District	Composition	Population (1958)	No. Seats
1	Dade	846,800	20
2	Duval	427,200	10
3	Hillsborough	359,300	8
4	Pinellas	296,100	7
5	Broward	265,900	6
6	Orange	237,600	6
7	Palm Beach	214,300	5
8	Polk	176,000	4
9	Escambia	166,400	4
10	Volusia	102,100	2
11	Brevard	86,200	2
12	Santa Rosa, Okaloosa	84,700	2
13	Alachua	80,500	2
14	Leon	78,000	2
15	Bay	63,600	2
16	Pasco, Hernando, Citrus, Sumter	60,500	1
17	Sarasota	59,000	1
18	Manatee	56,300	1
19	Lake	52,200	1
20	Clay, St. Johns	51,000	1
21	Marion	47,500	1
22	Gadsden	46,700	1
23	St. Lucie, Martin	46,700	1
24	Monroe	46,300	1
25	Seminole	46,200	1
26	Liberty, Franklin, Wakulla, Gulf, Jefferson, Taylor	46,000	1
27	Baker, Union, Bradford, Nassau	43,000	1
28	Hardee, De Soto, Highlands	42,000	1
29	Jackson, Calhoun	41,900	1
30	Lee	40,800	1
31	Madison, Hamilton, Lafayette, Dixie, Levy	39,600	1
32	Osceola, Indian River	39,400	1
33	Putnam, Flagler	38,600	1
34	Walton, Holmes, Washington	36,700	1
35	Collier, Hendry, Glades, Charlotte, Okeechobee	36,500	1
36	Suwannee, Columbia, Gilchrist	36,000	1

*Under this plan 50.5 per cent of the population would elect 52 representatives—a majority of the house.

Appendix B

The Conservative-Liberal Range

THE following scale represents a "conservative" rank order of the Florida house of representatives (1957 session) in terms of six major legislative issues. Each *x* indicates a conservative vote—that is, conservative in the special Florida sense which we have attempted to develop in Chapters 1 to 4—and each *0* indicates the countervailing "liberal" vote on one of these issues. The six issues are as follows:

1. H.C.R. 174—Interposition—Roll call on motion to defer temporarily. Nays (x) indicate favorable to interposition.
2. H. B. 671—Last Resort—Roll call vote on final passage. Yeas (x) indicate favorable to last resort, under which the public school system could have been closed in event of integration.
3. S. B. 241—Governor's Racial Commission—Roll call on final passage. Nays (x) indicate unfavorable to establishment of governor's commission on race relations.
4. S.B. 48—Small Loans—Roll call on amendment by Hopkins and Turlington to reduce interest on second $300 from 2.5 per cent to 1.5 per cent. Nays (x) indicate support for higher monthly interest rates on small loans.
5. Committee Substitute for H.B. 721—Highway Rights of Way—Roll call on amendment to apply the formula for distributing the seventh cent of the gasoline tax to the allocation to the counties of state highway right of way funds. Yeas (x) indicate opposition to allowing funds to be applied as needed rather than on the basis of a formula dating from the early 1930's.
6. H.J.R. 2116—Revision of the Legislative Article—Roll call on

final passage. Yeas (x) indicate favorable to an unchanged apportionment, since this was the major point in contention over this version.

The difficulties of selecting issues that are representative of the thinking of Florida legislators is greatly complicated by the fact that legislative procedure becomes so complicated that the recorded vote on many issues is meaningless without an understanding of the reason behind each vote of the individual members. Although some allowance must be made for bias, it is thought that the six issues used herein reflect the attitudes of the individual legislators as basically as any we have analyzed and that the spread is fairly wide. The fact that no clear set of issues could be uncovered in the senate which would be suitable to this type of analysis shows the ease with which basic divisions can be played down through procedural involvements. We have taken two votes on straightforward segregation issues (the central social problem of the state) and a third on a question of administrative study and handling of the racial problem, which also involves executive-legislative relations. In addition, questions concerning the regulation of business, finance and taxation (cutting across the rural-urban pattern), and apportionment are included. If the results are not a complete reflection of the legislative line-up, they are at least an illustration of the kind of analysis that has led to some of our conclusions.

Since the scale (Figure 11) could not be arranged in geometric descent by ordering the votes under specific subject-matter columns, footnotes are included to show the issues on which each member deviated from his "normal" voting pattern. The basic rural-urban, North Florida-South Florida division manifests itself quite clearly in this arrangement.

Figure 11
"Conservative" Rank Order
of the Florida House of Representatives, 1957 Session

Name	County	Rural-Urban+ North-South						
Anderson	Jefferson	R - N	x	x	x	x	x	x
Beck	Putnam	R - S	x	x	x	x	x	x
Chaires	Dixie	R - N	x	x	x	x	x	x
Chappell	Marion	U - S	x	x	x	x	x	x
Hathaway	Charlotte	R - S	x	x	x	x	x	x
Jones	Taylor	R - N	x	x	x	x	x	x
Kimbrough	Santa Rosa	R - N	x	x	x	x	x	x
Manning	Holmes	R - N	x	x	x	x	x	x
Mitchell, R. O.	Leon	U - N	x	x	x	x	x	x
Mitchell, Sam	Washington	R - N	x	x	x	x	x	x
O'Neill	Marion	U - S	x	x	x	x	x	x
Peacock	Jackson	R - N	x	x	x	x	x	x
Peavy	Madison	R - N	x	x	x	x	x	x
Peters	Calhoun	R - N	x	x	x	x	x	x
Putnal	Lafayette	R - N	x	x	x	x	x	x
Roberts, H. W.	Suwannee	R - N	x	x	x	x	x	x
Rowell, E. C.	Sumter	R - S	x	x	x	x	x	x
Russ	Wakulla	R - N	x	x	x	x	x	x
Stewart, E. L.	Hendry	R - S	x	x	x	x	x	x
Strickland	Citrus	R - S	x	x	x	x	x	x
Williams, G. W.	Hardee	R - S	x	x	x	x	x	x
Lancaster	Gilchrist	R - N	*	x	x	x	x	x
McAlpin	Hamilton	R - N	*	x	x	x	x	x
Stewart, C. D.	Okaloosa	R - N	*	x	x	x	x	x
Wise	Okaloosa	R - N	*	x	x	x	x	x
Ayers	Hernando	R - S	*	*	x	x	x	x
Conner	Bradford	R - N	*	*	*	x	x	x
Cross	Alachua	U - S	0^4	x	x	x	x	x
Daniel	Lake	U - S	0^4	x	x	x	x	x
Griffin, J. J.	Osceola	R - S	0^4	x	x	x	x	x
Horne	Leon	U - N	0^3	x	x	x	x	x
Marshburn	Levy	R - N	0^5	x	x	x	x	x
Roberts, C. A.	Union	R - N	0^4	x	x	x	x	x
Stone	Escambia	U - N	0^4	x	x	x	x	x
Wadsworth	Flagler	R - S	0^4	x	x	x	x	x
Williams, B. D.	Columbia	R - N	0^5	x	x	x	x	x
Peeples	Glades	R - S	0^5	*	x	x	x	x
Sheppard	Lee	U - S	0^3	*	*	x	x	x
Papy	Monroe	U - S	0^1	*	*	*	x	x
Arrington	Gadsden	R - N	0^3	0^4	x	x	x	x
Duncan	Lake	U - S	0^4	0^5	x	x	x	x
Inman	Gadsden	R - N	0^3	0^4	x	x	x	x

Figure 11—(Continued)

Name	County	Rural-Urban+ North-South						
Livingston	Highlands	R - S	0^1	0^3	x	x	x	x
Mattox	Polk	U - S	0^5	0^6	x	x	x	x
Patton	Franklin	R - N	0^1	0^3	x	x	x	x
Rowell, M. H.	Martin	R - S	0^5	0^6	x	x	x	x
Smith, S. C.	DeSoto	R - S	0^3	0^4	x	x	x	x
Williams, J. R. A.	Pasco	R - S	0^4	0^6	x	x	x	x
Walker	Collier	R - S	0^3	0^6	*	x	x	x
Askins	Nassau	R - N	0^1	0^2	*	x	x	x
Alexander	Liberty	R - N	0^2	0^3	0^5	x	x	x
Beasley	Walton	R - N	0^1	0^2	0^3	x	x	x
Cleveland	Seminole	U - S	0^3	0^4	0^5	x	x	x
Costin	Gulf	R - N	0^2	0^3	0^6	x	x	x
Grimes	Manatee	U - S	0^3	0^4	0^6	x	x	x
Muldrew (Repub.)	Brevard	U - S	0^4	0^5	0^6	x	x	x
Peterson (Repub.)	Pinellas	U - S	0^4	0^5	0^6	x	x	x
Saunders	Clay	R - S	0^3	0^5	0^6	x	x	x
Barron	Bay	U - N	0	0	0	*	x^5	x^6
Crews	Baker	R - N	0	0	0	0	x^5	x^6
Frederick	Seminole	U - S	0	0	0	0	x^1	x^5
Griffin, B. H.	Polk	U - S	0	0	0	0	x^1	x^2
Karl	Volusia	U - S	0	0	0	0	x^4	x^5
Moody	Hillsborough	U - S	0	0	0	0	x^1	x^2
Pratt	Manatee	U - S	0	0	0	0	x^1	x^2
Roberts, E. S.	Palm Beach	U - S	0	0	0	0	x^1	x^5
Shaffer (Repub.)	Pinellas	U - S	0	0	0	0	x^2	x^3
Surles	Polk	U - S	0	0	0	0	x^1	x^2
Sweeny	Volusia	U - S	0	0	0	0	x^2	x^4
Usina	St. Johns	U - S	0	0	0	0	x^1	x^6
Zelmenovitz	Okeechobee	R - S	0	0	0	0	x^4	x^6
Porter	Monroe	U - S	0	0	0	0	*	x^5
Shipp	Jackson	R - N	0	0	0	0	*	x^4
Blank	Palm Beach	U - S	0	0	0	0	0	x^1
Carney (Repub.)	Pinellas	U - S	0	0	0	0	0	x^5
Harris	Bay	U - N	0	0	0	0	0	x^5
Mathews	Duval	U - S	0	0	0	0	0	x^1
Sutton	Orange	U - S	0	0	0	0	0	x^1
Weinstein	St. Johns	U - S	0	0	0	0	0	x^4
Bartholomew (Repub.)	Sarasota	U - S	0	0	0	0	0	*
Vocelle	Indian River	R - S	0	0	0	0	0	*
Westberry	Duval	U - S	0	0	0	0	0	*
Gibbons	Hillsborough	U - S	0	0	0	0	0	0
Herrell	Dade	U - S	0	0	0	0	0	0
Hollohan	Dade	U - S	0	0	0	0	0	0
Hopkins	Escambia	U - N	0	0	0	0	0	0

Figure 11—(Continued)

Name	County	Rural-Urban+ North-South						
Land	Orange	U - S	0	0	0	0	0	0
Maness	Duval	U - S	0	0	0	0	0	0
Mann	Hillsborough	U - S	0	0	0	0	0	0
Musselman	Broward	U - S	0	0	0	0	0	0
Orr	Dade	U - S	0	0	0	0	0	0
Ryan	Broward	U - S	0	0	0	0	0	0
Smith, R. J.	St. Lucie	U - S	0	0	0	0	0	0
Turlington	Alachua	U - S	0	0	0	0	0	0
Youngberg (Repub.)	Sarasota	U - S	0	0	0	0	0	0

[1]Interposition.
[2]Last Resort.
[3]Governor's Racial Commission.
[4]Small Loans.
[5]Highway Rights of Way.
[6]Legislative Article Revision.
+Classifications: U-Urban, R-Rural, N-North, S-South (based on classification explained in Figure 5).
*Not Voting.

Notes

Chapter II

[1]V. O. Key, *Southern Politics in State and Nation* (New York, 1950), 82.

[2]The actual vote was: Eisenhower, 53,481; Stephenson, 53,127. See Ray A. Gray, Sec. of State (comp.), *Tabulation of Official Votes Cast in the General Election* (Florida, Nov. 6, 1956), 1.

[3]H. D. Price, *The Negro and Southern Politics* (New York, 1957).

[4]*Ibid.,* map, 101.

[5]Herbert Doherty, Jr., "Liberal and Conservative Voting Patterns in Florida," *Journal of Politics,* XIV, No. 3 (1952), 403-15.

[6]Price, *The Negro and Southern Politics,* 44.

[7]House Concurrent Resolution No. 174 (1957); although the record vote in the senate was twenty-one to seventeen, Sen. Pope's "nay" was changed from an "aye" in order to put him on the prevailing side, so that he could move for a reconsideration of the vote—a motion which can only be put by a member of the winning side and which automatically carries the matter over to the succeeding legislative day. See Orlando *Sentinel,* April 18, 1957.

[8]Senate Bill 9-X (1955 special session).

[9]House Bill 6-X (1955 special session).

[10]Key, *Southern Politics,* 102 f.

[11]Tampa *Tribune,* April 4, 1957, p. 1.

[12]E. E. Schattschneider, *Party Government* (New York, 1942), 193.

[13]Key, *Southern Politics,* 94 ff.

[14]Price, *Negro and Southern Politics,* 83.

[15]*Ibid.,* 95-96.

[16]Jasper Berry Shannon, *Toward a New Politics in the South* (Knoxville, 1949), 14-15.

[17]Price, *Negro and Southern Politics,* 82-83; much of this analysis is derived from Price's perceptive study.

[18]See n. 2, *supra.*

[19]Price, *Negro and Southern Politics,* 75 ff.

[20]*Ibid.,* 60 ff.

[21]*Ibid.,* 106.

[22]Bryant moved to revert to the consideration of the introduction of house bills and resolutions so that he could introduce the interposition resolution. However, Rep. Tom Beasley forestalled this by moving successfully for a

fifteen-minute recess, during which the governor's adjournment order was prepared. See *Journal of the House of Representatives, State of Florida* (Special Session, 1956), August 1, 1956, 173, 177. Hereinafter cited as House *Journal.*

[23]House Concurrent Resolution No. 174 (1957). Hereinafter cited as H. C. R.

[24]House Bills Nos. 523-528; hereinafter cited as H. B.; Senate Bills Nos. 345-350 (1957); hereinafter cited as S. B.

[25]H. B. No. 671; S. B. No. 331 (1957).

[26]He did veto the "last resort" school closing bill (H. B. No. 671; S. B. No. 331); the veto message is contained in the House *Journal* (1957) for June 7, 1957.

[27]Data are from *The Florida Sheriff, 1957,* but since the information contained therein is not always comparable for each member of the legislature there is a probability that some members have held county offices which are not listed in the source.

[28]Shannon, *Toward a New Politics,* 38-53.

[29]*Ibid.,* 44-45.

[30]*Ibid.,* 45.

[31]*Ibid.,* 47.

[32]*Ibid.,* 48.

[33]*Ibid.,* 50.

[34]*Ibid.,* 50.

[35]H. B. Nos. 452, 461, 684; S. B. Nos. 276, 277 (1957).

[36]Committee Substitute for H. B. No. 721 (1957).

[37]H. B. No. 871 (1957); it is fair to add that the law was strengthened in 1959.

Chapter III

[1]*Constitution of the State of Florida, 1885,* Art. VII, sec. 3; hereinafter cited as *Constitution.*

[2]*Ibid.,* Art. VII, sec. 4.

[3]*Ibid.,* Art. VII, sec. 3.

[4]Manning J. Dauer and Robert G. Kelsay, "Unrepresentative States," *National Municipal Review,* Dec., 1955, pp. 572-74. A composite ranking is more interesting, perhaps, for its symptomatic revelations than for any other reason because a serious distortion in either house can serve as a barrier to the passage of legislation. Even so, one well-apportioned house in a bicameral system may have important effects on both the legislative activities of its sister chamber and in exerting pressure to secure reapportionment in the other house.

[5]For instance, Brown v. Saunders, 159 Va. 28, 166 S.E. 105 (1932); Sherrill v. O'Brien, 188 N.Y. 185, 81 N.E. 124 (1907); Shoemaker v. Lawrence, 31 Pa. D. & C. 681 (1938); Tishman v. Sprague, 293 N.Y. 42, 55 N.E. 2d 858 (1944); Donovan v. Holzman, 8 Ill. 2d 87, 132 N.E. 2d 501.

[6]See Fergus v. Marks, 321 Ill. 510, 152 N.E. 557 (1926); State *ex rel*

Martin v. Zimmerman, 249 Wis. 101, 23 N.W. 2d 610 (1946); Fergus v. Kinney, 333 Ill. 437, 164 N.E. 665 (1928); People *ex rel* Fergus v. Blackwell, 342 Ill. 223, 173 N.E. 750 (1930); Waid v. Pool, 255 Ala. 441, 51 So. 2d 869 (1951).

[7]Courts are authorized to compel (or have compelled) reapportionment in Arkansas, Missouri, Ohio, Oregon, Texas, Washington, Hawaii, and Alaska. Information from Anthony Lewis, "Legislative Apportionment and The Federal Courts," *Harvard Law Review,* LXXI, No. 6 (April, 1958), 1089.

[8]Lewis, "Legislative Apportionment," *loc. cit.,* 1091.

[9]Baker v. Carr, 82 S. Ct. 691 (1962).

[10]See Jacksonville *Florida Times-Union,* April 7, 1959; New York *Times,* October 11, 1959, p. 44.

[11]New York *Times,* May 14, 1962, pp. 1, 20.

[12]For a description of these early developments, see Dorothy Dodd (ed.), *Florida Becomes a State,* with a foreword by W. T. Cash, (Tallahassee, Florida, 1945), 37.

[13]*Constitution of the State of Florida, 1838,* Art. IX.

[14]A more detailed acount of these historical developments is to be found in: Douglas S. Gatlin and Bruce B. Mason, *Reapportionment: It's History in Florida {sic}* ("Civic Information Series," No. 23 [University of Florida: Public Administration Clearing Service, 1956]), 6.

[15]Bruce B. Mason and Penrose Jackson (eds.), *Reports of the Governor's Citizens' Committees* ("Studies in Public Administration," No. 15 [University of Florida: Public Administration Clearing Service, 1956]), 13-26.

[16]*Report of the Secretary of State of the State of Florida,* 1955-56, pp. 88-389.

[17]Even this measure *(Laws of Florida,* Extraordinary Session, 1955, chap. 31378) was not allowed to have effect without extensive controversy. The representatives from Brevard County brought suit testing the constitutionality of the act on the grounds that the reapportionment of the house was inoperative until the senate was reapportioned in accordance with Art. VII, sec. 3 of the constitution. The circuit court ruled that the house apportionment act was constitutional and the decision was upheld by the supreme court; Brewer v. Gray, Fla., 86 So. 2d 799 (1956).

[18]At one point certain legislators publicly stated that the gubernatorial veto power did not extend to reapportionment legislation, whereupon the governor requested an advisory opinion on the subject from the Florida Supreme Court. In a four to one opinion the court advised that the veto was operative, Fla., 81 So. 2d 782 (1956).

[19]Fla., 81 So. 2d 782 (1956).

[20]Fla., 88 So. 2d 131 (1956).

[21]House *Journal* (Extraordinary Session, 1955-1956), 48.

[22]*Ibid.,* 119-20.

[23]*Ibid.,* 114.

[24]Messages of Governor LeRoy Collins to the joint session of the senate and house of representatives of the state of Florida, Tallahassee, April 2, 1957.

[25]Florida Constitution Advisory Commission, *Recommended Constitution for Florida,* Art. III, sec. 4, 5, 6, 7, 8.

[26]*Revised Florida Constitution Proposed by the Legislature and Explanation of Changes* (Tallahassee: Issued by the Secretary of State, undated), Art. III.

[27]Rivera-Cruz v. Gray; Pope v. Gray, 104 So. 2d 501 (Fla. 1958). In restraining the placement of the constitutional proposals on the ballot the Florida Supreme Court held that the commission-legislative method of revision was an improper circumvention of the constitutional requirement that complete revision take place through a convention and that the "daisy-chain" technique eliminated the right of the people to originate revision.

[28]Senate Joint Resolution No. 660 (1959); hereinafter cited as S. J. R.

[29]Designation of an amendment as an emergency measure requires approval of three-fourths of the elected members of each house; *Constitution*, Art. XVII, sec. 3.

[30]S. J. R. No. 660 (1959).

[31]Quoted in St. Petersburg *Times*, May 5, 1959, p. 9-A.

[32]John M. Maclachlan, *Florida's Population, 1920-1950* ("Civic Information Series," No. 11 [University of Florida: Public Administration Clearing Service, 1952]), 1.

[33]For a clever turning of the tables see: Richard L. Neuberger, "The Country Slicker Versus the City Yokel," *New York Times Magazine*, July 31, 1949, pp. 17, 36 ff.

[34]Figures on personal income are either taken directly or adapted from: Wylie Kilpatrick, "Personal Income Received in Florida Counties: 1957," *Economic Leaflets* (University of Florida: Bureau of Economic and Business Research), XVIII, No. 2 (Feb., 1959).

[35]The concept of *anomie* is used here in the sense that it was developed by Durkheim and applied to contemporary politics by Sebastian DeGrazia in *The Political Comunity, A Study of Anomie* (Chicago, 1948); i.e., to denote a situation in which diversity becomes so complete as to make for a disintegrated social condition with no apparent common purpose.

[36]Much consideration has been given by some Democratic members of the legislature to the problem of controlling the growth of the Republican party in Florida, and one of the fears of reapportionment has been that it would increase the size of the Republican delegation because the strength of the party is in the more populous, underrepresented areas. The fear is not of a Republican program (except on issues of governmental organization the differences do not seem very great in Florida), but of the institutionalizing effect that the development of the party might have on Florida politics. The replacement of interpersonal ties by organization and the thrashing out of broader issues within the organization rather than suppression through exclusive localism would radically alter politics as the present in-group knows it.

[37]The large-county representative in Florida is often strongly business-oriented so that even if the present tacit community of interest between the business groups and small-county representatives should be upset by reapportionment, no hardship would be worked on the business interests. At present, certainly, organized labor gives no indication of being able to make appreciable direct gains in the representative sense even if the number of urban seats should be vastly enlarged. For an excellent discussion of the

way in which this particular question is affected by malapportionment in many states see: Gordon E. Baker, *Rural versus Urban Political Power* (New York, 1955), 24. Baker's study is probably the most comprehensive treatment available of the complex and interrelated consequences of malapportionment.

[38]Charles W. Shull, "Political and Partisan Implications of State Legislative Apportionment," *Law and Contemporary Problems* (Spring, 1952), 431-37. It is interesting to note that the respondents to the last question gave the following as the shifts most likely to occur as a result of reapportionment in Florida: the political balance would shift from North to South Florida, tax distribution would be affected, and the possibility of executive reorganization and general constitutional revision would be enhanced.

[39]The popular vote on the issue was interesting in itself, especially since Florida was the first state to enact a "right-to-work" law. The vote on the amendment was small relative to the vote on candidates in the general election but large compared to votes on other amendments, the margin of victory was narrow (about 25,000 in a total vote of 270,000) and the urban areas (where the issue was probably better understood) voted very narrowly against the proposal, while two-thirds of the rural vote favored it. See: John G. Shott, *How "Right-to-Work" Laws are Passed: Florida Sets the Pattern* (Washington, 1956), especially pp. 38-39.

[40]See Appendix A for a proposal of a method of systematic reapportionment.

Chapter IV

[1]The main outlines of the suffrage qualifications appear in the *Constitution,* Art. VI. After each biennial session of the legislature, the secretary of state issues a *Compilation of the Election Laws of the State of Florida* containing the entire body of law regulating elections. For a discussion of most aspects of suffrage and elections in Florida, see Bruce B. Mason, *Florida Voter's Guide* ("Civic Information Series," No. 21 [University of Florida: Public Administration Clearing Service, 1955]).

[2]Committee Substitute for S. B. 105 (1957).

[3]S. B. 3 (1959).

[4]*Laws of Florida,* General Laws (1951), Vol. I, chap. 26819. For a good summary of the law and its early effects on statewide campaigns see: Elston E. Roady, "Florida's New Campaign Expense Law and the 1952 Democratic Gubernatorial Primaries," *American Political Science Review,* XLVIII (1954), 465-76.

[5]Prior to 1957, the candidate for nomination had to swear or affirm that he had voted for and would vote for a majority of his party's candidates. The change was one of a series of measures to strengthen the Democratic party and prevent raids on it by "new" Republicans. The Democratic party first attempted to get through a loyalty oath based on 100 per cent support for party candidates, a party loyalty oath for all members of the party, and an increase in filing fees from 3 to 4 per cent. The latter measures failed, and even when the senate had watered down the candidates' loyalty oath

to 90 per cent, it did not at first pass in the house of representatives. The legislative chairman of the State Democratic Executive Committee presided over a Democratic house caucus on May 27 and strongly criticized the attitude of the house towards the Democratic party. The following day the house passed the 90 per cent candidate's oath bill (S. B. 277).

[6]Requirements reduced from one-eighth to 5 per cent in 1957 (S. B. 105).

[7]Wilson K. Doyle, Angus M. Laird, and S. Sherman Weiss, *The Government and Administration of Florida* (New York, 1954), 50-51.

[8]In 1957 these were: three house seats from Pinellas (St. Petersburg), two house seats from Sarasota, a house seat from Brevard, and the senate seat from Pinellas. The Brevard seat was a 1956 acquisition; a Republican was elected from Orange for the 1955 session, but the Democrats recaptured the seat in 1956. The 1961 seats were the five from Pinellas and Sarasota plus one each from Orange and Charlotte.

[9]The Republicans formulated a legislative program for the 1957 session, consisting mainly of "good government" proposals such as constitutional revision, but also including measures such as a severance tax, which by Florida standards is very liberal. In fact the best hope for Republican advancement in the state would seem to lie in taking a liberal stand on issues of governmental reorganization and civil liberties, thereby challenging Democratic conservatism in these areas without compromising the general Republican stand on economic matters.

[10]In addition to measures described above, several other attempts were made to control formal defection from the Democratic ranks, including a proposed time limit on changes in party registration.

[11]See: Belle Zeller (ed.), *American State Legislatures* (New York, 1954), 66-67.

[12]Although the figures on tenure and turnover given here are for the 1957 session only, they seem to follow the general trend of the post-war period. See the chart on previous legislative experience of Florida legislators in Lorace E. Catterson, "The Legislative Process in Florida," *Florida State University Studies,* Number Four (Tallahassee, Florida, 1951), 85.

[13]Former Senator Harry King, the man in question, was convicted and sentenced to a term in prison by the lower courts.

[14]Dixie, Franklin, Gulf, Holmes, Lafayette, Liberty, Martin, and Suwannee.

[15]Alachua, Brevard, Broward, Dade, Hillsborough, Palm Beach, Pinellas, Polk, and Sarasota.

[16]The data summarized here were taken from registration and election data tables prepared for this study which are, unfortunately, too cumbersome for reproduction here. The data which went into these tables were compiled from the files in the office of the secretary of state and from his biennial reports.

[17]It is preferable to be able to tie local and state-wide issues together. A typical appeal (based on actual campaign literature) includes a proposal to improve state buildings (with emphasis on the type of institution prevalent in the county), a specified increase in welfare payments, a program for improvement of the tourist trade (which might also suggest the build-up of small business), a school improvement plank, and a plan for develop-

ment of recreation areas (preferably including the fishing sites in the particular county).

[18]Two bitter newspaper condemnations of senators in the 1957 session were made by the Tampa *Tribune* and the Orlando *Sentinel*. The former's action was in relation to a bill allowing the city of Tampa to condemn for public use some riverfront property of the Atlantic Coast Line Railroad. The paper published at least two strongly worded editorials (April 5 and April 7, 1957) deploring Sen. Kickliter's proposal to attach a provision to the bill requiring a referendum to be held in two and one-half years. Since this was an old issue, it was also subtly intimated by the paper that favoritism towards the Atlantic Coast Line in the past had cost other legislators their seats. The *Sentinel* headed an editorial of May 3, "Senator Rodgers Digs His Own Political Grave"; the reference was to the senator's vote on a bill (which was being pressed by private power companies) providing for taxation of publicly-owned power facilities located outside the county served by them. Orlando had arranged for an auxiliary power plant in Brevard County which, by agreement, was not taxable by the latter. The senator concerned had tried without success to obtain permission from the senate to reconsider his vote on the measure, but the senate, in an unprecedented action, did pass a resolution commending Sen. Rodgers in order, as one fellow-senator put it, "to soften the blow."

[19]The data digested here were taken from the campaign finance reports in the office of the secretary of state. Full information has been tabulated and analyzed, but the results are too voluminous for complete reproduction here. Information for 1958 and 1960 was not available; there is no reason to think expenditures have changed greatly.

[20]Henry J. Ford, *Representative Government* (New York, 1924), 154.

[21]The following personal data were computed mainly from the biographical information in *The Florida Sheriff, 1957,* an annual publication of the Florida Sheriffs Association, Inc., together with the scattered newspaper reports. Allen Morris took a poll of the personal characteristics of the house members and reported the results in his column "Cracker Politics," St. Petersburg *Times,* April 7, 1957. His totals vary slightly from some of those offered here. It is our feeling that these figures are average for recent sessions.

[22]Morris's figures on the house, n. 21, *supra,* are somewhat more complete than those reported in *The Florida Sheriff.* He discovered, among a scattering of others, twenty-eight Baptists, twenty-four Methodists, twelve Presbyterians, eight Episcopalians, and six Catholics. Morris found it "politically astounding" that five members reported no religious affiliation. In the senate, according to our computation, there were fifteen Baptists, nine Methodists, five Episcopalians, three Presbyterians, one Catholic, one member of the Christian Church, and four unreported.

[23]Quoted in the *Florida Times-Union,* March 8, 1957.

[24]Jim Hardee, "He'd Rather Be Governor Than Anything Else in the World," Orlando *Sentinel Florida Magazine,* May 5, 1957, p. 5-E. Interestingly enough Beasley went on to say that he thought the governor's first duty was to the state as a whole.

[25]Tampa *Tribune,* April 28, 1957; Hopkins did run in the 1958 election for Beall's seat and was defeated.

[26]John McDermott's column in the Miami *Herald,* April 28, 1957.

[27]There is an excellent description in W. J. Cash, *The Mind of the South* (New York, 1941), especially Book II, chap. 1, of the way in which the Negro question was used by the would-be Southern Bourbons after the Civil War to prevent the discontent of the hill farmer from manifesting itself in political mass movements. Some analogy may be drawn between these practices and the technique of influence described here.

[28]These awards are based on "outstanding service to all of Florida rather than only the confines of his own district or section, . . . [and] the personal and public integrity of the recipient as well as ability and courage in promoting progressive legislation" determines the choice. Winners are selected by secret ballot of the newspaper, radio, and television reporters and the editors of the daily newspapers in the state. See the St. Petersburg *Times,* March 31, 1957, sec. D.

[29]See the profile by Lowell Brandle, "Voice of Valor" in the magazine section of the Miami *Herald,* March 31, 1957. Orr was defeated in 1958 for re-election.

Chapter V

[1]*Constitution,* Art. III, sec. 2.

[2]Zeller (ed.), *American State Legislatures,* 93.

[3]The budget for the 1957 legislature was $1,400,000 out of a total state budget approximating $700,000,000; see: Tampa *Tribune,* April 28, 1957.

[4]*Constitution,* Art. III, sec. 2; in 1957 the legislature extended the session one week, adjourning June 8.

[5]*Constitution,* Art. III, sec. 2.

[6]*Ibid.*

[7]*Ibid.; Constitution,* Art. IV, sec. 8.

[8]*Constitution,* Art. VII, sec. 3.

[9]*Constitution,* Art. III, sec. 29.

[10]Although Sen. Harry King of Polk County was originally chosen as 1957 president, he failed of re-election to the senate and Sen. William Shands of Alachua replaced him.

[11]Jim Hardee in Orlando *Sentinel,* April 14, 1957. It also seems possible that the failure of the 1957 nominee to be re-elected, which forced a second selection by all the thirty-seven Democratic senators, may have set a precedent.

[12]*Rules and Manual of the House of Representatives,* House Rule No. 22 (1957), 9; hereinafter cited as House Rule.

[13]*Ibid.,* 53.

[14]Senate Rule No. 4; House Rule No. 1 (1957).

[15]Robert Luce, *Legislative Procedure* (Boston, 1922), 455.

[16]It should also be noted that much Florida revenue is dedicated to the use of the counties, for various purposes such as highways, in fixed proportions which cannot be altered by the appropriations committees.

[17]When chided on the floor of the house about being chairman of the aeronautics committee in 1957 (its name had been changed from "aviation"), Henry Land replied that the aeronautics committee was simply the old aviation committee "cleaned up."

[18]Five members of the House Citrus Committee in 1957 listed themselves as citrus growers; the number is actually probably somewhat higher.

[19]*Florida Times-Union,* May 9, 1957.

[20]House Rule No. 47 (1957).

[21]See Chapter 8 on lobbying for discussion of these bills; Senate Rules Nos. 32 and 53 (1957).

[22]House Rule No. 27 (1957).

[23]Senate Rule No. 66 (1957).

[24]See Tampa *Tribune,* April 4, 1957; House Rule No. 64; St. Petersburg *Times,* April 4, 1957; Senate Rule No. 58 (1957).

[25]Tampa *Tribune,* April 4, 1957.

[26]Cited in Luce, *Legislative Procedure,* 478.

[27]House Rule No. 70; Senate Rule No. 51 (1957).

[28]St. Petersburg *Times,* April 4, 1957.

[29]See House Rule No. 75 (1957).

[30]Zeller (ed.), *American State Legislatures,* 95.

[31]Luce, *Legislative Procedure,* 122.

[32]House Rule No. 67 (1957); in the 1955 session there were fifty-six committees with 599 seats, an average of well above six for each member.

[33]Since the 1955 senate had only 38 committees, totaling 346 seats, the average senator held about 9.5 committee assignments.

[34]St. Petersburg *Times,* April 4, 1957.

[35]Doyle, Laird, and Weiss, *Government and Administration of Florida,* 62.

[36]Zeller (ed.), *American State Legislatures,* 125.

[37]Doyle, Laird, and Weiss, *Government and Administration of Florida,* 63 f.; see Jacksonville *Florida Times-Union,* March 7, 1957.

[38]Industrial fumes, drugs designed to avert mental illness, the milk commission, the poultry industry, and the state's tax structure.

[39]See Doyle, Laird, and Weiss, *Government and Administration of Florida,* 79-81; *Laws of Florida,* General Laws (1949), Vol. I, chap. 25369.

[40]House Rule No. 25 (1957).

[41]Zeller (ed.), *American State Legislatures,* 128.

[42]*Ibid.,* 133-34.

[43]Doyle, Laird, and Weiss, *Government and Administration of Florida,* 66-67.

[44]See the summary of qualifications for a bill-drafter in Zeller (ed.), *American State Legislatures,* 144-45.

[45]Florida Statutes Annotated, sec. 16:44; hereinafter cited as Fla. Stat. Annot.

[46]See S. B. No. 38-XX (1956 Special Session); S. B. No. 347 (1957).

[47]It was so described in newspaper articles; see Orlando *Sentinel,* May 7 and 8, 1957, for examples; it apparently had subpoena powers, see Miami *Herald,* May 5, 1957.

[48]See Gainesville *Sun,* July 28, 1957.

[49]*Constitution,* Art. III, sec. 29.

Chapter VI

[1]For all members except the holdover senators this roll is the one prepared by the secretary of state in certification of the election returns.

[2]House Rule 28 (1957).

[3]Senate Rule 14 (1957).

[4]Senate Rule 15; House Rule 42 (1957).

[5]In the house this rule is applicable also to extended sessions and special sessions convened by the governor.

[6]*Constitution,* Art. III, secs. 12-19.

[7]Although there is no rule against reintroducing a defeated bill, there are precedents for refusing to consider bills of the same substance as one already rejected. See the separately printed *Rules and Manual of the House of Representatives of the State of Florida,* 1957, which contains a section on "Significant Precedents in the House of Representatives" compiled by Allen Morris, especially precedents 7 and 8, pp. 60-61. It is not unusual, however, for bills varying only slightly in content to be introduced simultaneously.

[8]House Rule 25 (1957) permits bills to be introduced into the house by the legislative council without further sponsorship by a member of the house. Senate Rule 32 (1957) specifies that standing committees may introduce bills, and if a bill is one within the introducing committee's competence it may go directly on the calendar; House Rule 47 (1957) contains a similar provision.

[9]Senate Rule 33 (1957).

[10]The number of copies and certain other requirements vary slightly in the case of measures other than bills.

[11]Senate Rule 32 (1957).

[12]Printing of bills is independent of the legislative process and the absence of a printed copy cannot be used to delay the progress of a bill.

[13]Senate Rule 53 (1957).

[14]House Rule 47 (1957).

[15]House Rule 68 (1957).

[16]Amendment on third reading requires a two-thirds vote in the house and unanimous consent in the senate.

[17]House Rule 37 (1957).

[18]In an article in the St. Petersburg *Times* of March 24, 1957, Frank Trippett offered an amusing glossary of the more hackneyed cliches which have become standard legislative language in Florida. He notes, for example, that the phrase, "would you believe me if I told you . . . ,"may fairly be interpreted to mean, "could you conceivably be gullible enough to swallow the fictions I am about to foist on this body." By the same token, "I'm going to vote for this bill, but . . ." means, according to Trippett, that "the legislator has made a pledge to win a friend, but has arranged for other of his colleagues to bury the legislation forever."

[19]Both houses also permit a standing vote if a question is raised regarding a voice vote, but since it takes only five members to call for a record vote the standing vote is seldom, if ever, used.

[20]House Rule 31; Senate Rule 11 (1957). Both houses also have strict

rules compelling attendance of all members at each session. Members may, of course, request permission to be absent. As a matter of fact, there is no real problem of absenteeism in the Florida legislature.

[21]The house rule on reconsideration (House Rule 38 [1957]) is fairly strict: no motion to reconsider a secondary matter is permitted to remove the main question from consideration by the house, and a motion to reconsider a collateral matter must be decided at once and is out of order once the house has passed from the collateral matter to other business connected with the main question.

[22]Senate Rule 47 (1957).

[23]House rules require that all general bills and joint resolutions, whether amended or not, be referred to the engrossing clerk for examination. If no amendments have been adopted the measure may be returned as engrossed without being rewritten (House Rule 51 [1957]). In the senate, bills may be placed on the calendar for third reading as engrossed without reference to the engrossing secretary (Senate Rule 39 [1957]). When one house amends the bills of the other, the amendments are separately retyped and not incorporated into the body of the bill.

[24]James W. Ayers, "Local Legislation for Florida Municipalities" (Master's thesis, Florida State University, 1953), 31.

[25]Power to draft charters and amend them locally (thus providing a limited form of legislative home rule) dates from 1915: Laws of Florida, 1915, chap. 6940.

[26]Manning J. Dauer and George John Miller, "Municipal Charters in Florida: Law and Drafting," University of Florida Law Review (Fall, 1953), 430.

[27]Constitution, Art. III, sec. 24.

[28]Manning J. Dauer and William C. Havard, "The Florida Constitution of 1885—A Critique," University of Florida Law Review (Spring, 1955), 63.

[29]Constitution, Art. III, sec. 20.

[30]Constitution, Art. III, sec. 21.

[31]Constitution, Art. VIII, sec. 11.

Chapter VII

[1]Alexis de Tocqueville, Democracy in America, ed. Phillips Bradley (Vintage ed.; 2 vols.; New York, 1954) I, 126.

[2]Constitution, Art. III, sec. 28.

[3]Constitution, Art. IV, sec. 18.

[4]Constitution, Art. IV, sec. 9.

[5]Constitution, Art. IV, sec. 7, 16.

[6]Constitution, Art. IV, sec. 15.

[7]Constitution, Art. IV, sec. 2.

[8]Constitution, Art. IV, sec. 5, 27.

[9]Coleman B. Ransone, The Office of Governor in the South (University, Ala., 1951), 79.

[10]Ibid.

[11]Fla. Stats. Annot., chap. 110.06.

[12]Florida Highway Code of 1955, sec. 31.

[13]*Constitution*, Art. IV, sec. 17.

[14]*Constitution*, Art. XII, sec. 3.

[15]*Constitution*, Art. IV, sec. 12.

[16]*Constitution*, Art. IX, sec. 16 (b). This board administers the parcelling out of two cents of the state gasoline tax.

[17]Fla. Stats. Annot., chap. 216.01.

[18]*Ibid.*, chap. 373.01.

[19]*Ibid.*, chap. 321.02.

[20]*Ibid.*, chap. 253.02.

[21]S. B. 217 (1957).

[22]Fla. Stats. Annot., chap. 517.03; the governor is not even a member of this agency.

[23]Ransone, *Office of Governor in the South*, 67.

[24]*Ibid.*, 69.

[25]*Ibid.*

[26]*Constitution*, Art. IV, sec. 6.

[27]Zeller (ed.), *American State Legislatures*, 173.

[28]*Ibid.*, 173-74.

[29]House Rule No. 47 (1957).

[30]Senate Rule No. 53 (1957).

[31]See Zeller (ed.), *American State Legislatures*, 176-77.

[32]*Constitution*, Art. IX, sec. 16.

[33]Doyle, Laird, and Weiss, *Government and Administration of Florida*, 113-14, treat briefly the development of the constitutional and statutory earmarking of the gasoline tax. The motor vehicle license tax is also partly dedicated as are the cigarette tax, the intangibles tax, the insurance premiums tax, and the citrus tax; see *ibid.*, 114-20.

[34]Zeller (ed.), *American State Legislatures*, 179.

[35]See Zeller (ed.), *American State Legislatures*, 182-83; and Doyle, Laird, and Weiss, *Government and Administration of Florida*, 136-38. For a statement of the need of budget execution review, see Zeller, *supra.*, 180-82, for a brief description of Florida legislative practice, see Doyle, Laird, and Weiss, *supra.*, 128-29.

[36]See Zeller (ed.), *supra.*, 185-86.

Chapter VIII

[1]Arthur F. Bentley, *The Process of Government*, as quoted in David B. Truman, *The Governmental Process* (New York, 1951), 263.

[2]*Ibid.*, 321.

[3]Truman, *Governmental Process*, 325.

[4]Dayton D. McKean, *Pressures on the Legislature of New Jersey*, as paraphased in Truman, *Governmental Process*, 334.

[5]*Ibid.*, 340.

[6]*Ibid.*, 345.

[7]Belle Zeller, *Pressure Politics in New York* (New York, 1937), 275.

[8]For instance, see *Florida Times-Union*, May 9, 1957 and May 14, 1957.

[9]S. B. 1035, 1036, and 1037 (May 16, 1957).

[10]George B. Galloway, *The Legislative Process in Congress* (New York, 1955), 509.

[11]Statistics compiled from *The Florida Sheriff, 1957*.

[12]Alexander Hamilton, James Madison, and John Jay, *The Federalist* (Modern Library ed.; New York, 1937), No. 10, p. 56.

[13]Orlando *Sentinel*, April 14, 1957.

[14]Tampa *Tribune*, May 8, 1957; *Wall Street Journal*, June 5, 1957, p. 1.

[15]Truman, *Governmental Process*, 265.

[16]Galloway, *Legislative Process in Congress*, 513.

[17]These figures were compiled from the House *Journal*, April 8, 15, 22, 29; May 6, 13, 20, 27; and June 4, 1957. Due to difficulties of classification and interpretation of the data, the figures are approximate rather than precise.

[18]The atmosphere of the legislature was such that the reception of NAACP delegates would not have been friendly and might have harmed rather than helped the group. There appear to be circumstances in which it is wiser *not* to lobby.

[19]*Wall Street Journal*, June 5, 1957, p. 1.

[20]Truman, *Governmental Process*, 352.

[21]*Ibid.*

[22]*Ibid.*, 353.

[23]*Ibid.*, 354.

[24]H. B. No. 75, S. B. No. 59; and H. B. No. 367, S. B. No. 217 (all 1957).

[25]Jim Hardee in Orlando *Sentinel*, June 16, 1957.

[26]Cited in Truman, *Governmental Process*, 355.

[27]John McDermott in Miami *Herald*, April 28, 1957.

[28]Allen Morris in St. Petersburg *Times*, April 21, 1957.

[29]Truman, *Governmental Process*, 340.

[30]Quoted by Allen Morris in St. Petersburg *Times*, April 28, 1957.

[31]*Wall Street Journal*, June 5, 1957, p. 1.

[32]Miami *Herald*, April 14, 1957.

[33]In St. Petersburg *Times*, April 28, 1957.

[34]Fla. Stats. Annot., chap. 11, sec. 11.05.

[35]House Rule No. 74, House *Journal*, April 3, 1957.

[36]E. P. Herring, *Group Representation Before Congress* (Washington, 1929), 247.

[37]Galloway, *Legislative Process in Congress*, 513.

[38]*Ibid.*

[39]*Ibid.*

[40]*Ibid.*

[41]Paul H. Douglas, *Ethics in Government* (Cambridge, Mass., 1952), 64.

[42]George A. Graham, *Morality in American Politics* (New York, 1952), 134.

[43]Douglas, *Ethics in Government*, 103.

Chapter IX

[1]George A. Graham, *Morality in American Politics* (New York, 1952), 119.

[2]See the comments by Senator Richard Neuberger in *Streamlining State Legislatures* (Berkeley, California, 1955), 63-65.

[3]Michael Oakeshott, *Political Education,* Inaugural Lecture at the London School of Economics and Political Science (Cambridge, 1951), especially p. 8.

[4]In addition to the resignation of Sen. Rodgers (with a plea for longer sessions and higher pay) mentioned in Chapter 5, other legislators have expressed themselves publicly on the inadequacies of the present system of remuneration. Sen. Fred O. Dickinson, for example, recently advocated annual salaries of $3500, saying that the legislator's job is already practically a full-time one. Gainesville *Daily Sun,* August 7, 1957. Others have expressed themselves privately along the same lines. The older members seem able to shift their private responsibilities more easily and usually argue that the present expense allowance is quite adequate to live on during the session—which it probably is if other financial considerations are left aside.

[5]Zeller, (ed.), *American State Legislatures,* 168-69.

[6]E. E. Schattschneider, *Party Government* (New York, 1942), 11.

[7]Thomas C. Desmond, "Those Dinosaurs—The State Legislatures," *New York Times Magazine,* Jan. 16, 1955, p. 15.

Appendix A

[1]A definitive treatment of the entire question, including all the methods and their mathematical proof, is found in Laurence Schmeckebier, *Congressional Apportionment* (Washington, 1941). All of the so-called "modern methods" were either developed or advocated after the discovery of the "Alabama Paradox" whereby the use of a fixed ratio of representation may produce a decrease in the size of the house despite an increase in population. To avoid this possibility the "modern methods" do not start with a fixed ratio, but assign seats, in effect, on the basis of proportionate claims of each state to each seat that is added after each state is assigned its one guaranteed representative.

[2]In the case of congressional districts, for instance, Schmeckebier suggests "that a 20 per cent deviation from the average, for all districts, is a fair and workable tolerance." *Ibid.* 130.

Index